The middle years of the twentieth century marked a particularly intense time of crisis and change in European society. During this period (1930-1950), a broad intellectual and spiritual movement arose within the European Catholic community, largely in response to the secularism that lay at the core of the crisis. The movement drew inspiration from earlier theologians and philosophers such as Möhler, Newman, Gardeil, Rousselot, and Blondel, as well as from men of letters like Charles Péguy and Paul Claudel.

The group of academic theologians included in the movement extended into Belgium and Germany, in the work of men like Emile Mersch, Dom Odo Casel, Romano Guardini, and Karl Adam. But above all the theological activity during this period centered in France. Led principally by the Jesuits at Fourvière and the Dominicans at Le Saulchoir, the French revival included many of the greatest names in twentieth-century Catholic thought: Henri de Lubac, Jean Daniélou, Yves Congar, Marie-Dominique Chenu, Louis Bouyer, and, in association, Hans Urs von Balthasar.

It is not true — as subsequent folklore has it — that those theologians represented any sort of self-conscious "school": indeed, the differences among them, for example, between Fourvière and Saulchoir, were important. At the same time, most of them were united in the double conviction that theology had to speak to the present situation, and that the condition for doing so faithfully lay in a recovery of the Church's past. In other words, they saw clearly that the first step in what later came to be known as *aggiornamento* had to be *ressourcement* — a rediscovery of the riches of the whole of the Church's two-thousand-year tradition. According to de Lubac, for example, all of his own works as well as the entire *Sources chrétiennes* collection are based on the presupposition that "the renewal of Christian vitality is linked at least partially to a renewed exploration of the periods and of the works where the Christian tradition is expressed with particular intensity."

In sum, for the *ressourcement* theologians theology involved a "return to the sources" of Christian faith, for the purpose of drawing out the meaning and significance of these sources for the critical questions of our time. What these theologians sought was a spiritual and intellectual communion with Christianity in its most vital moments as transmitted to us in its classic texts, a communion that would nourish, invigorate, and rejuvenate twentieth-century Catholicism.

The *ressourcement* movement bore great fruit in the documents of the Second Vatican Council and deeply influenced the work of Pope John Paul II.

The present series is rooted in this renewal of theology. The series thus understands *ressourcement* as revitalization: a return to the sources, for the purpose of developing a theology that will truly meet the challenges of our time. Some of the features of the series, then, are a return to classical (patristic-medieval) sources and a dialogue with contemporary Western culture, particularly in terms of problems associated with the Enlightenment, modernity, and liberalism.

The series publishes out-of-print or as yet untranslated studies by earlier authors associated with the *ressourcement* movement. The series also publishes works by contemporary authors sharing in the aim and spirit of this earlier movement. This will include any works in theology, philosophy, history, literature, and the arts that give renewed expression to Catholic sensibility.

The editor of the Ressourcement series, David L. Schindler, is Gagnon Professor of Fundamental Theology and Dean Emeritus at the John Paul II Institute in Washington, D.C., and editor of the North American edition of *Communio: International Catholic Review,* a federation of journals in thirteen countries founded in Europe in 1972 by Hans Urs von Balthasar, Jean Daniélou, Henri de Lubac, Joseph Ratzinger, and others.

VOLUMES PUBLISHED

Mysterium Paschale
Hans Urs von Balthasar

***Joseph Ratzinger in* Communio**
Volume 1: The Unity of the Church
Pope Benedict XVI

***Joseph Ratzinger in* Communio**
Volume 2: Anthropology and Culture
Pope Benedict XVI

The Heroic Face of Innocence: Three Stories
Georges Bernanos

Maurice Blondel: A Philosophical Life
Oliva Blanchette

The Letter on Apologetics* and *History and Dogma
Maurice Blondel

Prayer: The Mission of the Church
Jean Daniélou

On Pilgrimage
Dorothy Day

We, the Ordinary People of the Streets
Madeleine Delbrêl

The Discovery of God
Henri de Lubac

Medieval Exegesis*, volumes 1-3: *The Four Senses of Scripture
Henri de Lubac

Opening Up the Scriptures:
Joseph Ratzinger and the Foundations of Biblical Interpretation
Edited by Jose Granados, Carlos Granados Jr.,
and Luis Sanchez-Navarro

Letters from Lake Como:
Explorations in Technology and the Human Race
Romano Guardini

The Epiphany of Love:
Toward a Theological Understanding of Christian Action
Livio Melina

Divine Likeness: Toward a Trinitarian Anthropology of the Family
Marc Cardinal Ouellet

The Portal of the Mystery of Hope
Charles Péguy

In the Beginning:
A Catholic Understanding of the Story of Creation and the Fall
Joseph Cardinal Ratzinger

In the Fire of the Burning Bush: An Initiation to the Spiritual Life
Marko Ivan Rupnik

Love Alone Is Credible:
Hans Urs von Balthasar as Interpreter of the Catholic Tradition
David L. Schindler, ed.

Hans Urs von Balthasar: A Theological Style
Angelo Scola

The Nuptial Mystery
Angelo Scola

Joseph Ratzinger in *Communio*

VOLUME 2

ANTHROPOLOGY AND CULTURE

Pope Benedict XVI

Edited by

David L. Schindler *and* Nicholas J. Healy

William B. Eerdmans Publishing Company
Grand Rapids, Michigan / Cambridge, U.K.

Published 2013 by
Wm. B. Eerdmans Publishing Co.
2140 Oak Industrial Drive N.E., Grand Rapids, Michigan 49505 /
P.O. Box 163, Cambridge CB3 9PU U.K.

Printed in the United States of America

19 18 17 16 15 14 13 7 6 5 4 3 2 1

Library of Congress Cataloging-in-Publication Data

Benedict XVI, Pope, 1927-
Essays in communio / Pope Benedict XVI;
introduction by David L. Schindler.
p. cm. — (Ressourcement)
ISBN 978-0-8028-6417-8 (pbk.: alk. paper)
1. Catholic Church — Doctrines. 2. Theology. I. Title.

BX1751.3.B453 2013
230′.2 — dc22
2009043676

www.eerdmans.com

Contents

From the Editor

Anthropology and Culture is the second volume of *Joseph Ratzinger in* Communio, which will bring together in three volumes the articles by Cardinal Joseph Ratzinger published in the North American edition of *Communio* since its inception in 1974. The articles are grouped very roughly into three themes: church, anthropology, and theological renewal. The lines between the themes are of course not clean. Cardinal Ratzinger (Pope Benedict XVI) rarely writes on any churchly matter that does not manifest its implications for man and culture, and vice versa. Indeed, this indissoluble linking is one of the main distinguishing features of his theology. Grouping the articles into three volumes as we have done nevertheless provides a larger unity of theme that may be helpful for readers.

As is well known, Ratzinger, along with Hans Urs von Balthasar, Henri de Lubac, and others, was one of the founders of the international Catholic journal *Communio,* which began in Germany (and Italy) in 1972. Most of the articles published in this and the other volumes, however, especially those written after Ratzinger left his professorship at Regensburg to become archbishop of Munich-Freising in 1977, were not written expressly for the journal. The articles consist rather of papers, book reviews, interviews, lectures, and the like completed for various occasions and made available to the national editions of *Communio.*

I am grateful to Emily Rielley and Agata Rottkamp of the American *Communio* for their work in editing the volumes, and to Nicholas Healy for his help in arranging the themes.

1 November 2012 DAVID L. SCHINDLER
Feast of All Saints

Beyond Death

The question of what lies beyond death has long been a dominant theme of Christian thought. Today it has fallen under that suspicion of Platonism which, originating in different ways in Marx and Nietzsche, weighs more and more oppressively on the Christian mind. The "beyond" looks like a flight from the distress and tasks of this world, which are deliberately encouraged and held out as a hope by those holding power here below. Consequently, even the general attitude to life today almost completely blocks access to the question. Furthermore, at a time when the defense of Christian essentials in the face of the "principalities and powers" of this world has become a central concern, the theme may appear secondary even to those who are far from accepting that the Christian message should be recast into mere social action or criticism.

There are other barriers as well. The next world is not only beyond the range of our action, it is inaccessible to rational thought and therefore questionable. It looks as though any statement about it cannot be more than a pious conjecture or wish. Even among theologians what was apparently quite clear has become nearly inaccessible – though in this connection it must be taken into account that the kind of theological problems emerging are essentially determined by the shift in general attitude to life, as well as by the loss of a philosophy

---

This article first appeared as "Jenseits des Todes," in *Internationale katholische Zeitschrift Communio* 3 (1972): 157-165.

capable of mediating between the facts of revelation and the positive findings of science. The situation is largely characterized by the clash of two positivisms, theological and scientific; this often produces a sort of short-circuit philosophy which does not recognize itself for what it is and consequently is all the more self-confident in its assertions. Here, then, we have a wide-ranging task, and one which will also help with the urgent problem of the political and social responsibility of the Christian faith, for even on that subject people will be able to speak on a firmer basis and more effectively if its relation to Christian hope as a whole is clarified. Without an intelligible answer to the question of death, no light can be thrown on the question of man's life and purpose. For this life is in fact marked by death and cannot be planned as though that were not so. And the question of death includes the problem of what is beyond death, the whole problem of being and nothingness.

1. The Resurrection or Immortality of the Soul Antithesis

a. The Thesis

Only a few remarks can be offered here on this wide-ranging task. Moreover, they will be essentially theological and consequently nothing more than a first stimulus to further thought. The question has been considerably complicated for Catholics in the course of the last decade by the fact that it was increasingly impossible for them not to pay heed to those Protestant theologians who regard "immortality of the soul" as a thoroughly unbiblical concept. Oscar Cullmann has been particularly insistent here, and we must recall at least one of his most striking expressions: "If we ask an average Christian, Protestant or Catholic, what the New Testament teaches about the individual lot of man after death, with few exceptions we will receive the answer, 'The immortality of the soul.' In this form this opinion represents one of the greatest misunderstandings of Christianity."[1] Cullman speaks in this connection of the incompatibility of the biblical belief in resur-

1. O. Cullmann, *Unsterblichkeit der Seele und Auferstehung der Toten* (1956), 19; English trans. *The Immortality of the Soul, or the Resurrection of the Dead* (1958).

rection with the Greek doctrine of immortality. This rejection of the idea of an immortal soul in favor of recognizing the resurrection of the body as alone biblical, is of course the result of reading the Bible in the light of a particular hermeneutics. The central content of the latter seems to me to consist in establishing an antithesis between the biblical and the Greek, which once again includes various dimensions. It has a long history,[2] but in modern theology it is more or less consciously regarded as one of the weapons by which Christianity is to be cleared of the imputation of Platonism. In the form in which we find it in Cullman and the earlier volumes of Kittel's monumental *Theological Dictionary of the New Testament,* it seems to me to be associated, in the tradition of Protestant thought, with two main decisions of principle: on the one hand the decision to banish philosophy as far as possible from the domain of faith, and, on the other, an extremely radical view of the divine action of grace, a way of thinking "from above," which knowingly and decidedly opposes the philosophical schema of ascent.[3] The terms "soul" and "immortality" are suspect by the mere fact that they are the product of philosophical reflection, while the affirmation of an immortality of the soul flowing from man's essential constitution appears to express something naturally belonging to man as opposed to the raising from the dead, which can only be effected by God, in other words, by sheer grace. As a result, not only the idea of immortality but also that of "soul" itself falls under the suspicion of Platonism and has to make way for a doctrine of man as a totality which will have nothing to do with the distinction of "soul" and "body" in man.

2. On the history of the question, cf. A. Grillmeier, "Hellenisierung und Judaisierung des Christentums als Deuteprinzipien der Geschichte des kirchlichen Dogmas," *Scholastik* 33 (1958): 321-355, 528-558. The influence and background of the idea in recent theology would need a whole study to themselves.

3. The classical presentation of an antithesis between the ascent and descent schemas is that of A. Nygren, *Eros und Agape. Gestaltwandlungen der christlichen Liebe* (1930, 1937); Eng., *Agape and Eros* (Chicago: University of Chicago Press, 1982). For a discussion of this, cf. J. Pieper, *Über die Liebe* (1972), 92-106 (*Faith, Hope, Love* [San Francisco: Ignatius Press, 1997]); valuable indications (in the sense of a Christian rehabilitation of Eros) in H. de Lubac, *Histoire et Esprit* (1950) (*History and Spirit* [San Francisco: Ignatius Press, 2007]).

b. The Problems

At this point we also see the connection with the modern mentality or attitude to life, and the trend of the modern scientific study of man. There is a rediscovery, a new feeling for the human body; science has everywhere found confirmation of the unity of man and his complete indivisibility. This is precisely what corresponds to the fundamental tenor of biblical thought, and contradicts the dualism that with some justification can be attributed to Platonism.[4] But if this gets rid of one difficulty, that of Platonism, another no less grave takes its place. For now one would have to say that if the immortality of the soul as a substance independent of the body contradicts the Bible as well as modern knowledge, what about the raising of the dead? If this is not to be relegated to the sphere of the purely miraculous but to be thought of in reasonable terms, even greater difficulties arise. Are we to think of it happening for everyone "on the Last Day"? If so, what lies between? A sleep of the soul? Or total death? And if so, who exactly can be raised from the dead? What constitutes the identity between the dead and the resurrected if complete non-being intervenes? And what is resurrected? The doctrine of man as a totality seems to demand a body, and basically can recognize only a body as the bearer of identity (if the soul is completely rejected); but how is human identity to be maintained in the body alone? How can man's restoration be intelligibly conceived at all? How are we to picture the life and mode of existence of those raised from the dead? It is obvious that without rational thought along the logical lines of the biblical statements, that is to say without philosophical mediation — without "hermeneutics" — no further advance can be made. But in that case it can no longer be forbidden to ask whether something like the concept of the soul is not needed after all as a hermeneutical connecting link, whether it is not in fact suggested by the data themselves, even if the latter take reflection in this direction no further than a step or two.

For the moment, however, let us continue to establish the state of

4. "Platonism" has sunk here to a mere catchword that has no longer anything to do with the historical reality of Platonic philosophy, the great political relevance of which has recently been forcefully brought out by U. Duchrow, *Christenheit und Weltverantwortung* (1970), 61-80.

the question. It was widely recognized that a general postponement of the solution of the problem of death to the "end of time" is unsatisfactory, and that, together with the question of the intermediate state and the preservation of identity, it involves a further series of practically insoluble problems. Consequently a philosophy of time is in many cases introduced here, of the kind, for example, worked out by Karl Barth in his early days, drawing on Ernst Troeltsch in regard to the problem of eschatology. Troeltsch had expressed the idea that the Last Things really stand in no relation to time.[5] To say that they will come "at the end of time," "after our time" is, Troeltsch claims, merely a makeshift way of speaking in such terms as our time-bound minds can manage. In reality the otherness of the Eschaton is simply incommensurable with our time. Consequently, it is argued, one might say that every wave of the sea of time breaks in the same way on the shore of eternity. The early Barth could accordingly write that to wait for the parousia is equivalent to "taking our actual situation in life as seriously as it really is." Similarly, the parousia is made identical with the resurrection, which is not a phenomenon in time but an emanation of eternity, and symbolizes what is ultimate in the metaphysical sense.[6] Here the question inescapably arises concerning the actual real content of such formulations. Do they turn eschatology into a rather more elaborate formulation of men's day-to-day responsibilities? Or what do they actually state?

In Catholic theology ideas from this philosophy of time and eternity gained increased acceptance in connection with the discussion of the dogma of Mary's bodily assumption into heavenly glory. Here a raising from the dead which had already taken place was explicitly affirmed, even if only directly in regard to one human being, the mother of the Lord. Nevertheless this raised quite generally the question of what constitutes the resurrection of the body and its relation to time. And so this dogma appeared, in the perspective of the discussions that had been going on, as a downright challenge to correct a purely linear representation of the end of time and, instead, to think of the Last

5. I am following here the account given by F. Holmström, *Das eschatologische Denken der Gegenwart* (1937); on Troeltsch, cf. 131ff. Cf. also F. M. Braun, *Neues Licht auf die Kirche* (1946), 93-132.

6. K. Barth, *Der Römerbrief* (^{2}1922), 240ff.; English trans. 1933. Cf. F. Braun, *Neues Licht,* 113f.

Things, death and resurrection, as coextensive with time.[7] This made it possible to remove the particular stumbling block of this dogma, which could now be regarded simply as the paradigm case of the fundamental correlation of time and eternity; similarly, eschatological problems could be clarified by a new understanding of what "end" means in relation to time. The view that each man's death is entry into the wholly other, into what is not time but eternity, gained wide acceptance. Eternity does not come *after* time (that would mean it was itself in time); it is rather time's counterpart, ever present and contemporaneous with it. Consequently, dying in each case means dying into eternity, into the "end of time," into the total Eschaton, the already present resurrection and fulfillment. Just as the spatial conception of the Beyond as a sort of upper storey of the world was only slowly and not without opposition being replaced by a personal and metaphysical view, so in the same way a temporal conception of it as an end coming "after" world-time must be got rid of. For this view, we are told, is no less naïve and misses no less radically the essential structure of the time-eternity relation.

This philosophy of time and eternity abandons the attempt to be satisfied with a simple biblical positivism, and by reflection on the different levels of reality some progress is undoubtedly achieved. At the same time the idea of the resurrection of the dead is considerably modified, unfortunately mostly without sufficient consideration. For the dead man laid in his earthly grave is simultaneously said to be already risen, on the other side of the line of time. What does that mean? Is there after all a human existence separable from the body? Something like the "soul," in fact? Or what kind of concept of time is it that seems to make it possible to think of man as both risen and as lying in the grave? Either way, further questions are inescapable.

2. In Search of New Answers

a. Physical Time — Human Time — Eternity

Let us continue with the problem of time. The distinction between time and eternity, which has been adopted as a sort of magic key to

7. One of the first attempts to interpret the dogma of the Assumption in this way was that of O. Karrer, "Über unsterbliche Seele und Auferstehung," *Anima* 11 (1953): 332-336.

solve the problem, makes possible some progress, as we have noted, as compared with an unanalyzed linear extension in which an end, which as such is no longer time, is nevertheless simply located "after" time and so turned into time. But it remains far behind the stage of reflection reached by Augustine and pursued in the Middle Ages in various forms. Augustine's fundamental insight in his considerations on human memory consists in the distinction he draws between physical time and time as humanly experienced. The latter in fact offers a model on which eternity can at least be thought about. Physical time denotes the successive moments of a process of movement which can be ascertained and dated by reference to a particular parameter (sun or moon, for example). Its essential features are uniformity and irrevocability. The movement in question (revolution of a body, etc.) can be repeated, yet the movement that has once taken place is irrevocably past and as such can only be verified as the date when something did happen. In short, physical time might be defined as the measurable course of corporeal movement. Now man, because corporeal, is tied to physical time. The stages of his bodily and, therefore, indirectly, of his mental existence can be fitted into the general course of the movement of bodies and dated in days and years by the course of the sun. But it is obvious that man's personal experience is not wholly identical with measurable corporeal movement. While it is true that even human processes of intellectual decision are connected with the body and to that extent, as we have said, can be dated indirectly, in themselves they are something different from corporeal movement and to that extent transcend the measures of physical time. What is "present" for each human being is not determined solely by the calendar, but much more by his mental attention, the section of reality which he grasps as present, as effectively Now. To this present belong his hopes and fears, that is, what is chronologically future, as well as his fidelity and gratitude, what is chronologically past. "The present" in this sense is a strictly human phenomenon, differing from one human being to another (in different human beings different "presents" intersect); physical time has only moments. Augustine tried to designate this specifically human phenomenon by the term "memory." Memory unites an element determined by my vital decisions, from the chronological past or future, with my human present. This human time possesses neither the uniformity nor the absolute irrevocability of the physical time process. Human acts with their unique character cannot be repeated as a particular physical movement can; on the other hand they do not simply pass away, but "remain." Love in its very essence endures, truth, once discovered, abides; my human experiences are a real part of my living self. Present consciousness, which is able to summon what is past into the present of recollection, thus makes possible some notion of what "eternity" is: pure *memoria* bearing the whole changing movement of the world in the all-inclusive present of the creative mind, yet comprehending each detail exactly as it is at its own chronological moment.

If we apply this to our previous considerations, the shortcoming of the time-eternity philosophy described above appears to me to be that it presents only a single alternative: physical time or pure eternity; moreover, it conceives the latter quite negatively as the non-temporal. Death then appears simply as the change from physical time to eternity. But this overlooks precisely the specifically human element. Consequently the answer turns out to be quite insufficient. For if one were rigorously to follow up the idea that beyond death a pure Now prevails, that resurrection, end of the world and Last Judgment are already present, because there is no time there, this would mean that in each instance men would enter into the whole of completed history and into the complete timelessness that prevails there, thus finding there all those people who think they are still living in the course of time or in general still belong to the future. This absurd consequence inescapably follows from the conception of time and eternity in question. It would also mean that, viewed from the other side, history would be an empty spectacle in which people think they are striving and struggling, whereas simultaneously in "eternity," in the already ever present Now, everything is long since decided. The result of thinking in terms of a sole antithesis between physical time and eternity would thus be a shoddy "Platonism" such as Plato and the Platonists never knew. In contrast to this a correct description of what happens at death would have to say, for example, that specifically human time is detached here from its physical-chronological context, and thereby receives a definitive character. But that means that the two sides of man and history neither stand to one another in a relation of simple succession, nor are absolutely incommensurable. Which also means that the unfolding history of the world and its definitive theological future most certainly stand in a real relation to one another, that the activity of the one is not at all a matter of no account to the genesis of the other. The common future of creation, of which faith speaks, and the future of the world toward which our activity is directed, cannot be calculated in terms of one another, but are nonetheless inseparable.

b. Rehabilitation of the Soul

There remains the question of the soul. It cannot be denied that this term was accepted into Christian tradition with some hesitation, even though the transition of biblical faith into the domain of Greek thought was prepared and in part carried out much earlier than the harsh antithesis to which we referred earlier would suggest. I need only recall that intertestamental Judaism already had very elaborate conceptions of the life and conditions of men after death, and that these for a very long time gave their stamp to the mental world of the ancient Church, and even in Augustine were still exercising more influence than Plato's schemata.[8] The prayer of the Roman Canon that the dead may have a place of light, peace, and refreshment (literally, of running water) preserves to this day an expression from that world of Jewish beliefs that survived in the Church. Continuity of this kind provides a precise indication of how to read the New Testament correctly on this question. The apostolic preaching presupposes in principle that Israel's faith is its own, with, of course, the one decisive proviso that it must be viewed and lived in its entirety with Christ as its basis and in relation to Christ; in him it receives a new center, and this slowly pervaded its various elements. But this process of reshaping the various elements through faith in Christ took time, proceeding slowly. The difference this relation to Christ made to particular elements of Jewish belief did not necessarily have to be decided straight away, only in central matters. Consequently for a very long time eschatology remained, so to speak, in a largely Jewish condition, but this testifies in fact to the con-

8. On the development of the doctrine of the "intermediate state" in the ancient Church cf. in particular A. Stuiber, *Refrigerium interim* (1957); J. Fischer, *Studien zum Todesgedanken in der alten Kirche*. There is a good collection of materials in Y. Trémel, "Der Mensch zwischen Tod und Auferstehung nach dem Neuen Testament," *Anima* 11 (1953): 313-331.

tinuity of the ancient Church with the original Jewish Christian community. The new emphasis consists in the fact that Jesus Christ is proclaimed as having already risen. The real point of reference for immortality is less some time or other to come than the living Lord now. Thus Paul gave a radically christological and personal interpretation to the late Jewish doctrine of intermediate realms, in the words "to depart and be with Christ" (Phil 1:23). The Lord is where our indestructible life is, and there is no need to ask questions about or seek any other place. In the synoptic gospels two sayings of Jesus have been preserved in more archaic formulations of a more Jewish coloring. In the context of the story of Lazarus at Luke 16:19-29, mention is made of Abraham's bosom as the place of salvation, as contrasted with the place of torment, separated from it by an unbridgeable abyss. The good thief receives the answer from the dying Lord, "This day thou shalt be with me in Paradise" (Lk 23:43).[9] This recalls the late Jewish theology of martyrdom, also echoed in the account of the first Christian martyrdom: "Lord Jesus, receive my spirit," is Stephen's dying prayer (Acts 7:59). Already in the words to the good thief, "with me" introduces a christological nuance into the idea of Paradise, and in the prayer of the Christian martyr, the Lord himself is the Paradise into which the dying man knows his life is taken up. No longer is the bosom of the patriarch Abraham the place of shelter for the believer's existence, but the risen Lord in whom those who are his own live.

Thus in relation to the risen Lord there was now an awareness of a life bestowed on men even in the death of the body and before the final accomplishment of the world's future. It was thus realized that there is a human continuity that extends beyond the identity of man's corporeal existence, even though he is fully himself in his body, as a single indivisible creature. How was this factor of continuity and identity to be thought of? Even in earthly life it is more than the sum of the material parts of man (which of course change even during his earthly existence), and its real significance only really becomes apparent in the possibility of an existence beyond death. Greek had the term "soul" to offer, which for that matter had already here and there in the New Testament carried the meaning of this factor of identity transcending cor-

9. Cf. J. Jeremias, παράδεισος, in *Theologisches Wörterbuch zum Neuen Testament,* V, 763-771, esp. 768f.

poreality.[10] Of course this expression had the drawback of being associated with a dualistic world-view and was therefore dangerous and could not be used without clarification. But that was fundamentally the case with all words, even the word "God." The Greek "God" was not at all the same as the biblical Yahweh, the Father of Jesus Christ, so that the common use of the name "God" involved a no less serious possible danger. On the other hand, it must not be forgotten that the words of the Bible themselves did not fall from heaven, but were turned into ways of expressing faith by molding and clarifying words taken from Israel's religious and secular environment. It is possible to observe how hesitantly and gradually that reshaping took place, not without relapses, and never actually ceased. Except by the slow transformation of words and thoughts that man has discovered during history, it is impossible to preach the faith at all. To that extent, therefore, the dualist origin of the term "soul" says something about the danger but nothing about the impossibility in principle of using it. More recent studies have conclusively shown how intensively Christian thought, especially at the height of the Middle Ages, endeavored to achieve the necessary purification and transformation of the concept.[11] Unfortunately it is impossible to go into details, but it could be shown that the doctrine of the immortality of the soul as Thomas Aquinas formulated it represents something radically new in comparison with the immortality doctrines of antiquity. Aristotle, whom Aquinas makes use of in his own thinking, actually denies that the *forma corporis* (the integrative force of the body) is immortal, just as he denies that the immortal element (the *intellectus agens*) belongs to the individual as such. Similarly Plato would never have admitted that the "immortal soul" is so linked

10. J. Schmid, "Der Begriff der Seele im Neuen Testament," in *Einsicht und Glaube,* ed. J. Ratzinger and H. Fries ([2]1963), 128-148, minimizes this as far as he can, but cannot eliminate it entirely. Cf. also on the different levels of meaning, P. van Imschoot, "Seele," in *Bibellexikon,* 2nd ed., ed. H. Haag (1968), 1567f.

11. Cf. the unpublished Bochum thesis of T. Schneider, *Die Einheit des Menschen. Die anthropologische Formel "Anima forma corporis" im sogennanten Korrektorienstreit und bei Petrus Johannis Olivi. Ein Beitrag zur Vorgeschichte des Konzils von Vienne.* Cf. also the unpublished Regensburg thesis of H. J. Weber, *Die Lehre von der Auferstehung der Toten in den Haupttraktaten der scholastischen Theologie von Alexander von Hales zu Duns Scotus.* Cf. also the references given by J. Pieper, "Tod und Unsterblichkeit," *Catholica* 13 (1959): 81-100 (*Death and Immortality* [New York: Herder and Herder, 1969]).

to the body, belongs to it in such a way and is so one with it, that it must be called its "form" and cannot subsist except in closest relation to it.

There is no doubt, of course, that a dualistic element has repeatedly imposed itself to a considerable extent on the public mind. To that extent a new endeavor to purify the concept or even to seek to formulate it better is certainly not out of place. But the reality itself cannot be bypassed, certainly not if the message of the New Testament is to be preserved without diminution. Perhaps some light can be shed on what is meant from another side. Talk of the immortal soul has a suspicious ring about it today because people have the impression that it refers to an objectifying metaphysics of substance, whereas in contrast to this a dialogical, personal concept is regarded as more appropriate. Accordingly, the question of what actually makes man immortal appears to call for a different kind of answer. For that matter, it is identical with the question of what is distinctive and specific in man, what makes man human. In a dialogical conception, the answer would be that this distinctive feature lies in his capacity for God, in the fact that he is addressed by God and is in principle called upon to respond. Anyone who speaks with God does not die. God's love gives eternity.[12] But this thought differs from the true sense of an authentic concept of the "soul" only in mode of formulation and approach. Augustine deduced man's immortality from his capacity for truth. Aquinas follows him in this: Anyone who has commerce with truth shares in its indestructibility.[13] Nowadays we should lay more emphasis on the dialogue of mutual love, but the line of thought is the same. But this means that "soul" and "capacity for truth" or "to be called to indestructible dialogue with eternal truth and love" are all expressions for one and the same thing. Soul is not an occult entity that one *has,* a partial substance hidden somewhere in the human being; it is the dynamism of an unlimited openness, which at the same time means participation in infinity, in the eternal. On the other hand, however, it is also the case that this dynamic character of human personal life, the thirst for truth and

12. I tried to formulate the idea of immortality on these lines in my *Introduction to Christianity* (English trans. 1960).

13. Cf. references in J. Pieper, "Tod," 96f.; Augustine, Solil. 2, 19 (PL 32, 901); Aquinas, *ST* I, q. 62, art. 2 ad 3 (here applied to the angels: . . . "ex hoc quod habent naturam per quam sunt capaces veritatis, sunt incorruptibiles").

indestructible love, is not a disconnected, merely factual succession, but, most fragile as that dynamism is, is also the most authentic and enduring reality. This dynamism is substance and this substance is dynamism. This fundamental, enduring, and essential human reality is called to mind by the term "soul." This presupposes, of course, that we do not think of substance from below, in terms of "mass" (which in any case is itself becoming more problematic) but from above, in terms of the dynamism of mental activity, and that we cease to regard solid "mass" as what is most incontrovertibly real – the contrary is the case.

A radio program under the title "Is the soul immortal?" was recently introduced with the remark that the question – if unexpanded and left without comment – sounds absurd and even "indecent." Now there is in fact a kind of shame which ought to impel us not to rob great things of their dignity by frivolous use. To that extent everyday misuse of elevated language can in fact become in a certain sense "indecent," and it cannot be denied that there have been cases of this in everyday Christian language. On the other hand, in an age in which the shame which ought to protect the dignity and grandeur of the human body is increasingly scorned, things should not be allowed to come to such a pitch that man is ashamed of his spirit, his "soul," in a way that threatens to degenerate into a total (and very ominous) taboo. It seems to me that it is high time theology set about rehabilitating the taboo concepts of "immortality" and "soul." Certainly they raise problems, and the shock of the last few years may prove to have been salutary or even necessary. It will no longer be possible to use the words as simply and unthinkingly as formerly. But simply to outlaw them is at bottom just as naïve, and bars access to the whole problem. It makes no difference to object that they go beyond biblical terminology. Anyone who regards that as putting an end to the matter would be denying the whole problem of hermeneutics, the whole function of reflective mediation.

3. Belief in Immortality and Secular Responsibility

The problem remains: What is the point of it all? The biblical question, "What does it profit a man if he gain the whole world but suffers the loss of his own soul?" appears nowadays to be inverted into the question of what it profits a man to gain his whole soul if the world is not served thereby. A lot might be said on this; perhaps this kind of inversion of the question represents the main problem of Christian life today. In accordance with the fragmentary character of these reflections, only a suggestion or two can be attempted, certainly inadequate, but enough perhaps to help open up a line of thought. As is well known, Dietrich Bonhoeffer once formulated the thought that the believer today must live *quasi Deus non daretur* – as though God did not exist. I fully agree with what this saying is intended to express, namely, that we must avoid an egotistical and primitive notion of God that misuses him as a stopgap in our earthly failure. Nevertheless, I think that for the conduct of life it would be more appropriate to suggest the opposite. Even the skeptic and the atheist should live *quasi Deus daretur* – as though God really exists.

What does this mean? To live as though God exists means to live as though one had an unlimited responsibility; as though justice and truth were not only programs, but a living existent power to which one has to render an account; as though what one does now would not disappear like a drop in the ocean, but was of lasting, even permanent consequence. To act as though God exists would also mean to act as though the human being next to me were not just some chance product of Nature, of no great ultimate importance, but an embodied thought of God, an image of the Creator whom he knows and loves. That would mean acting as though each human being were destined for eternity and as though each were my brother because created by the same God. To act *quasi Deus daretur,* as though God exists, seems to me to be the only meaningful replacement for Kant's categorical imperative in an age when the conditions required for its application have been destroyed. Kant had tried to solve the ethical problem by the simple maxim: Act in such a way that the maxim of your conduct could at all times serve as a law for all. The idea is that by putting this procedure into practice one will always hit on the good. What can be generalized can be justified in relation to the whole. This at first very clear solution is in fact only practicable as long as people remain more or less agreed about *what* can be generalized and what forms of action are appropriate as general laws. Kant's imperative therefore presupposes a society in which a definite value structure exists and in which people are to some degree certain what serves the well-being of the whole and what does not. But this is precisely what we have become so disunited about today, in a way that Kant could not have imagined. According to what theory of society is held, exact contraries will be regarded as a possible general law. The point of reference that provided the basis of Kant's thought, namely universality, human society, is too uncertain for human action to be securely built on it alone.

To act as though God exists – anyone who tries this reaches without much further reflection the kernel of belief in the immortality of the soul. Even if perhaps he can never get further than the "As if," and remains a life-long questioner, he has accepted what is really in question much more than someone who affirms immortality as a formula but lives as though there were no one but himself. An important point emerges here which has not been mentioned so far: The real import of Christian belief in the immortality of the soul is not to posit some theory or other about things we can know nothing about and subsequently declare to be certain; it makes a statement about the standards and scope of human life. It is intended to inculcate the fact that man is never a means but always an end in himself. It seeks to impress on the mind the reality of values, especially those of justice and truth, which are not mere abstract goals but life and life-giving. To that extent it is a thoroughly practical statement, a decision about the status and dignity of human life.

Once this has been said we can go a step further. Human life cannot ultimately be based on an "As if." That may work quite well for an individual if the "As if" has strong enough support; it may suffice for long stretches of human life during which theoretical solutions are suspended and people simply push on in the darkness. But it cannot be the fundamental form of human personal existence as such. If it is the case that human existence can actually be constructed on the basis of this "As if," this implies something about the validity and reality of the hypothesis. The same thing may be approached from another angle. Anyone who patiently trusts to this "As if," taking it constantly as the maxim of his life, can see that he is not living by a fiction, that what he at first adopted as a hypothesis is true, the authentic truth about man and reality itself.[14]

14. This section was delivered in the course of the above-mentioned broadcast from Radio Free Berlin. The producers (L. Dilzen and H. Wöller) commented that "to save the principle of life which we call 'soul'" I had "demanded an intellectual effort and the ca-

Truth and justice are not simply ideas, they *are*. In other words, God *is*. This, however, basically implies immortality. For God is a God of the living. The idea of God, to my mind, already includes that of man's immortality. For a creature who is looked upon and loved by him who is eternity has thereby a share in eternity. How exactly one is to formulate this, or even how one is to think it, are *ultimately* secondary, though by no means unimportant, questions. All the concepts we employ – and so also the affirmation of the immortality of the *soul* – are in the last resort mere aids to thought (in part of course irreplaceable) with which we try on the basis of various anthropological models to define the whole more concretely. Such conceptual advances are unquestionably necessary for us to see more clearly and firmly maintain the demands and responsibility of rational thought. But they are not the essential. And above all there is no question of obtaining descriptions of the beyond, thus extending the range of our vain curiosity. In essence the confession of belief in immortality is nothing else than a profession of faith that God really exists. It is a statement about God, and precisely for that reason it is a statement about man who is to find in it the way and manner of his personal life.

Translated by W. J. O'Hara

---

pacity for rational abstraction, which (was) rewarded by belief in the possibility of eternal existence." It would be impossible to imagine a more absurd misinterpretation of what I said. I was simply trying to bring out the reference to practice which is inherent in religious cognition, and which is impossible without a context of experience.

Conscience in Time

Is conscience really a power we can count on? Is it not rather the case that we must equip ourselves with weapons that are less abstract? Reinhold Schneider, in his story of Bartolomé de las Casas, impressively presents the mystery of conscience in the nameless girl of the Lucayos, who gradually brings the unscrupulous Spanish soldier of fortune, Bernardino, to understand the mystery of suffering and thereby awakens the soul that was dead in him.[1] This frail young creature, who has no strength left but to suffer, represents conscience among these soldiers of fortune for whom all that counts is gold and the sword, sheer economic or military power. She stands there negligible in her frailty, and that is how conscience stands in the world to this very day, helpless like that girl, doomed to an early death in the face of gigantic economic and political interests. What is it but folly to rely on conscience, when we see

1. The novel *Las Casas vor Karl V. Szenen aus der Konquistadorenzeit* is quoted here from the paperback edition (Ulstein-Verlag, 1968). The story of Lucaya appears on pages 81-94. "My soul?" he asked, "I do not know whether it still was my soul. Perhaps it has lived for many years in another being and was only given back to me after that one's death" (81). For an interpretation of R. Schneider's work, cf. Hans Urs von Balthasar, *Reinhold Schneider. Sein Weg und sein Werk* (1953); new edition: *Nochmals Reinhold Schneider,* 1991 (*Tragedy Under Grace: Reinhold Schneider on the Experience of the West,* trans. Brian McNeil [San Francisco: Ignatius Press and Communio Books, 1997]).

This article is based on a lecture given at the Annual Meeting of the Reinhold Schneider Society in Freiburg, 13 May 1972. This article first appeared as "Das Gewissen der Zeit," in *Internationale katholische Zeitschrift Communio* 1, no. 5 (1972) (first series) and republished in *Communio* 19, no. 4 (Winter 1992).

what really counts in the world. Is it not an empty, meaningless daydream, in view of the threats of the present day, to look up to those who bore witness to conscience, and whose only possible contribution was but to suffer? Are we – it will be objected – to go into politics and solve the problems of the age with lyricism?

1. The Nature and Significance of Conscience

But another more serious objection crops up. What is conscience in actual fact?[2] Is there any such thing? Or is it not merely an interiorized super-ego which transforms the taboos of education into divine commands and so makes them insuperable? Do not those in power, for example, use the idea of conscience to transpose their power into the very minds of the human beings whom they shamelessly exploit, by such constant inculcation of all their demands on their victims, that the latter actually come to hear them within as the "voice of God"? In that case, Hitler would have been right after all in saying that conscience is a slavery from which man must above all be freed. But we must go on to ask, what direction really remains for a human being who has freed himself from his conscience? What is he actually set free for? Is he no longer bound by respect for the humanity of others, if the higher interest of future society demands it should be disregarded? Can crime, murder for example, become a legitimate means of creating the future?

It is not easy to answer all these questions. There is no doubt that the term "conscience" can conceal the canonization of a super-ego which hampers a human being in truly becoming himself; the absolute summons of the person to assume his own responsibility is covered over by a layer of conventions which falsely claims to be the voice of God, whereas in fact it is only the voice of the past, the fear of which bars the way to the present. Conscience can become an alibi for bigotry and unteachability in which stubborn incapacity for self-correction is justified by fidelity to the inner voice. Conscience then becomes the

2. On the question of the nature of conscience, which cannot be pursued here, see in particular J. Stelzenberger, *Das Gewissen. Besinnliches zur Klarstellung eines Begriffes* (1961); *Das Gewissen. Studien aus dem C. G. Jung-Institut Zürich,* vol. 7 (1958), especially the contribution of H. Zbinden, "Das Gewissen in unserer Zeit," 9-51. See also J. Messner, "Morality in a Secularized Society," in *Communio: International Catholic Review* 2 (1972): 94-106.

principle of a subjective willfulness posited as absolute, just as in the other case it becomes a principle which places the person under the tutelage of the anonymous crowd, or of another ego. Consequently the concept of conscience constantly needs purification; its claim and the appeal to conscience demand a sober, honest awareness that it is an abuse to invoke too readily what is great. Those who have the word "conscience" all too easily on their tongue are as suspect as those who degrade the holy name of God by making it commonplace, practicing idolatry in fact, not serving God.

But the vulnerability of conscience, the possibility of its misuse, cannot abolish its greatness. Reinhold Schneider has said: "What is conscience, if not the knowledge of responsibility for the whole of creation, before him who created it?" Conscience, to put it quite simply, means acknowledging man, oneself and others, as created, and respecting the Creator in his creation. That sets a limit to all power and at the same time gives it a direction. Consequently perseverance in the powerlessness of conscience remains the fundamental condition and innermost core of all true control of power. Where this innermost core is not maintained, there can no longer be any question of the control of power, but simply of a balance of interests in which man and human society are reduced to the model of natural selection: good is what prevails; to exist means to survive. Man no longer lives as a creation but as a product of natural selection, and the power which he set out to control becomes his sole criterion. His humanity is destroyed. Consequently we need those human beings who stand by conscience like the poor, frail girl Lucaya, who embody the power of powerlessness and protest against the exploitation of man simply by sharing the sufferings of oppressed humanity and siding with suffering. That is why the sonnets of Reinhold Schneider – "lyricism" – were a power that the dictators feared as a formidable weapon. Schneider suffered from the abuse of power for the sake of conscience. To suffer for the sake of conscience sums up in fact his whole life. But, it may be said, what is the use of merely suffering? Yet ultimately injustice can be overcome only by the voluntary suffering of those who remain true to their conscience and thereby really testify to the end of all power by their suffering and their whole life. We are slowly beginning to realize once more something of what it means that the redemption of the world, the overcoming of power, is found in the suffering of an executed man, that precisely where power ends in suffering, the salvation of man appears.

2. Las Casas and the Problem of Conscience

Using the example of the Las Casas material as Schneider handles it, I would like to try to develop this thought that the kernel of the necessary control and limitation of power in this world consists in the courage to follow conscience. First of all, a short reflection on the historical background. With the discovery of America, the question of men's rights as men, human rights, emerged anew. In the course of the Crusades and the increasing contact with the Arab world, it had indeed demanded attention with mounting urgency since the thirteenth century; it now assumed its full acuity through the powerlessness of the newly discovered peoples in the face of Spanish arms. The problem of the limits of power had previously presented itself mainly among Christians in the conflict between *sacerdotium* and *imperium.* In the Christian world these two clashed as powers which were both, in intention, absolute: as Christian power wholly subject to the *sacerdotium,* as secular wholly to the *imperium.* As Christian and secular, that is to say in the coincidence of world and Church, it raised for both the question of self-limitation. Now, however, a largely new problem arose. The Christian faith understands itself as absolute, as the revelation of the one saving truth for man; it is aware of original sin by which man's reason is obscured, and only enlightened and restored again by faith. Consequently reason can find the foundations of genuine law only in faith, and cannot really recognize legal construction outside faith as true law – or at least this is what Augustine seemed to have said in the *Civitas Dei.* He denied the character of justice to pagan states that do not know God and thereby neglect an essential half of true justice. He defined them for practical purposes as a mere community of interests which as such serve a limited purpose in keeping the peace and to that extent are legitimate.[3] Now, however, the question arose of what criteria and possibilities for limiting power exist when two peoples meet and superior-

3. On the problems connected with these developments, cf. U. Duchrow, *Christenheit und Weltverantwortung* (1970).

ity of arms is linked with consciousness of superiority in possession of the sole obligatory truth. Do the missions and colonialism together form the hybrid that is responsible for the distress of the Third World? Where could a corrective come from in this case? Reinhold Schneider's answer in his novel is that the corrective could come only from faith itself – in the suffering and struggling conscience which such faith itself awakens. That faith is alone justified as truth by the fact that its very basis forbids it to be a multiplication of power; it is a summons to awaken conscience, which limits power and protects the powerless, for its absolute character consists in protecting others as created beings.

We must take another look at the historical facts. Did this conscience appear at all? Was it a real power or was there only that false absolute of faith in which faith operates as an ideology of power instead of proclaiming the absolute character of the Creator in the absolute dignity of the powerless? Las Casas in 1542, in his *Brevisima Relación de la Destrucción de las Indias Occidentales,* framed the most terrible indictment of the impotence of conscience and the brutality of unscrupulous power that we know. We are aware today that this work was largely based on extremely unreliable sources, that is, "extremely one-sided and often exaggerated and distorted"; that it is completely silent about the monstrous features of the other side, for example that Aztecs sacrificed twenty thousand human hearts in a religious service.[4] There nevertheless remains an enormous indictment of the Spanish conquerors, who enslaved and despoiled human beings without restraint and condemned whole tribes to extinction by brutally exploiting their labor. It is in fact the case that conscience really did just stand there like a lamenting Lucaya, who could only watch the horror as she wept in unspeakable grief. Nevertheless, conscience was there, and Las Casas is not by any means the only witness to it; its traces can be followed from the first laws of Queen Isabella, who declared all the Indians to be free subjects of the crown and forbade their enslavement, through the *Leyes de Burgos* (1512), to the *Leyes Nuevas* of 1542, which were decisively influenced by Las Casas and represented a comprehensive attempt to liberate the Indians and ensure them full legal protection; the regulation

4. On the question of Las Casas, cf. the view of G. Kahle, *Bartolomé de las Casas* (1968), especially 18 and 32 for the present point. Cf. also B. M. Bierbaum, *Las Casas und seine Sendung* (1968).

that they should with all care and love "be instructed in our holy Catholic faith" was not intended to dominate them, but to put them on an equal footing and protect them from the arbitrary will of those in power.[5]

The fact that here, too, very limited success was achieved does not alter the fact that conscience was recognized in principle as setting a limit to power, and that an attempt was thereby made to make faith effective as a political force without transforming it into one more power factor among others. This is precisely what must remain its characteristic note: that the power of conscience consists in suffering, in the power of the Crucified; only in that way can it be kept from inaugurating yet another kind of enslavement. It redeems only as the power of the Cross; its mystery lies in this powerlessness and it must remain powerless in this world in order to remain itself. I think that the attitude of the New Testament to political power can be correctly understood only in this perspective. A brief remark on this. Anyone who reads the Sermon on the Mount or in general takes up the New Testament with the political distress of our time in mind, and the Christian's responsibility for it, is most disappointed. The whole thing looks like a flight into non-political interiority; there is scarcely any mention of shaping the world, but rather of a loyalty which looks to us like criminal passivity and an authoritarian mode of thought; whether one thinks of Romans 13:1-7 or of 1 Peter 2:13-25, in each the key word is *úpostasis,* subjection, patience, obedience – and 1 Peter even refers to the example of Christ's sufferings. And the only statement of Jesus about the state, Mark 12:17: "Render to Caesar the things that are Caesar's," remains within loyalty as a principle. Jesus in fact was not a revolutionary, and anyone who asserts the contrary falsifies history. It is also the case that the New Testament in its own particular situation did not feel impelled to develop more positively and fully a Christian political ethics; mere biblicism here in fact gets one nowhere. The New Testament was written from the minority standpoint of the slowly growing Christian Church, and is consequently concerned with preserving Christian essentials despite the powerlessness of the Christians, not with the right ordering of a Christian power. Nevertheless it contains the deci-

5. Kahle, 10ff.; J. Höffner, *Christentum und Menschenwürde. Das Anliegen der spanischen Kolonialethik im Goldenem Zeitalter* (1947).

sive element to which one must always return as the basic starting point. By his statement that to Caesar must be given what belongs to Caesar and to God what belongs to God, Jesus separates Caesar's power from God's power. He removes the *ius sacrum* from the *ius publicum* and thereby cuts to pieces the fundamental structures of Greco-Roman antiquity, and indeed of the whole pre-Christian world. By separating the *ius sacrum* from the imperial *ius publicum,* he makes room for freedom of conscience where all power ends, even that of the Roman god-emperor, who thus becomes merely a human emperor and is transformed into the beast of the Apocalypse, where he nevertheless wants to remain God and denies the inviolable domain of conscience. This pronouncement therefore sets a limit to all earthly power and proclaims the freedom of the person, which exceeds all political systems. For this limit, Jesus goes to his death, attesting the limit of power by suffering. Christianity does not begin with a revolutionary, but with a martyr.[6] The increase in freedom that mankind owes to the martyrs is infinitely greater than what revolutionaries have been able to bring.

Reinhold Schneider's fundamental theme, the relation between power and conscience, is depicted with particular force in his Las Casas novel. Along with Lucaya, Las Casas himself and Charles V appear as living representatives of conscience; all three together represent its function on different levels, orchestrating the theme over its whole range. Without a doubt its purest form is symbolized by the girl Lucaya. In the humility of her suffering and the simplicity of her belief, conscience is present unalloyed, as it were, in its pure essence. The Lucayos nation to which she belongs and which she embodies is described by the knight Bernardino as follows: "They were as defenseless and unsuspecting as if Adam's sin had not affected them."[7] To them, the islands they inhabited were the entire human world; they thought that just beyond their borders lay the world of souls, the abode of the dead. When the Spaniards arrived, they could think only that the strangers came from beyond the world of men, from the land of souls. Consequently they followed them readily, without any suspicion, ex-

6. On Mk 12:17 and the reception of this saying in the political catechesis of the primitive Church, cf. Duchrow, *Christenheit und Weltvorantwortung,* 137-80. On the whole problem, cf. the precise account by O. Cullmann, *Jesus und die Revolutionäre seiner Zeit* (1970).

7. Schneider, *Las Casas vor Karl V. Szenen aus der Konquistadorenzeit,* 81.

pecting these strangers to lead them to the souls of their ancestors. On this Bernardino says: "And today I cannot but think how clear the conscience of these human beings must have been since they looked forward so sincerely to being reunited with the dead, whereas we . . . would perhaps have to fear this reunion, because much hidden guilt would be revealed and we would not dare to look our relatives in the face."[8] Human beings in fraternal familiarity with eternal life, whose world stands open to the other world, whose sole standard is to be with what is to come – conscience therefore – encounter brutal power, force which knows no conscience and has lost its soul. They think they are coming to heaven and find themselves in hell. It seems to me that this scene in particular shows how profoundly Reinhold Schneider had understood and endured the abysses of human life and the world of experience long before his last book, *Winter in Wien.* Reality is not smoothed over here in edifying apologetics; this is not the world of Job's rationalist friends, who have a pious refrain for everything and can explain everything. We hear the cry of Job himself: People think they are going to heaven and are led into hell. Reality as it is makes light of faith and no *Deus ex machina* appears to set everything right in the end. All that remains is "the dull lament and crying" of the tortured mass of humanity,[9] the exhausted sobs of the woman who has been deceived, and the face of the Crucified. There remains the grief of this woman who has suffered for the conqueror just as she has for her oppressed and enslaved brothers. For Lucaya, the conqueror in his blindness is no less worthy of compassion than her brothers in their torment, even if he does not realize how needy his delusion has made him, how much he needs deliverance if he is to become himself again. It seems to me that in the whole novel this mysterious woman character best expresses what Schneider obviously recognized as his own function and his own destiny: it was not given to him to intervene in the field of power. All that was left to him was to speak for conscience, to endure the evil of the time by suffering, and thereby to authenticate the voice of conscience.

8. Ibid., 85.

9. "We were not afraid of the crowd under the decks, and I was just as used as my companions from previous voyages to hearing the dull wailing and crying underneath me; it affected me just as little as the noise of cattle crammed together. It didn't occur to me at all that I was hearing the voice of my guilt" (ibid., 92).

Las Casas embodies a second possible way in which conscience can become a mission. Besides the suffering conscience, he represents the prophetic conscience that shakes the power of the powerful, establishes the right of the dispossessed, and calmly persists in disturbing the complacency of those whose power endures at the expense of others' rights.[10] Las Casas had been a soldier and *encomendero* himself; even after his ordination he had been far more concerned about his income than about the Indians in his charge. Then something happened which we find more than once in the story of the saints. He suddenly realized that a particular passage in Scripture, which he happened to come across, is meant quite literally and that he must take it literally. Las Casas read Ecclesiasticus 34:25-27 and knew that it concerned him: "The bread of the needy is the life of the poor; he that defraudeth them thereof is a man of blood. He that taketh away the bread gotten by sweat is like him that killeth his neighbor. He that sheddeth blood and he that defraudeth the laborer of his hire are brothers." From that moment Las Casas became the bad conscience of those in power – hated, execrated, but no longer to be silenced. It is part of the inherent greatness of the Christian faith that it can lend conscience its voice, that it can inexorably oppose the world which believers have built for themselves and which they justify on grounds of faith, that it has room for the prophetic No, and in general that it gives birth to prophets, men who are not the voice of some particular interest but the voice of conscience against chicanery. Las Casas became at the same time a witness to the sovereignty of right: "Right needs no human attestation; it stands above man, not in him. But if men disagree, they can consult their conscience, and if they do so without hatred and passion, their conscience will help them."[11]

A third element enters in the form of the emperor Charles V: the conscience of a man to whom power is committed and who must endeavor to exercise it responsibly. The scene on a cold evening when the friar meets the tired emperor, who has only the *Imitation of Christ* lying on the table in front of him, is extremely impressive. The key words are

10. For forceful observations in this regard, see Balthasar, *Reinhold Schneider,* 177ff., 178: "The saint not as leader of the State, but as the conscience of the king: that would be the realization of the transcendent ethics which does not weigh with two scales."

11. Schneider, *Las Casas,* 153 (Las Casas is speaking to Bernardino).

conscience and the Cross. Schneider, prophetically addressing his own age here, portrays a ruler who does not desire to conquer but to reconcile, who is ready to abandon greatness, who is marked by the burden of guilt and who recognizes true greatness in responsibility for man. He represents a man in power for whom power is a painful burden and who for that reason can bring out the meaning of power.[12] This idea is sharply focused when a Mexican bishopric is conferred on Las Casas. The prophet has to assume power and thus undergo his most severe test – whether in power he will remain true to the prophetic word. Power as suffering and thereby as healed power – the first and third of these characters merge in this vision. The absolute monarch stands under the control of conscience, without which all other checks on power would be ineffectual.

Only power which comes from suffering can be salutary to power; power shows its greatness in the renunciation of power. André Malraux' account of his last conversations with de Gaulle contains a remarkable parallel to these ideas. In these dialogues, which constantly turn on de Gaulle's central theme, France and greatness, we can see how the concept of greatness was finally transformed for this remarkable ruler-figure of our century. To a question about his speech on Napoleon's jubilee, de Gaulle replied, "He left France smaller than he found it, it is true, but a nation is not defined in such terms. It was necessary for France that he should have existed. . . ."[13] Malraux comments that de Gaulle did not think of France in terms of strength. "He regarded as silly Stalin's remark that 'France has fewer divisions ready for action than the Lublin government.'" Even less did he think in terms of loss or gain of territory. When he decided on the independence of Algeria, "he decided for the soul of France, against everything else and in the first place against himself." Malraux must have been certain of his agreement when he remarked that France would find its soul only if it found it for others: "the Crusades and the great Revolution . . . much more than Napoleon." The upshot of these strangely melancholy conversations is quite clearly recognizable. The greatness the general was

12. For excellent observations on the connection between power and ability to suffer according to Luther, relevant to the present context, see Duchrow, *Christenheit und Weltverantwortung,* 547 and 552.

13. A. Malraux, *Les chênes qu'on abat.*

able to bestow upon his country consisted in leaving it smaller, in giving away an empire. It did not consist in the vain attempt to become a great power of the old kind again, but in the renunciation which he taught himself and his nation. In the end the general no longer measured himself against the conqueror Napoleon, but by the emperor in exile, in his saying that greatness is sad. Without the ambiguity which of course inevitably persists, this would surely mean that power attains greatness when it allows itself to be moved by conscience. That is Reinhold Schneider's legacy to our time. And it is the opportunity and the task of Christian faith amid the clash of powers in which we find ourselves today.

Translated by W. J. O'Hara

On Hope

Paul reminds the Christians of Ephesus of the time when they were not yet Christians. Their situation was characterized by the lack of a promise.[1] They lived in this world without hope and without God (Eph 2:12). A similar observation is found in 1 Thessalonians. Paul speaks here to the Christians of this Greek port city of a hope that looks beyond death so that they will not have to live "like those who do not have any hope" (4:13). Therefore, one can conclude from these two passages that for Paul hope defines the Christian, and inversely that the absence of hope defines the atheist. To be a Christian is to be one who hopes; it is to situate oneself on the foundation of a sure hope. According to these texts, hope is not just one virtue among others; it is the very definition of Christian existence.

Casting a glance over the horizon of modern thought, one is tempted to contradict this last statement. True enough, hope has al-

1. The text of this article returns to one of the lectures given in the framework of the jubilee of the Franciscan college of Rome, the Antonianum. The common theme of these lectures was "Francis, witness and guardian of hope." This is why I have tried to develop the theme of hope particularly in the perspective of Francis and the Franciscan tradition. It seems to me that this point of departure, which has caused me to give more emphasis to certain aspects, remains to be completed, but it is also in a position to put in concrete form certain aspects of the theme.

This article first appeared as "Über die Hoffnung," in *Internationale katholische Zeitschrift Communio* 12, no. 1 (Spring 1985), and was reprinted in *Communio* 35, no. 2 (Summer 2008).

ways been listed in the catalogue of Christian virtues, but was it not fear rather than hope that marked the average Christian? And even if there was hope, was it not much too narrow, far too restricted because it was restricted to the self alone? The question arises of whether one may purely and simply deny the hope of others. Ernst Bloch, in his *Das Prinzip Hoffnung*, has emphatically revived this long-forgotten theme by defining it as the central question of all philosophy. The world represents for him "a laboratory of possible salvation." With convincing eloquence he attempts to make it clear to us that the regeneration and reign of man would have precisely as a precondition the fact that "there is no God above, that there is not one now, and there never has been any."[2] Thus for Bloch the opposite of what we have heard in Paul is true; the atheist is the only one who hopes and, as long as the Marxist way of transforming the world was unknown, human beings lived in this world without true hope and therefore had to try to be content with an imaginary hope.

1. The Anthropological Basis: Hopes and Hope

Who, in this controversy, is the real guardian and witness of hope? This is the question. To find an answer we have to look at the matter a bit more closely. What do we really mean by the word "hope"? What is hope and what is it that those who hope are hoping for? One thing is obvious from the start: hope has to do with the future. It signifies that man expects of the future some joy, some happiness that he does not now have. Hope therefore rests on the experience of temporality according to which man never totally possesses his own being. He is himself only within the tension between the past and the future as he passes through the present. Naturally the hopes tied to this temporality can be of varying quality. A child can hope for the next holiday, a good report card with its pleasant consequences, a piece of cake, or a nice picnic. Many such hopes mark our whole life and give it color. Paul for his part would not contest that pagans have such hopes; nor will

2. Ernst Bloch, *Das Prinzip Hoffnung* (Frankfurt, 1959), 1524. See Josef Pieper, *Hoffnung und Geschichte* (Munich, 1967), 85 (*Hope and History* [San Francisco: Ignatius Press, 1994]).

Bloch deny them to Christians. But all these hopes cannot be for either of them the one hope which is our basic concern. So what is it then that is meant by this?

It will perhaps become clearer if we consider a little more precisely hope's opposite, which is fear. At first, of course, there are the thousand and one fears that weigh upon us in everyday life, from the fear of a vicious dog, to the fear of the daily annoyances that occur in our contact with others in the workplace and at home. Here again, it is not these small fears that particularly threaten man and lead him to despair. Behind them lies what we properly call fear – fear of ruining one's life, fear that life may become gloomy and difficult to the point of being unlivable.

After a confirmation, a professor once told me what he had said to a child, "You must be grateful to your parents for having given you life!" And the boy responded, "But I am not at all thankful for having to live. I would much rather not be alive!" This shocking comment from the mouth of a child of our day, far from being unique, could be taken as the definition of hopelessness. Life itself is not good; one can only take a stand against everything that is responsible for the evil of having to live. Destruction is the sole good that can be produced because being is itself evil. Here it is no longer a question of fear – there is always an element of possible hope hidden in fear – but rather a question of pure resignation, of despair, doubt about being itself. Being is not good, especially if you have not experienced it as welcome, have not had "Yes" said to you, that is, if you have not been loved. This indicates that the fear which transcends all fears is the fear of losing love altogether, fear of an existence in which the little daily disturbances fill everything, without anything large and reassuring coming along to keep the balance. Then these little fears, if they constitute everything that can be expected of the future, will pass over into the great fear – fear of an unbearable life – because hope no longer dwells in it. In this case, death, which is the end of all hopes, becomes the only hope.

Through an analysis of fear we are back again to the key word, hope. If the fear that transcends all fears is in the last resort fear of losing love, then the hope which transcends all hopes is the assurance of being showered with the gift of a great love. One could then say that simple objects become hopes by taking on the coloration of love, by more or less resembling it, each according to its uniqueness. Inversely, in fears one always finds the feeling of not being loved, a hope of love, but a trampled one. 1 John is, from the viewpoint of anthropology, perfectly logical when it says, "Perfect love casts out fear" (1 Jn 4:18).

In another sentence from the same epistle we also see the importance for the question of hope. It concerns one of the greatest expressions of the whole history of religions, "God is love" (1 Jn 4:16). A perspective opens up that allows a better understanding of the words of Paul with which we began. Up to now we have said that hope has for its ultimate goal the fulfillment of love. If therefore hope and love on the one hand, and God and love on the other, are inseparable, then it ought to be clear that God and hope go together; and that finally the one who is without hope is truly one who "lives without God in the world." But we are not far enough along to be content with such a statement. For there remains the question of knowing whether passing from love to God is not crossing the frontier in vain.

What kind of love does the hope that transcends all hopes await? This is the genuine hope which Dr. Herbert Plugge of Heidelberg, on the basis of his contacts with the terminally ill and the suicidal, calls the "fundamental hope."[3] Without any doubt man wants to be loved by others. But is there not anything further to be hoped for in the last hours of life, when death has long since carried off dear ones leaving behind a terrible loneliness? And inversely, is there nothing lacking in the great moments of life, in the great "Yes" of one who knows he is loved? We need the answer of a human love, but this response reaches farther out of itself toward the infinite, toward a world redeemed. Heinrich Schlier, following a tradition which is not only that of the philosophers, but of anyone's experience, has rightly said, "To hope indicates, properly speaking, hoping against death."[4] With incomparable clairvoyance, Plato, in the language of myth and mystical religions (and therefore in humanity's ancestral tradition), sets forth in his *Symposium* the perspective that we have tried to follow. The hope of man is at first, he says, to find for himself the beloved who complements him. But at the very moment when he finds that person, he realizes that the unity

3. Herbert Plugge, *Wohlbefinden und Missbefinden. Beiträge zu einer medizinischer Anthropologie* (Tübingen, 1962). The philosophical significance of this work and everything specifically related to our theme is explained in striking fashion by Pieper, *Hoffnung und Geschichte,* 30.

4. Heinrich Schlier, *Essais sur le Nouveau Testament* (Paris: Cerf, 1968), 165.

for which his whole being yearns is impossible. And so it is that the experience of love awakens at first "great hopes," hope in the restoration of our original nature, but at the same time it teaches us that such wholeness is indeed possible "if we retain a deep respect for the gods."[5] It could also be said that from Plato onward, man waits in the depths of his being for something like a lost paradise. And here we return again to Bloch and Karl Marx who do not speak of anything but the restoration of the utopia to which they believe they can show the way.

At the same time of course the fundamental difference between Paul and Bloch or Marx reveals itself. Hope as described by Bloch is the product of human activity. Its realization is brought to fulfillment in the human "laboratory of hope." What one cannot do oneself is very consciously excluded. One could not hope for what one cannot control; there are directives only for what we ourselves can bring about.

Doing and hoping, however, are on two entirely different levels. If we need hope, it is because what is done and feasible does not satisfy.[6] Further, by its very essence hope refers to the person. True, it aspires to something that goes far beyond the person, to a new land, a paradise. But if it aspires to this, it is because the person has need of it; it is hope only to the degree that it is hope for the person concerned and not for anyone else anywhere else. The anthropological problem of hope therefore consists in the human need for something that goes beyond all human ability. Accordingly we must certainly wonder whether it does not happen to be the impossible that we need, and whether, consequently, we are absurd beings — an aberration in the evolution of the species.

2. Faith as Hope

This is exactly the question to which the aforementioned sentences of St. Paul refer; the expectation of this "paradise" which is lacking never leaves us, but this condition becomes despair when there is neither certitude about God nor certitude of a promise made by God. It is because

5. Plato, *Symposium,* 193d. See also the entire speech of Aristophanes from 189c to 193d.

6. This is what Pieper's rigorous analysis demonstrates in *Hoffnung und Geschichte,* 25ff.

the promise did not exist (and cannot exist) without the incarnation, death, and resurrection of this God, that Paul says the "others" are without hope. It is because Jesus is this hope that being a Christian consists of living in hope. In the New Testament as with the apostolic fathers, the concepts of hope and faith are, to a certain extent, interchangeable. Thus 1 Peter speaks of rendering an account of our hope, where it is a question of becoming the interpreter of faith to the pagans (3:15). The epistle to the Hebrews calls the confession of the Christian faith a "confession of hope" (10:23). The epistle to Titus defines faith that has been received as a "blessed hope" (2:13). The epistle to the Ephesians poses as a premise of the fundamental affirmation "one Lord, one faith, one baptism, one God and Father of all," that there is "only one hope to which you are called" (4:4-6). These quotations could be multiplied,[7] as could those from the apostolic fathers. In the first letter of Clement of Rome, as in Ignatius of Antioch, or in Barnabas, "hope" can be substituted for "faith." Ignatius, for example, is "imprisoned for his name and for his hope." Christians are those "who hope in the Lord."[8]

So, where do we now stand on the subject of hope? Hope rests first of all on something missing at the heart of the human condition. We always expect more than any present moment will ever be able to give. The more we follow this inclination, the more aware we become of the limitations of our experience. The impossible becomes a necessity. But hope means also "the assurance that this longing will find a response." If this experience of a void, of a desire which carries one outside oneself, comes to move the person to despair over self and over the rationality of being, then inversely this hope can be transformed into a secret joy that transcends every experienced joy and suffering. In this way a person is enriched by the very need which causes him to conceive a happiness that he would never be able to experience without this decisive step. Hope could accordingly be described as an anticipation of what is to come. In it, the "not yet" is in a certain sense already here, and so is the dynamism that carries one beyond oneself and prevents one from ever saying, "Linger a while: you are so beautiful."[9]

7. See also, for example, 2 Cor 3:12; Gal 5:5; Eph 1:19; Col 1:23.

8. Ignatius, *To the Ephesians* 1, 2; *Epistle of Barnabas* 19, 7; cf. Clement, *Epistle to the Corinthians,* 11, 1; 22, 8; 27, 1; Ignatius, *To the Magnesians* 9, 1; *To the Ephesians* 21, 2, etc.

9. Goethe, *Faust.*

This means, on the one hand, that to hope belongs the "dynamism of the provisional," going beyond all human accomplishment. On the other hand, it means that through hope, what is "not yet" is already realized in our life. Only a certain kind of present can create the absolute confidence which is hope.[10] Such is the definition of faith given in the epistle to the Hebrews: faith is the substance *(hypostasis)* of what is hoped for, the certitude of what one does not see (11:1). In this basic biblical text both an ontology and a spirituality of hope are affirmed. It is recognized today even in Protestant exegesis that Luther and the exegetical tradition that followed him are misguided when in their search for a non-Hellenistic Christianity they transformed the word *hypostasis* by giving it a subjective meaning and translating it as "firm confidence." In reality this definition of faith in the epistle to the Hebrews is inseparably linked to two other verses of the same epistle which also use the term *hypostasis.* In the introduction (1:3), Christ is presented as the splendor of the glory of God and the image of the *hypostasis.* Two chapters further on, this christological and fundamentally trinitarian affirmation is expanded to the relation between Christ and Christians — a relation established by faith. By faith Christians have become participants in Christ. Now everything is going to depend upon maintaining their initial participation in his "hypostasis."[11] These three texts fit together perfectly: the things of this world are what pass away; the self-revealing God who speaks in Christ is what endures, the reality that lasts, the only true *hypostasis.* Believing is leaving the shadowy play of corruptible things to reach the firm ground of true reality, *hypostasis* — quite literally therefore, what stands and that on which one can stand. In other words, to believe is to have touched ground, to approach the substance of everything. With faith, hope has gotten a footing. The cry of waiting wrung from our being is not lost in the void. It finds a point of solid support to which we for our part must hold fast.

Here ontology gives way to spirituality. This will be apparent if we consider the context of the definition of faith in the epistle to the He-

10. On this point I am not in complete agreement with Pieper (see *Hoffnung und Geschichte,* 35ff.), who rejects all anticipation as contradicting hope. While there does exist a manner of anticipating which is incompatible with hope, there is also an attentive gift without which even hope is impossible. For the Christian this attentive gift is faith.

11. On the interpretation of Hebrews 11:1, cf. H. Koster, *Theologisches Wörterbuch zum Neuen Testament,* VIII, 584-587.

brews. As a matter of fact we are prepared for it in the preceding chapter (chapter 10) by a kind of subtle word play, by an accumulation of terms that all begin with the prefix "hypo-" ("under"): *hyparchein, hyparxis, hypomene, hypostellein, hypostole.*[12]

What is the point here? The author is reminding his readers that for the sake of their faith Christians have lost *ta hyparchonta,* that is, their money, their possessions, and what appears in ordinary life to be the "substance" upon which a life can be constructed. Here the Franciscan dimension of hope shows through, if I may so express myself. We shall have to come back to this. So the text now begins to play upon the words by saying that it is precisely through the loss of what ordinarily constitutes "substance," the basis of daily living, that Christians are shown that in fact they have a better *hyparxis.* This one endures; no one can take it away. The lexical meaning of *hyparxis* is "that which is there, on hand." This is what it means: We Christians have another mode of being; we are standing upon another foundation that can never be pulled out from under us – not even by death. The chapter concludes with the exhortation not to reject the full assurance in the confession of faith, which obviously implies *hypomene* – a word commonly translated "patience," in which the objective and spiritual aspects are mingled. We have a solid foundation, more solid than the goods immediately within our grasp. The author makes still clearer the essence of this attitude by evoking the opposite in a passage from Habakkuk: *hypostole,* an attitude of levity, of dissimulation, of adaptation at any price. This attitude corresponds to the baselessness and falsity of an empty life which seeks only to save its own skin and by that very fact is lost (10:32-39).

3. The Dimensions of Hope: Its Franciscan Element

a. Hope and Possession

At first glance it could seem that the statements of the epistle to the Hebrews belong to a Platonic vision of the world in which the visible world of appearances stands in opposition to invisible substance, the sole and

12. On *hypostellein, hypostole,* see the important developments of K. H. Rengstorf, *Theologisches Wörterbuch zum Neuen Testament,* VII, 598ff.

unique reality to which one must attach oneself. When we follow the progression of this thought, however, it appears that this schema has been put at the service of a dynamism of hope which could grow only from an encounter with the risen Christ (with the promise that he not only expresses, but which he, himself, is). As we have already seen, it is to this dynamism of hope that the Franciscan spirit belongs – a spirit which is freed from the absolute power of possession, from that basic defect of the need to possess which regards possessions as the true substance of existence. Where possession in itself appears as a guarantee of the future, what develops is a pseudo-hope that can only deceive man in the end. The law of possession constrains him to *hypostole,* to the game of hide and seek, of compromises by which one tries to assure oneself of the sympathy of the powers that be, by hanging on to one's "substance." The person who tries to safeguard himself by lying may save his position *(ta hyparchonta),* but he pays too high a price. He destroys himself and loses his real foundation *(hypostasis).* Hope founders in cynicism. Francis is the witness and guardian of hope because he has helped us "accept with joy" (Heb 10:34) the loss of rank, of position, of possessions, and has made visible, behind the false hopes, the true, the genuine hope – the one that no one can confiscate or destroy.

In this connection I should like to refer to the closing prayer of the *Gelasianum Vetus* evoked for the feast of the Ascension in the missal of Paul VI: "With the Church we pray that our hearts may strive toward the place where our substance already dwells – with the Father of Jesus Christ, with our God."[13] And in point of fact no other feast of the liturgical year expresses as well as the Ascension of Christ does the essence of Christian hope: with Christ our substance abides in God. It is now going to be our concern to ground our daily life in our substance, not ignoring the substance of our very selves, not leaving our life outside its substance, not letting it sink into nothingness, chance, the accidental. And how easy it is to spend one's whole life missing the point, falling into alienation, drowning in the secondary. In the end such a life will have become empty of substance and therefore empty of hope. The hope that sustains us is that our substance is already in paradise. To live like someone who hopes is to have our life enter into reality itself,

13. Cf. J. Pascher, *Die Orationen des Missale Romanum Papst Pauls VI,* vol. 3: *Temps pascal* (St. Ottilien, 1982), 117ff.

to live in and by the body of Christ. This is *hypomene,* enduring patience, just as *hypostole* is living for the moment, hiding from the truth, and thus avoiding life.

b. Hope and the Recollection of Being

In order to rediscover here from a different point of view the Franciscan dimension of our theme, I would like to demonstrate it by a passage drawn from St. Bonaventure's sermons for Advent, a treasury of the theology and spirituality of hope. The saint is commenting on that sentence of the Canticle of Canticles so important to the mystic tradition: "I sat down in the shadow of the one I have longed for" (2:3). The shadow of Christ, says Bonaventure, is grace, which for us is a cool retreat from the scorching heat of the world. "To be seated" signifies composure of the spirit, recollection, the opposite of a thought going round and round endlessly and without purpose. To enter into the domain of the One toward whom our interior expectation tends, we must stop "being open to the outside and be recollected interiorly. Let nothing prevent the taste of eternal goodness from penetrating one's being."[14] If these words sound a bit abstract, they are clarified when we consider them in conjunction with what the legends of St. Francis tell us of the origin of the Canticle of the Sun. In the midst of almost unbearable pains of illness, and in an inhospitable lodging, Francis becomes aware of the treasure that he has already received. God's voice says to him: "Live henceforth in serenity, as if you were already in my kingdom."[15] In his last years Francis had lost everything – health, possessions, his own foundation, *ta hyparchonta.* And it is precisely from this man that the most delightfully joyous words issue. With all his hopes taken away, all his disappointments, there shines forth the "fundamental hope" in its invincible grandeur. Francis had truly left the "accidental" to enter into "substance." Free of the multiplicity of hopes, he has become the great witness that man has hope, that he is a being of hope.

14. For the first Sunday of Advent, sermon no. 2 in *Opera Omnia,* IX, 29a.

15. See, for example, *Speculum perfectionis,* 100 (Fonti francescane, Assisi, 1978, no. 1799); *Legenda perugina,* 43 (ibid., no. 1591ff.). On the dating of the *Canticle of the Sun,* cf. C. Esser, *Opuscula Sancti Patris Francisci Assisiensis,* Bibl. Franc. Medii aevi XII (Grottaferrata, 1978), 47.

Still more concretely, do we not all run the risk of losing the grace of hope amid everyday vexations? The more our life is turned toward the exterior, the less the great and true hope can counterbalance the havoc caused by daily worries. Gradually these become the only reality, existence is depressing, hopes wear thin, initial optimism is exhausted, and ill humor becomes an insidious form of despair. We can remain people of hope only if our life is not contentedly grounded in the everyday but is solidly rooted in "substance." The more we recollect ourselves, the more hope becomes real and the more it illumines our daily work. Only then can we perceive the brightness of the world which otherwise withdraws farther and farther from view.

c. The Social and Cosmic Dimension of Hope

One question remains. An objection could be raised about what we have just said, that once more all this would tend toward escape into interiority and that the world *qua* accident would be condemned to hopelessness. What we should do is create living conditions such that the flight into interiority becomes unnecessary, since suffering would be eliminated and the world itself would become paradise. Obviously we cannot attempt within the framework of these reflections to explain Marxist and evolutionist theories of hope.[16] Let it suffice to counter with two questions that may to some extent put the whole matter back into the right light. First of all, as to the advent of paradise in this world, is it not more certain to begin when people are freed from the greed of possession and when their interior freedom and independence from the domination of possession have awakened in them a great goodness and serenity? Besides, where do we begin transforming the world if not with our own transformation? And what transformation could be more liberating than one that engenders a climate of joy? Here we are at the second question already. Let us begin with a statement: The hope for which Francis stands was quite a different thing

16. For the essential, cf. Pieper, *Hoffnung und Geschichte,* 37-102. Cf. also U. Hommes and J. Ratzinger, *Das Heil des Menschen: Innerweltlich — christlich* (Munich, 1975); some important indications (in spite of the unsatisfactory conclusion) in W. Post, "Hoffnung," in *Handbuch philosophischer Grundbegriffe,* ed. H. Krings et al., vol. 2 (Munich, 1973), 672-700.

from a retreat into the interior and the individualistic. It created the courage to be poor and the disposition for community life. On the one hand, it set new principles of common life in the community of brothers, and on the other hand, through the Third Order, it applied to the everyday life of his time that anticipation of the world to come already lived in common.[17]

Here again, in one of his Advent sermons, Bonaventure was able to translate into marvelous images this broad human dimension of hope. He says that the exercise of hope must resemble the flight of birds, who spread their wings and mobilize all their strength to move, to become wholly movement, to climb. So the one who hopes must, according to Bonaventure, mobilize all his forces, become motion himself with all his members in order to rise, to respond to the need of hope. Bonaventure presents in detail a sublime intertwining of interior and exterior meanings. *"The one who hopes must lift up his head,"* directing himself upwards, lifting up his eyes "for the circumspection of his thought and of his being; his heart for revealing his feelings, but also his hands through his working. To the dynamism of hope, to the comprehensive movement of man that hope wants to realize, belongs the physical and practical work without which one cannot raise oneself."[18]

Let us restate it, this time without the imagery. In the Franciscan pattern of hope, which takes up exactly the model traced by the epistle to the Hebrews, it is a question of surmounting the wish to possess. Possession as a foundation of being is surpassed by a new foundation so that man is freed of the former. It is precisely this greed for possession that shuts man out of paradise. Here is the key to the economic as well as the ecological questions which are both without hope unless a new "fundamental hope" comes to free man. This is why the way to the interior traced by the New Testament is the only way to the exterior, to free air.

Here the thematic of hope expands by internal necessity to the

17. See my article, "Eschatology and Utopia," *Communio: International Catholic Review* 5, no. 3 (Fall 1978); A. Rotretter, "Der utopische Entwurf der franziskanischen Gemeinschaft," *Wissenschaft und Weisheit* 37 (1974): 159-69; C. del Zotto, *Visione francescana della vita,* Quaderno I and II, Settimana di Spiritualità Francescana (Santuario della Verna, 1982).

18. For the first Sunday of Advent, sermon no. 16 in *Opera Omnia,* IX 40a. On the Franciscan attitude toward work, cf. C. del Zotto, *Visione francescana,* II, 187-97.

question of the relation between man and creation. Human beings are so deeply tied to creation that there cannot be any salvation for them that would not equally entail the salvation of creation. Paul has explained this connection in chapter 8 of the epistle to the Romans. The creature waits too. It is important to remember that the hope of creation does not extend, for example, to the capacity of shaking off the human yoke one day. Creation waits for man transfigured, man who has become the child of God. This man gives back to creation her freedom, her dignity, her beauty. Through him creation herself becomes divine. Heinrich Schlier makes this comment: every creature is oriented toward the expectation of this event. It is an infinite responsibility that is thus entrusted to humans — to be the accomplishment of every aspiration of earth and heaven.[19]

But for the moment creation undergoes the opposite experience. She is subjected to vanity, not that she would have wished it but because of the one who subjected her to it (Rom 8:20). That one is Adam, who delivers himself over to the thirst for possessing and for lying.[20] He reduces creation to slavery; she groans and awaits the true man who will return her to herself. She is "subjected to vanity," that is, she is herself implicated in the ontological lie of man. Instead of witnessing to the Creator, she presumes to pass for God. "One no longer meets her in her truth; she no longer appears to be what she is, that is, creation."[21] She participates in the fall of man and only the new man can be her restoration. He is the one she hopes for. It is from this source that the sermon of St. Francis to the birds takes its theological and profoundly human meaning, his whole being turned toward the creature. Here too Francis was perfectly right to take the Bible literally: "Announce the Gospel to every creature" (Mk 16:15). Creation herself awaits the new man, and when he appears she is again recognizable as a creation and thus becomes new. Only the "fundamental hope" can heal the relation between man and nature.

While I was rereading my *Catechismus Romanus* in preparation for my lecture on catechesis, I was struck by a curious statement on the subject of hope which had hitherto escaped me. The four principal parts of

19. H. Schlier, *Das Ende der Zeit* (Freiburg, 1971), 254.
20. Ibid., 255. See also his *Der Römerbrief* (Freiburg, 1977), 261.
21. Schlier, *Römerbrief*, 260.

catechesis (creed, commandments, sacraments, the Our Father) are associated here with the different dimensions of the Christian life. The Our Father is said to teach us what the Christian must hope for.[22] This association of the Our Father with our subject of hope surprised me at first. This does not square with our familiar ideas on a theology of prayer. However, it seems to me that this remark cuts deep into the matter. Just what hope is becomes clear in the prayer. We understand what prayer signifies as we come to understand the subject of hope. And as the Our Father gives us the model of all prayer, it provides also the rule that governs the link between prayer and hope. It is therefore worthwhile to follow the line of thought opened up by this remark of the *Catechismus Romanus,* which at first sight appears curious and somewhat arbitrary. First the Our Father by its very content has something to do with hope. In the second place, it responds to the daily anxieties of people and encourages them to transform these through prayer into hopes. It is a matter of each day's subsistence; it is a matter of the fear of evil which menaces us in multiple ways; a matter of peace with our neighbor, of making peace with God and protecting ourselves from the real evil, the fall into lack of faith, which is also hopelessness. Thus the question of hope goes back to hope itself, to our longing for paradise, for the Kingdom of God with which our prayer begins. But the Our Father is more than a catalogue of subjects of hope; it is hope in action. To pray the Our Father is to deliver ourselves to the dynamism of what is asked for, to that of hope itself. One who prays is one who has hope, for such a person is not yet in the position of one who has everything. Otherwise we would have no need to ask. But we know that there is someone who has the goodness and the power to give us anything, and it is to him that we stretch out our hands. The one who prays, says Josef Pieper, "keeps himself open to a gift which he does not know; and even if what he has specifically asked for is not given him, he remains certain, however, that his prayer has not been in vain."[23] This is why teachers of prayer would not be able to be merchants of false hopes in any case; they are on the contrary true teachers of hope.

Translated by Esther Tillman

22. *Catechismus Romanus,* Preface, XII.
23. Pieper, *Hoffnung und Geschichte,* 136, n. 32.

Technological Security as a Problem of Social Ethics

For a theologian to speak on questions of technological security may appear from the outset strange and unprofessional: security as a factor in technological constructions is a problem to be solved by technology, a problem for which only the engineer can offer a concrete contribution. Of course, we can reply right away: It is because security presents itself as an ethical task to technology in the first place that security appears as a technological problem for technology to solve. In this context we can address the very general question of the relationship between ethics and technology.

In the first phase of modern technology, the question hardly seemed to be asked. Capability of itself meant right, even necessity; nor was technological ability to be restrained by external concerns, by "irrelevant" moral objections. Technology justified itself as the realization of human potential and human freedom itself. To exercise the spirit freely up to the limit of one's capability and with no other limit than precisely this appeared to be the way man's ethical nature manifested itself. To fulfill oneself, to achieve one's freedom, the freedom of knowing and of acting from knowledge free of taboo and prohibition – such was the new morality. This was supposed to set one free from primitive forces and fears disguised as morals, free for the autonomy of the man

---

This article first appeared as "Technische Sicherheit als sozialethisches Problem," in *Internationale katholische Zeitschrift: Communio* 11, no. 1 (January 1982): 51-57. English publication in *Communio: International Catholic Review* 5, no. 3 (Fall 1982): 238-246.

bound simply to the logic of the scientific enlightenment. Technology and physics had, as it were, absorbed ethics. "Scientific-technological thinking is actually able to free us from that dominion which nature exercises over us insofar as it helps us to have dominion over nature. . . . Traditional morality, guided by the concepts of good and evil, has not been able to bring about this liberation. It turned pale beside the brilliant reality of this liberation, then appeared superfluous and finally detrimental and 'reactionary.' Liberation itself appeared as the new morality; the scientific-technological enlightenment was considered identical with enlightenment itself."[1]

But then, in the second half of the twentieth century, what Horkheimer and Adorno have called "the dialectic of enlightenment" became evident.[2] We began to feel the threat in technology to man and the world. The dependence of man on great technological systems had brought with it his dependence on central administrations and thus simultaneously the impotence of the individual, his incorporation into impenetrable and inescapable anonymous systems of government, against which an even louder cry of revolt then arose. Morality, which had previously become identified with technology, now turned unexpectedly against it. Surprisingly, our situation today is characterized by the fact that technology is denied any morality and moral revolt alone is seen as ethical behavior, which now either sets the limits for technology or fully damns it. To oppose fully or simply "to drop out": these present themselves as the new ways to behave. In this situation the question of the morality of technology and of technology as moral art becomes a question of survival. The total identification of old has been shattered, an identification which had actually come

1. M. Kriele, *Befreiung und politische Aufklärung* (Freiburg, 1980), 76f. Kriele works out impressively the destructive consequences of an identification of the ethical-political and the scientific-technological enlightenment over the technological: "The 'seed for regress,' however, does not lie in scientific-technological thinking in itself. It lies rather in the reversal of the primacy, that is, in scientific-technological thinking's claim to rule over morality, a claim which can intensify to a restless absorption of all morality" (76).

2. M. Horkheimer and T. Adorno, *Dialectic of Enlightenment,* trans. Edmund Jephcott, ed. Gunzelin Schmid Noerr (Palo Alto: Stanford University Press, 2007); compare critically with Kriele's work, 172-178; R. Spaemann, "Die christliche Religion und das Ende des modernen Bewußtseins," *Internationale katholische Zeitschrift: Communio* 8, no. 3 (May-June, 1979): 251-270, especially 268ff.

about from a previous total separation, insofar as morality had been eliminated from the calculation as an immaterial, unexplained remainder. The modern re-establishment of a total separation under reversed signs only demonstrates how urgent it is to seek a responsible synthesis of practical and theoretical reason, of ethical and scientific enlightenment, as opposed to the models of separation and identification – which are ultimately identical and which mutually call forth one another. The topic of "security" presents itself as a starting point because the newly erupting elemental fear of the destructive insecurity in modern technology directly accounted for the turn described above in the relationship between ethics and morality in the second half of the twentieth century.

1. The Theme of "Security" as a Question about the Structure of What Is Ethical According to the Moral Tradition

Of course, when we ask of classical ethics what it has to say concerning the theme of security, we find that the problem was not posed as the ethical problem of technological ability because it did not exist as such (although serious problems of technological security did come up in the context of such constructions as bridges and cathedrals, which nevertheless differed qualitatively from ours, as we intend to show). We must further note that the issue was developed as a fundamental problem of ethical principles, not in social ethics but in the ethics of the individual.

Let us nevertheless take a brief look at this context, for it illustrates in any case a basic framework of values which may remain important for our question. It is of interest, first of all, that the Magisterium felt compelled in the seventeenth century to condemn a teaching concerning the fundamental orientation of moral behavior that has come down in history under the title of "tutiorism." Tutiorism maintains that man, in making a decision, must guide himself according to given laws and thus must always choose that option which corresponds most surely to the law in each case. Thus it is not a conformity to reality that leads to a decision but the positivistic security of a direction derived from the law. This conception, binding man completely to an alien will – that of the law-giver – and fundamentally denying him his own capacity for ethical insights, was rejected by the Magisterium as opposed to the Christian vision of man, to the personal moral responsibility of the individual, and to the objectivity of his decision – with the reservation, to be sure, that, in the case of the validity of the administration of the sacraments (where the salvation of another comes into play) and in the case of the duty-bound protection of others' rights, tutiorism may be applied.[3] Here we have an exemplary balance of viewpoints: on the one hand, man cannot dispose of another's salvation or his rights and is thus limited in his right to take risks when the other is vitally concerned. Here "security" becomes a guiding principle. But on the other hand, security cannot become the determining principle of human morality in general because the man who no longer risks anything, only holding his ground and protecting himself, behaves contrary to the ethical claim of his nature, directed as it is to the unfolding of his gifts, to self-giving, and thereby also to self-risking; only in this way will man find himself.

We see the same basic attitude also in the ancient ethical teachings further developed by Christian tradition. For these the determining idea is that virtue, that is, ethically appropriate behavior, always represents a middle ground between excess and renunciation. This *medietas,* this living-in-the-proper-middle, is not to be confused with *mediocritas,* with a lukewarm mediocrity that remains simply beneath the demands placed upon man. The middle can very well be a maximum, a peak, but exactly such a peak as will be found to be that center of gravity capable of bearing human existence between two abysses. Thus virtue stands, on the one hand, opposed to *hybris,* immoderation, in which man misses himself: misrepresenting the truth about himself and the truth about reality, he tries to be a god, and failing to respect his own limits and those of others, he becomes the destroyer of being rather than its shepherd.[4] On the other hand, the morality of the Desert Fathers emphasized that the greatest temptation for the monk was *acedia,* discouragement, which trusts itself with nothing and thus leads to inertia, to a deadening of the heart, a renunciation that parades as virtue, confusing itself with humility, but which is in

3. Compare P. Hadrossck, "Tutiorismus," *Lexikon für Theologie und Kirche* 10 (1966): 415ff.

4. Compare J. Pieper, *Auskunft über die Tugenden* (Zurich, 1970).

truth a renunciation of existing, a renunciation of morality, and so the real denial of God and man.[5]

Antiquity, in comparison, emphasized as the appropriate attitude of man *sophrosyne,* the reasonableness which recognizes man's limit, a reasonableness which is objectivity and rationality; rationality, however, with a sense for ethical responsibility. It seems important that in both the ancient and Christian moral systems the fundamental cardinal virtue, the essential cornerstone of ethics, is *prudentia* ("good sense"), that is, the objectivity which of course is not to be understood in the sense of a functional neutrality abstracted from what is human, but as the eye for what befits man and for what is the truth of things. In the Christian moral system, in which *caritas* becomes the real heart of what is ethical, the cardinal virtues (as opposed to the new order of the theological virtues) still remain the fundamental human basis, and in this sense human reasonableness, the human limit recognized by *prudentia,* remains the cornerstone of what is ethical.[6]

2. The New Formulation of the Question in Relationship to Man and Machine

With the appearance of technological systems, human work has reached new dimensions that necessarily entail a new dimension in the formulation of ethical, and particularly social-ethical, questions. From the viewpoint of ethics, what can we identify as the new and essential element of the machine and of the technological systems which the age of natural science has produced? I believe we can single out in a rough sketch three elements.

First, man has put into the machine his own spirit, so to speak, indeed a whole system of spiritual processes, so that it functions independently in the previously created chain of systems and is not in need of ever-new decisions. Indeed, once the system is operating, it excludes them. In this transferral of one's own spirit into the apparatus, a previ-

5. Compare G. Holzherr, *Die Benediktsregel: Eine Anleitung zu christlichem Leben* (Einsiedeln, 1980), 105ff., 206ff.

6. Compare J. Pieper, *Das Viergespann* (Munich, 1964), 13-64; also by Pieper, *Buchstabierübungen* (Munich, 1980), 39-65, 109-130.

ously established form of behavior becomes fixed or is multiplied with only a predetermined and limited number of variants included. Capacity for the ever-new ethical decision and its restraining function in the face of varying circumstances is not included. This means that, in the machine, tutiorism is in a certain sense introduced, for the machine does not offer a free, independent decision but rather the reproduction of a system of human insights concerning the functioning of natural laws.

Secondly, characteristic of the technological systems that result from the interaction of mechanical processes is the centralization of human achievements. On the one hand, these systems free the individual from the burden of ever having to master the whole set of tasks of a human life, and thus make specialization possible as freedom, also in the form of free time. On the other hand, these systems create a general dependence on centralized achievements, both for the individual, who is no longer responsible for himself, and for the society as a whole. It is well-known that with the individual's loss of power and his dependence upon vast systems, totally new forms of constraint and threats to the individual also appear, which must be balanced by new forms of responsibility and assurances of freedom and life.

Thirdly, with the greater control of nature and man through systems of technology there goes hand in hand a deeper intrusion into the inner structure of the universe and the energies shaping it and thereby a reaching out into the dimension of time, into the world in which future generations will live. Along with the increase of man's power, this reaching out also entails modes of correspondingly increased responsibility for the world entrusted to man and for the rights of others, especially those of coming generations. At the same time, it would certainly be an exaggeration to try to solve today the energy problems of coming generations and to carry out their task for them. That would be a denial of the human spirit's ever-new ability to discover. On the other hand, however, the preservation of the rights of the as-yet-unborn must also be a concern of every present generation.

To these three characteristics of machines and systems of machines as seen from the viewpoint of ethics there must correspond three modes of security.

First, human responsibility demands not only that man set up in the machine or systems of machines the ability to function, a *ratio technica,* but also that he structure into the systems of machines a responsibility for men, man's ethical sense. This means that those restraining mechanisms that would guarantee human responsibility for individual cases must be incorporated into the machine's functioning. Expressed differently, the *ratio technica* must incorporate into itself a *ratio ethica* so that we would speak of something as truly functioning only when a fully responsible functioning was assured. We must look for that reasonable balance of risk and security which fundamentally reflects the nature of human activity.

Secondly, the demands on the ethical dimension of the functional *ratio* set up in a system must grow proportionally with the dependence generated by the whole system and the danger entailed for a large group of people.

Thirdly, this incorporation of the *ratio ethica* into the *ratio technica* must correspond also to the degree of the intrusion into the fabric of the universe and into the future of life. This intrusion may never be of such a kind that it would eliminate the very foundation of life for an extended period of time. Here it is again valid that between tutiorism and *hybris* the limit of *prudentia* must govern that ethical and humanly determined objectivity which finds the correct middle, and thus the true height of human existence.

3. Security and Freedom as the Starting Point for Technological Activity

When security appears today as a principle opposed in a certain respect to technological advancement and as a restriction of technology which technology itself should exercise, it is worthwhile to consider that the origin of technology lay essentially in man's desire for security. Contrary to the notions of urban civilizations' pastoral poetry and of the technologically overcrowded regions' ecological romanticism, primitive man did not experience nature as a protective, peaceful homeland, as something virginal and original. For him the experience of nature was rather the experience of the unfamiliar and threatening, of uncontrollable danger, in which unknown forces were at work and against which he tried to protect himself in various ways. The whole realm of magic rituals attempted to meet these dangerous powers even if the religious phenomenon as a whole could certainly not be reduced to the dictum *timor fecit deos* (fear created the gods).

Technology thus appears as the reasonable way to protect man from the dangerous power of nature and to transform nature from a threat to a peaceful home for human existence. Technology does not meet the unknown with irrational conjuring, but rather recognizes the rationality of nature and joins it with the rationality of man. Thus, technology appears as the liberation of man from irrational fear, a fear which technology renders unfounded through a rationally grounded security. Accordingly, one can say that technology originally arose as the means for assuring man's security, that it wanted to be and should be liberation as the guarantee of security: man need no longer fear the cosmos because he knows it, and, in knowing it, he understands how to control it.

Technology was thus at first the banishing of fear, until the unexpected change came. What had triumphed over man's primitive fears now let loose a new danger of its own – the danger of the unbridled power of the human spirit that is not ethically formed. The work of man which should protect him now becomes the real danger to both man and world. In a remarkable paradox, the danger of the domesticated powers of nature is breaking through again on a different plane. Nature, gripped in its very core by man, now shows its final indomitability. It slips out of the hand of the magician's apprentice, who is unable to find the saving word of ethics that could bring to a halt his own work, once his actions and their unrelenting advance have been set in motion. Both the human intrusion into nature and nature's own power, a power that was elicited and set free in this intrusion, produce through their interaction a new kind of danger, one that extends far beyond the archaic dangers of old and can even make those seem idyllic in hindsight, regardless of how little idyllic they were for the man actually delivered up to those forces.

If it is correct that the essential starting point of technology lay in the acquisition of freedom by assuring security, then the essential demand and guiding principle of every technological development must be that greater insecurity and less freedom not arise from the increase of dependences. Technological developments must recognize that technological activity as such is not liberating – and thus ethical – behavior, as it seemed in the beginning. Rather, technological activity must be guided by ethical principles in order to satisfy its own origins, which lay in an ethical ideal.

4. The Inner Unity of the Ethical Guidelines for Individual and Society

This necessary dialectic of technological development can, of course, only be met if man grasps in general the dialectic of the Enlightenment and of progress – that is, if he does not misunderstand progress as the self-intensifying, limitless drive to satisfy all demands, or misunderstand the history of freedom as the continual increase of the freedom to move about. He must realize that the intensification of his external control over matter, with its assurance of greater material security and freedom, need not change into its opposite, into a fundamental threat to man's existence and to the world. He must realize that this change can only be avoided on the condition that he does not consider material security a goal in itself, but rather as the possibility for greater inner freedom and renunciation, which alone can lead him to himself. In other words: If the dialectic of progress is not to become a dialectical shift from liberation to destruction, then it must be lived as a dialectic of change from the external to the internal, from the freedom to move about to an interior freedom. This means that the question of security, which has changed with the rise of technological systems from a question of individual ethics to one of social ethics, still leads back to a common, responsible individual-ethical core without which the questions of social ethics cannot be resolved. Nothing can replace the individual moral conscience and personal decision. Here also is present a dialectic or reciprocity which we have obscured all too often with a kind of technological collectivism that would view man as really only a system within systems. We can control the problem of progress only when, in the correct *prudentia* and *sophrosyne,* the tension between risk and responsibility, between the expansion of life and the acceptance of a limit and of the possibility of renunciation, becomes the fundamental rule of our activity.

We could also say: One can never take without giving. To develop technological possibilities in proper harmony with the development of a security that always corresponds to these new possibilities costs something and calls for a restriction of the pure will to rule and to use. The control of progress and the corresponding problem of security involve more than merely a balancing of costs and benefits, however. It involves bringing the ethical content of the human dominion over the earth to bear on the theoretical and practical business of ruling. Man's progress lies not in having more, but in being more; progress that leads only to having more is not progress at all. Progress should never be understood simply in the sense of a material "more," nor in the sense of ethical independence. It must be understood in the sense of greater service among men, of deeper communication, and of liberation for what is real, which is essentially liberation for renunciation and liberation from purely material demands. To be set free from morality is not freedom, but rather the unlocking of the forces of destruction. The true security and freedom of man consists in the rule of morality *(ethos)*. This inner security of man teaches him also the paths to the right means of external security and gives him, within the tension between security and openness, the ability to judge the new claims upon his life.

Translated by Peter Verhalen, O.Cist.

Freedom and Liberation: The Anthropological Vision of the Instruction Libertatis conscientia

Public discussion about the new *Instruction on Christian Freedom and Liberation* (1986) has hitherto been limited almost exclusively to its fifth chapter, which, on the basis of the principles of Catholic social teaching, drafts an outline for a Christian praxis of liberation in the political and social realms. This was to be expected, since the alternative to the Marxist-inspired liberation praxis rejected by the Magisterium had not yet become very clear. It is also quite normal insofar as it is easier to discuss forms of political praxis in newspaper commentaries than to present fundamental philosophical and theological questions. But this non-consideration of the anthropological foundation certainly has deeper grounds. They come to light, for example, in the critically intended remark of a journalist to the effect that the Congregation has decided to treat the problem of freedom not in a historical, but in an ethical perspective. It is obvious that "ethical" is tacitly equated here with "individualistic" and even with "idealistic": in an "ethical" treatment, there seems to be a reduction of the problem to an appeal to the good will of the individual and to theological speculations. The latter are considered "idealistic," i.e., unrealistic; they can be ignored because they have no concrete consequences. Ethical appeals are likewise re-

---

This article first appeared as "Freiheit und Befreiung. Die anthropologische Vision der Instruktion 'Libertatis conscientia,'" in *Internationale katholische Zeitschrift Communio* 14, no. 1 (Spring 1987). The paper was presented 19 July 1986 on the occasion of the conferral upon Cardinal Ratzinger of an honorary doctorate by the Pontifical and State Faculty of Theology of Lima, Peru.

garded as powerless; they seem to be without social or political importance. Behind such a conception there lies hidden the conviction that man's doings are ultimately determined, not by his moral freedom, but by natural economic and social laws, which are also abbreviated as the laws of "history." Those who think this way usually do not want to abolish the ethical altogether. But it remains limited to the realm of the "subjective," whose place in reality cannot be established precisely: it may be useful and desirable for one's private life, but it has nothing to say to public life.

1. The Question about the Fundamental Conception of Freedom

a. Ethos and History

The "historical," as a kind of magic formula, is here opposed to the "ethical," conceived in the way just described. Only those who think historically get to the bottom of human affairs, for all reality is "history" in its essence. Yet, it often remains rather unclear what one really means by "history." Evolutionary ideas, Hegelian influences, Marxist thought, and observations in the human sciences have blended together here into a conceptual structure that is not easily defined. The whole of history appears as a process of progressive liberations whose mechanism we are gradually able to explain and which we are thus able to steer ourselves. A fascinating promise opens up here: man himself can become the engineer of his history. He need no longer wager on the always unsure and fragile character of his good will and moral decisions. He now sees into the inner texture of the process of freedom and can create the conditions in which the will is good of itself, just as we have hitherto lived in conditions in which it is bad of itself. By steering history ourselves, we can make ethical endeavors superfluous. The objection that the Instruction has chosen an "ethical" instead of a "historical" perspective thus means that it has withdrawn from the realm of history-transforming action into the realm of theological dreams and more or less ineffectual appeals to ethical behavior.

But precisely the opposite is correct: both the current Instruction and the prior *Instruction on Certain Aspects of the "Theology of Liberation"*

(1984) have demythologized the myth of the process of freedom and posed the question anew in a rational context. It is only in this way that they were able to arrive at better practical suggestions, which presuppose this new discussion of the foundational questions. Thus, it is nevertheless a good sign that this practical chapter is being read with such interest. It was not so long ago that Catholic social teaching was spoken of in disparaging terms as an ideology of the middle class and as mere "reformism." It was asserted that the only alternatives are capitalism and revolution, and that only revolution promises a new man and a new society, because it alone corresponds to the laws of progressive history. How the new man is to come about and how the new society is to work no longer needs to be figured out, because the laws of history themselves will do their part. Today, after so many abortive attempts, faith in the miracle of the new society emerging of itself from the dialectical impulse of revolution is gradually being extinguished. It is slowly becoming clear that we need alternatives, rational steps, in which we do what is possible rather than conjure up the impossible with a nebulous philosophy. It is becoming clear that "natural laws" of freedom are a self-contradiction. A freedom brought about by historical necessities, and in that respect imposed on man from without, is no freedom. Conversely, a definitively stable, irreversible social order can never exist within history because man remains free and thus retains his freedom to change the good into the negative. Were this freedom to be taken from him by some society, this society would be an absolute tyranny and thus not a well-ordered society at all.[1]

The myth of a necessary and at the same time steerable development of all history toward freedom is thus gradually beginning to dissolve. It is becoming clear that its perspective is not a "historical" perspective at all, for real history refutes it continually. It is only through strict disregard of real history that this myth can be further transmitted. In this respect, it is precisely the "ethical" perspective that is the truly historical and realistic perspective, one that takes our concrete experiences into account. Yet the question remains: how does the Christian alternative look upon closer inspection? In broad strokes, the fifth chapter of the Instruction has convincingly indicated that such practi-

1. See, for example, Günter Rohrmoser, *Zeitzeichen. Bilanz einer Ära* (Stuttgart: Seewald, 1977), on the currents addressed here.

cal alternatives do exist. But these practical alternatives would be mere faint-hearted pragmatism if they did not also rest on a vision of man and his history that is more than theological speculation and an appeal to the good will of the individual. The practical alternatives have hitherto been insufficiently formulated and have in many cases remained without political reverberation because Christians have no confidence in their own vision of reality. They hold fast to the faith in their private devotion, but they do not dare to presume that it has something to say to mankind as such or that it contains a vision of man's future and his history. From original sin to redemption, the whole traditional structure seems too irrational and unreal for them to dare to bring it into public discussion. Thus, it is not only the non-Christian readers who ignore the first four chapters of the Instruction as unimportant, but above all the Christians. They hold the opinion that theology is merely an internal affair. A religious authority can scarcely help propounding such a theological foundation, but it can hardly be of public and historical interest. Because Christians are so weak in faith, the search for new myths will continue. A vision without praxis is insufficient; but, conversely, a praxis that did not rest on a coherent view of man and his history would be groundless – an external system of rules that cannot do justice to the magnitude of the question. For this reason, the fifth chapter of the Instruction and the two Instructions together form an indissoluble unity that one only understands if one reads and considers them as a coherent whole. It is a question of learning to understand and live Christianity in its totality as an alternative to the liberation mythologies of the present.

b. Anarchy and Obligation

If one reads the document in this way, one will quickly recognize that it is much more than an appeal to the good will of the individual garnished with theological speculations. Behind the falsely formulated and falsely conceived opposition of ethical and historical perspectives there lie hidden two antithetical conceptions of history and freedom between which we have to choose. The two documents clarify the alternatives before which mankind stands today and ground an option that one must understand if one does not wish to miss what is essential to the text. I shall attempt to make these alternatives clear from some of their fundamental elements.

What does the average man of today expect when he cries out for freedom and liberation? Approximately what Marx gave as a vision of full freedom: ". . . hunting in the morning, fishing in the afternoon . . . and criticizing as suits my pleasure after dinner. . . ."[2] By "freedom" one generally understands today the possibility of doing everything one wants and of doing only what one would like. Thus understood, freedom is arbitrariness. The standard image by which liberation ideologies generally measure themselves today is anarchy. According to this vision, freedom would be complete if there were no longer any rule or any obligation to other persons or things, but only the unlimited arbitrariness of each individual who has everything he wants at his disposal and who can do everything he likes. In this view, liberation consists in throwing off all obligations. Every obligation appears as a fetter that restricts freedom; every obligation eliminated means progress in freedom. It is clear that in such a view, family, Church, morals, and God must appear as antitheses to freedom. God obliges man; morals are a basic form in which the obligation to him is expressed. Church and family are figures in which this obligation assumes a concrete social form.

Even the state, declared to be the "rule of men over men," becomes an opponent of freedom. The relation to the use of force here is necessarily changed. Hitherto, the use of force by the state, which stands in the service of law and opposes law-breaking caprice on behalf of the common good, appeared to be positive, precisely because it was a legal safeguard against caprice and a protection of the individual against the destruction of the community. Now things suddenly seem reversed: law appears as a means of maintaining obligations and thus unfreedom. "Law and order" are becoming negative concepts. The use of force in the service of law is thus a power of oppression, whereas the use of force against the legal order of the state is a struggle for liberation and freedom, and thus positive. The same holds in relation to morals. It is the breaking away from morals that now becomes truly "moral." Only *one* rule holds in the new moralism of the countermorality: everything that serves the destruction of obligations and

2. *Marx-Engels-Werke* (East Berlin: Dietz Verlag, 1967 (1974), vol. 3, 33; cf. Konrad Löw, *Warum fasziniert der Kommunismus?* (Cologne, 1980), 64f.

thus the struggle for freedom is good; everything that preserves obligations is bad. Behind all this there ultimately stands a thoroughly "theological" program. God is no longer recognized as a reality standing over against man; rather, man himself would like to become such as he imagines a deity would be if one existed: boundlessly free and unrestricted by any limit. He wishes to become "like God." Jesus may retain his place in this connection as a symbolic revolutionary figure; but now as then, Jesus is replaced by Barabbas, who also bore the name "Jesus."[3]

Not every detail in this vision is false. A pure error, without any admixture of truth, could never remain in force among men very long. There are unjust laws, and there is evil governmental rule, which calls for resistance. Officially promulgated law can be unjust, and the use of force, which serves the law, can thus become an unjust use of force. Furthermore, if correctly understood, "becoming like God" is essential to man, who is created in God's image. Hence, although truths are contained both in the basic point of departure and in the particulars, the vision as a whole is a distortion of truth, and thus also a distortion of freedom. A praxis of liberation whose secret measure is anarchy is in reality a praxis of enslavement, because anarchy is opposed to the truth of man and thus also to his freedom. The more one approaches anarchy, the less freedom there is. To a concept of freedom whose basic measure is anarchy and whose way is that of systematic elimination of obligations, the Instruction opposes a vision according to which ordered obligations are the true safeguard of freedom and the way of liberation. One can denounce the family as slavery, as is still done in the liberalistic and Marxist model, and thereby obtain easy results. But as a counter-check, one can study sufficiently well in today's society what kind of freedom results from this, first for the children, and then for the woman and the man. In reality, the family is the first cell of freedom. As long as it survives, a minimal sphere of freedom is still secured. For this reason, dictatorships will always aim at breaking up families in order to eliminate this sphere of freedom which is withdrawn from their control.

The liturgical community, as well as the larger communion of the

3. Mt 27:16, according to the reading of the Codex Koridethianus as well as the Syrian and Armenian readings. We find the same tradition with Origen. On the question raised by this, cf. Martin Hengel, *War Jesus Revolutionär?* (Stuttgart: Calwer Verlag, 1970); Eng., *Was Jesus a Revolutionist?* (Philadelphia: Fortress Press, 1971); Oscar Cullmann, *Jesus und die Revolutionäre seiner Zeit* (Tübingen: J. C. B. Mohr, 1970).

Church standing behind it, is a sphere of freedom. Where the state is forced by the inner strength of these spheres somehow to respect them in their proper being, they form protective zones of freedom, which serve the individual as well as the whole. Other communities prior to the state can also form such spheres of freedom, and even the state itself, when it sees its limits and constructs a genuine system of law from the moral forces prior to it, may become a safeguard against the caprice of the individual and thus a means of preserving freedom for all. The right coordination of obligations renders freedom possible. Freedom rests on a just order of obligations appropriate to man. Anarchy, the rule of caprice, is not appropriate to man because he is not ordered to isolation, but to relationship. He cannot arbitrarily call for the other when he happens to appear useful. He cannot arbitrarily let him go when he does not like him, precisely because this other is a self and not just a means for anyone. But he would have to be just that if the philosophy of anarchic freedom were to work. This philosophy is constructed from the standpoint of the ego and presupposes the slave status of all others. A correct vision of man, however, must proceed from a relationship in which each one remains a free person and is joined to the other precisely as such. It must be a doctrine of relationship and seek a type of relationship that is not that of a means-to-end relation but of the self-giving of persons.

c. Practical Consequences

It is not difficult to recognize the practical and political implications of such a vision of man. If this is the way things are, then the rupturing of relationships and the destruction of the ability to commit oneself are in no way a praxis of liberation but, on the contrary, a means of establishing tyranny. In fact, the dissolution of natural obligations, dependency on large anonymous systems, and the connected anonymization of individuals in relationless metropolitan mass societies are proving themselves more and more to be the presupposition of total dictatorship and of totalitarian equalization. In an exactly opposite way, therefore, a true praxis of liberation must consist in education in the ability to commit oneself and in the building up of the basic relationships appropriate to man. It likewise holds that it is not the struggle *against* institutions but the effort to create *just* institutions that renders freedom possible. Finally, the struggle against law and order is not a means to make men free. Rather, precisely the opposite is the case: the struggle for a system of law, for a moral system of law, is a struggle against lawlessness and injustice. Only a dependable and implementable justice guarantees freedom: freedom only takes shape where one succeeds in bringing justice – equal justice for all under the law – to bear against the caprice of individuals or of groups.

It is only against this background that one can correctly understand the concrete options that are expressed in the fifth chapter of the Instruction. It emphasizes the family as an original sphere of freedom because in it the basic forms of relationship grow, which are the relationships of freedom – the relationships on which the human person rests. The text emphasizes education as the core of every praxis of liberation. The less a man is able to do and the less he knows, the less discriminating he is and the more dependent. In order for dependency to be replaced by meaningful relationships between persons, man must learn that he needs education and training, i.e., ability. Yet, it is not only ability that he needs, but also discernment concerning that which is really at issue in human life. Mere ability with simultaneous atrophy of conscience makes men prey to seduction and can degrade them into the ideal instruments of dictatorship. It is the formation of conscience that first gives the individual his human center. Ability then creates a realm of independence and of rights from which a social life in freedom can arise. These two aspects of pedagogy as education in the ability to live a human life and training in professional ability have, beyond their individual forms, a social form which is addressed in the Instruction under the headings of culture and work. Idleness is not freedom, and even less does idleness lead to liberation. Rather, it is the form of work and cooperation appropriate to man that leads to freedom. In order for work to satisfy man and to be an instrument of freedom, it must be integrated into culture, in which the answer to man's deepest questions, the exchange of ideas, and community in authentic humanity become possible.[4]

4. Rocco Buttiglione's *L'uomo e il lavoro. Riflessioni sull'enciclica "Laborem exercens"* (Forli: CSEO Biblioteca, 1982) is important for the philosophical background of the fifth chapter of the Instruction as well as for the new reflection on the anthropological ground of Catholic social teaching in general.

From the logic of this vision there result both the right and the duty to resist the corruption of institutions and the abuse of rights. But this kind of resistance is ordered to a rational context. It is thus bound to rules and must be justified by concrete, reasonable goals. It is therefore something entirely different from that ideology of force that expects a new stage of history from revolution as such, for such an ideology does not believe it has to give an account of the realizability of this new stage of history. Whoever thinks that only petty casuistic distinctions are at issue here, distinctions which should carry no weight in the great struggle against tyranny, mistakes the gaping abyss between the two basic visions of freedom and human dignity by which differing kinds of praxis are directed. For that reason, it is very important not only to set up a few practical rules but also to keep in view the inner connection between a praxis and its theory.

At this point, I should like for the moment to break off this course of reflection, although we are in no way at the end. For the anarchical and historico-ideological conception of freedom, which we first presented, definitely has its theological depths; indeed, it ultimately lives from these depths. Speaking with Feuerbach, we would say that it is a question of retrieving the "projection" of God that man has released from himself and of actualizing the divinity in man, thus allowing man to become as free as the God he had imagined. The Christian position, which we then began to present, opposes this claim. It says that man is a relational being; he deceives himself with an anarchic idea of freedom. He must recognize his poverty of relationships, build up the right relationships, and transform dependence into common freedom: it was in these terms that we circumscribed the logic of this thought. This is in fact the proven truth of man. But where is God in all this? Has he become superfluous in the Christian vision of man, of all places? The temptation to omit God and thus to water down the Christian into the merely Western does, of course, exist. But one cannot do justice to the greatness of man in this way. The question about God cannot be omitted when it is a question of man. We shall come closer to an answer if, for the time being, we interrupt our previous course of thought and turn to the question of how the Instruction interprets the biblical witness on freedom, its history, and its actualization.

2. The Contribution of the Bible

a. Exodus and Sinai

The type of liberation theology proper to the "anarchic model" but rejected by the Magisterium has created both a political and a generally human interest in the Bible again by carrying out a "reversal of symbols." In even more general terms, one could call it an inversion of the relation between the Old and the New Testaments.[5] Christians had interpreted the Exodus of Israel from Egypt as a symbol *(typos)* of baptism and seen in baptism a radicalized and universalized Exodus. The lines of history ran from Moses to Christ. But to the theologians of today the road from the Exodus to baptism seems to be a loss of reality, a retreat from the political-real into the mystical-unreal and the merely individual. In order to attach a meaning again to baptism or to being Christian, the lines of history must now be reversed: baptism is to be understood in terms of the Exodus, not the Exodus in terms of baptism. Baptism is an introduction to the Exodus, i.e., a symbol of an act of political liberation to which the chosen "people," i.e., the oppressed of all lands, are called. Baptism becomes a symbol of the Exodus and the Exodus a symbol of political and revolutionary action in general. Jesus is interpreted backwards with reference to Moses. Moses, however, is interpreted forwards with reference to Marx. And this line of interpretation now becomes decisive for the reading of the Bible in general, whether it be a question of the Eucharist, the kingdom of God, the Resurrection, or even the figure of Jesus. The enactment of symbols, i.e., the celebration of the sacraments, is logically included in this political dynamics. In this way, the Bible and the sacraments are becoming topical again, even if their original meaning is hardly still interesting: they illustrate and strengthen a historical vision and a political option with the power of symbolic events. The objection that one thereby quite clearly falsifies the Bible frequently remains ineffective, especially because a faithful reading of the text seems to lead one astray into a no-man's-land of edification whose relation to the experienced reality of our lives remains obscure. Thus, in the end, one prefers an obviously false relation between the

5. See here the Instruction *Libertatis nuntius,* X, 14.

Bible and reality to an understanding of the Bible that appears entirely unreal.[6]

How, then, does the Instruction see the biblical witness? It is clear that it cannot agree with the inversion of symbols in which the main lines of the biblical witness are reversed. It travels the opposite road and attempts to understand the inner logic of these lines and the image of God, the world, and man contained therein. In doing so, of course, the text must limit itself to indications that call for further development in theological work. Here, I should simply like to attempt to clarify somewhat the view of the Exodus event. Where does the Exodus lead? What is its goal? Is it merely an autonomous state for Israel, so that it may finally be a people like all other peoples, with its own government and its own boundaries? And if so, what kind of freedom does this state offer? If an autonomous state were automatically an internally free state also, then the liberation problem would have already been settled for Latin America after the dissolution of the Spanish and Portuguese colonial governments. But matters are obviously not so simple. At what freedom, then, did the Exodus liberation aim?

In order to answer this question, it is important to observe that in his conversation with Pharaoh, Moses in no way gives the conquest of a land for Israel as the goal of the departure, but rather the search for a sacrificial site in order to worship God in the way willed by him.[7] Before and above all else, the goal of the Exodus is Sinai, i.e., the covenant with God from which the Israelite law proceeds. The goal is the discovery of a system of law that provides justice and thus builds up the right relationships of men with one another and with all creation. But these relationships, which are justice and thus freedom for man, depend on the "covenant." They *are* the covenant, i.e., they cannot be conceived and formed by man alone; they depend on the fundamental relationship that orders all other relationships: the relationship with God. Thus, one can definitely say that the goal of the Exodus was freedom. But one must add that the figure of freedom is the covenant and that the form in which freedom is realized is the right relation of men to

6. Instructive in this respect is Kuno Füssel, "Materialistische Lektüre der Bibel," in *Theologische Berichte XIII. Methoden der Evangelienexegese,* Josef Pfammater and Franz Furger (Einsiedeln: Benziger, 1985), 123-163.

7. Thus, Ex 5:3; cf. 5:17, 8:21-24, 9:13, et passim. The close connection between land and Torah becomes clear in Josh 1:7ff., 23:6, et passim.

one another described in the Law of the covenant, and this relation is derived from the right relation to God. One could also say that it was the goal of the Exodus to make Israel into a people from out of a gathering of tribes, and to give it as a people its freedom and its own dignity as well as its own mission in the world. But once again, one must also consider that an assemblage of men becomes a "people" through a common system of law, and that man does not live justly when he remains in an unjust relation vis-à-vis God.

From this perspective, one can definitely understand that the "land" is numbered among the goals of the Exodus. For it doubtless belongs to the freedom of a people to possess a land of its own. But at the same time, it becomes clear that in a certain respect Sinai remains superior to the land. For if Israel loses Sinai in its land, i.e., if it destroys the law and the covenant and dissolves the order of freedom through the disorder of caprice, then it has returned to its pre-Exodus condition; it then lives in its own land and yet is still in Egypt, because it destroys its freedom from within. The Exile merely makes visible in an external, political way the prior inner loss of freedom through the loss of justice. One must thus say that what is truly liberating in the Exodus is the institution of the covenant between God and man, which is concretized in the Torah, i.e., in the orders of justice that are the form of freedom. Accordingly, the Exodus is not made possible by the particular boldness or industry of Moses, but by a religious event, the paschal sacrifice, which anticipates an essential ingredient of the Torah. In this there is expressed a primordial knowledge of humanity, a truth encountered ever again in the history of religion: that freedom and the formation of community are ultimately not to be obtained through the use of force or through mere industry, but through a love that becomes sacrificial and that first binds men together in their depths because it lets them touch the dimension of the divine. Thus, at the core of the Old Testament liberation event, there is incipiently present that which later emerges openly in the figure of Jesus Christ and from him becomes the means to a new history of freedom.

b. The Universalization of the Exodus Through Christ, and Its Consequences

I should like to refrain from developing this theme in detail here, however necessary it may be to make these connections accessible to modern consciousness again. Let us content ourselves with looking at the consequence that the life, death, and resurrection of Jesus Christ had for mankind's history of freedom. The historically most conspicuous consequence consists in that the "covenant," which had previously been limited to Israel, is now extended in a renewed form to the whole of humanity. In its transformation through the figure of Jesus Christ, Sinai is imparted to all peoples, who now enter into Israel's history of liberation and become heirs of this history. If Sinai, the Torah, the covenant, and the Exodus are essentially the same, then we can say that the Exodus, which had previously been limited to Israel and, moreover, had always remained incomplete, now becomes an element of all history. This history thereby crosses the threshold of a fundamental liberation and becomes the history of freedom.

This process of universalizing the liberating forces of the Exodus/ Sinai includes, however, the need for the fundamental order of right relations on which freedom rests to emerge from Israel's national system of laws and, as an offer made to all peoples, to be no longer identified with any state system of laws. The religious order of the covenant can enter into the most diverse of state orders, but it coincides with none of them. A new people is taking shape that has a place among all peoples; it does not abolish them, but forms a force for unification and for liberation in them all. Let us say this with terms that are more familiar to us: the universalization of the covenant has as a consequence the fact that in the future the religious and civil communities, Church and state, are no longer identical, but clearly distinguished from each other.

This distinction of the two levels of human society, which represents the most conspicuous form of the Christian turn of events, is criticized by many. They say that things should not have gone this way, for this means the spiritualization of religion. It withdraws itself from the political into the interior. It no longer attains the political realm. One must restore – so they say – the full Old Testament Exodus dimension to Christian liberation. In doing so, they again take up an objection that Celsus, the great opponent of Christianity, had already formulated in the third century. He had ridiculed the Christian's claim to redemption and said: what has your Christ already accomplished? Nothing at all! For everything in the world is just as it always was. If he had wanted to bring about a true liberation, he would have had to found a state, he would have had to effect a political freedom. This objection was extremely serious during a time in which the Roman Empire — governed by ever more despotic emperors — was sensibly experienced as a power of oppression. It was Origen above all who formulated the Christian response to this reproach. He asks: what would really have happened if Christ had founded a state? Either this state would have to accept its boundaries, and then it would benefit only a few; or it would have to attempt to expand, and then it would be obliged to have recourse to the use of force and would soon resemble all other states. On the other hand, its boundaries could also be threatened by envious neighbors, and then it would once again be reduced to the use of force. A state would be a solution only for a few, and an extremely questionable solution at that. No, the Redeemer had to do something quite different. He had to found a society that can live everywhere. He had to create a kind of social life, a place of truth and freedom, that is not tied to any particular state order, but that is possible everywhere. In a word: he had to found a Church, and that is precisely what he did.[8]

The existence of a new society that does not coincide with the state is a fundamental factor in the liberation of man. Wherever this distinction is revoked, an essential sphere of freedom is lost, for then the state has to proceed again to regulate the whole of human life. It again draws the realm of the divine to itself, because it again becomes the bearer of religion. It thereby destroys that freedom of conscience which rests on the position of the new society of faith vis-à-vis the state. The distinction, consequent upon Christianity, between the universal religious community and the necessarily particular civil community in no way means a complete separation of the two realms so that religion would now withdraw into the merely spiritual and the state would be reduced to a purely political pragmatism without ethical orientation. It is, however, correct that the Church does not immediately prescribe political orders. To find the best answer in changing times is now entrusted to

8. See Endre von Ivanka, *Romäerreich und Gottesvolk* (Freiburg: K. Alber, 1968), 161-165.

the freedom of reason. That this freedom is instated with its full rights in the political realm, and that political solutions are to be sought only in the communal exertion of practical reason, is one of the aspects of Christian liberation, of the separation of the religious and civil communities. But practical reason is not simply left without orientation. Even if the Law of Sinai, which had traced out for Israel the orders of community, the liberating relational structure, is no longer a national law, it nevertheless remains an orienting moral force which is purified and deepened in the light of the message of Jesus. From this Law there results the praxis of the faith, which at the same time traces out the fundamental moral imperatives for the building up of human society. Because the praxis of faith based on the Word of God is open to reason, it is capable of development within the progress of human history. But at the same time, it always remains in advance of this history because of the awakening to liberation, the Christian Exodus. Catholic social teaching is the academic development of these orientations, which result from the lasting foundations of faith and its growing experiences with historical praxis. It is thus far more than an appeal to the good will of the individual. It is a historical program that comes from a fundamental understanding of human history; yet it is not ideologically determined, but open to continual rational development.

3. Political Rationality — Utopia — Promise

The realism of Christian social teaching shows itself most conspicuously in the fact that it promises no early paradise, no irreversibly and definitely positive society within this history. This is again criticized by many, for the great incentive of utopia seems to be lacking; everything is pruned back to a seemingly resigned realism. But what good is the utopian incentive when it misuses man for a promise that must prove deceptive in the end because its presuppositions are untrue? We already established earlier that an irreversibly positive, definitive society would presuppose the paralysis of human freedom. It would proceed from the presupposition that it is not man who determines the structures, but the structures that determine man, and that he must necessarily act well if the structures are right. His freedom then consists in the necessity of not being able to do otherwise. Happiness is imposed upon him from without. Such a definitively liberated society would therefore be definitive slavery. If, however, man remains free, then there is no definitive state within history. Then his freedom must be guided again and again in finding the right way. Catholic social teaching accordingly knows no utopia, but it does develop models of the best possible organization of human affairs in a given historical situation. It therefore rejects the myth of revolution and seeks the way of reform, which itself does not entirely exclude violent resistance in extreme situations, but protests against the recognition of revolution as a *deus ex machina* from which the new man and the new society are one day inexplicably to proceed.[9]

At this point, we are inevitably led back to the problem that we temporarily left aside earlier. The question had arisen as to whether Catholic social teaching, as depicted above, is too pragmatic and realistic. The question was: what place does God actually occupy in it? In the meantime, we have already encountered the first part of an answer, for it was shown that Catholic social teaching lives from the orientations provided by the praxis of faith and that this praxis is not simply self-devised, but in essence results from the encounter with the old and the new Sinai, the Sinai of Israel and the Mount of Jesus Christ. But this perspective turned backward toward the past history of faith is not the whole. A forward-directed view belongs here also. The Christian faith indeed knows no utopia within history, but it does know a promise: the resurrection of the dead, the Judgment, and the kingdom of God. No doubt, that sounds very mythological to the man of today. But it is much more reasonable than the mixture of politics and eschatology in a utopia within history.[10] The separation of the two into a historical commission that receives new dimensions and possibilities in the light of faith, on the one hand, and into a new world to be created by God himself, on the other, is more logical and more appropriate. No revolution can create a new man — that will never be anything more than constraint. But God can create him from within. That we may expect this gives a new hope to action within history.

9. On the questions touched on here, see Helmut Kuhn, *Der Staat* (Munich: Kösel Verlag, 1967), esp. 63-135, 315-341; on the concept of revolution, see his *Die Kirche im Zeitalter der Kultur-revolution* (Graz: Verlag Styria, 1985), 30-73.

10. See Joseph Ratzinger, "Eschatology and Utopia," *Communio: International Catholic Review* 5, no. 3 (Fall 1978): 211-227. Also available in the collection, *Joseph Ratzinger in* Communio, vol. 1: *The Unity of the Church* (Grand Rapids: Eerdmans, 2010), 10-25.

But, above all, no answer to the questions about justice and freedom is sufficient if it omits the problem of death. If only a far-distant future will one day bring justice, then all of history's dead prior to that will have been cheated. It does no good to tell them that they have collaborated in the preparation for liberation and in that respect have entered into it. They have not entered into it at all, but have exited from history without having received justice. The measure of injustice always remains, then, infinitely greater than the measure of justice. For that reason, such a consistent Marxist thinker as Theodor Adorno has said that, if there is to be justice, then there must also be justice for the dead.[11] A liberation that finds its definitive boundary in death is not a true liberation. Without the solution of the question of death, everything else becomes unreal and contradictory. For that reason, faith in the resurrection of the dead is the point from which one can first conceive of justice for history and fight meaningfully for it. It is meaningful even to die for justice only if there is a resurrection of the dead. For only then is justice more than power; only then is it reality; otherwise it remains a mere idea. For that reason, the certainty of the Last Judgment is also of the greatest practical importance. For centuries, knowledge of the Judgment was ever again the force that put the powerful in their place. We all stand under this measure, each one of us – that is the equality of men from which no one can escape. The Judgment does not relieve us of the effort to create justice in history; it first gives this effort its meaning and removes its obligatory character from all arbitrariness. Nor does the kingdom of God simply lie in an indeterminate future. Only if we already belong to the kingdom in this life will we also belong to it in the next. It is not eschatological faith that displaces the kingdom into the future, but utopia, for *its* future has no present, and its hour will never come.

11. Theodor Adorno, *Negative Dialektik* (Frankfurt: Suhrkamp, 1966), 205 (*Negative Dialectics,* trans. E. B. Ashton [New York: Seabury Press, 1973], 203); cf. Joseph Ratzinger, *Eschatologie* (Regensburg: F. Pustet, 1977), 159 (*Eschatology: Death and Eternal Life,* trans. Michael Waldstein, ed. Aidan Nichols, O.P., enlarged ed. [Washington, D.C.: Catholic University of America Press, 1988], 142ff.).

4. Closing Remarks: Likeness to God and Freedom

We must still add a final comment. We had said that in the anarchic concept of freedom man wishes to become the God who is no longer to exist outside of man. Does the realism of the Christian idea of freedom mean, then, that man is to withdraw resignedly into his finitude and wish to be only a man? Not at all. In the light of the Christian experience of God, it becomes clear that the unlimited arbitrariness of the ability to do all has an idol as its model, and not God. The true God is self-obligation in triune love and thus pure freedom. To be an image of this God, "to become like him," is the vocation of man.[12] Man is not inescapably enclosed in his finitude. He must recognize that he is not self-sufficient and autonomous. He must give up the lie of unrelatedness and of arbitrariness. He must say "yes" to his neediness, "yes" to the other, "yes" to creation, "yes" to the limits and precepts of his own essence. He who can merely choose between arbitrary options is not yet free. Only he who takes the measure of his action from within and who need obey no external constraint is free. Therefore, he is free who has become one with his essence, one with the truth itself. For he who is one with the truth no longer acts according to external necessities and constraints; essence, willing, and acting have coincided in him. In this way, man can touch the infinite in the finite, unite himself to it, and thus become infinite precisely in the recognition of limits. Thus, in closing, it becomes clear once again that the Christian doctrine of freedom is not a petty moralism. It is led by a comprehensive vision of man; it sees man in a historical perspective which, at the same time, transcends all history. The *Instruction on Human Freedom and Liberation* wishes to be a help in discovering this perspective anew in order to bring it to bear in full force in the present day.

Translated by Stephen Wentworth Arndt

12. On man's likeness to God, see Johann Auer, *Die Welt — Gottes Schöpfung*, vol. 3 of *Kleine katholische Dogmatik* (Regensburg: Pustet, 1975), 217-227. Also see Joseph Ratzinger, *In the Beginning . . . A Catholic Understanding of Creation and the Fall* (Grand Rapids: Eerdmans, 1995).

Man between Reproduction and Creation: Theological Questions on the Origin of Human Life

1. Reproduction and Procreation: The Philosophical Problem of Two Terminologies

What is a human being? This perhaps all too philosophical-sounding question has entered a new phase since it became possible to "make" a human being, or, as the technical terminology has it, to reproduce one *in vitro*. This new ability man has acquired has also brought forth a new language. Up to now the origin of a human being has been expressed in terms of begetting and conception; in the Romance languages there is also the word "procreation," with its reference to the Creator, to whom ultimately each human owes his or her being. But now it seems that the word "reproduction" instead describes the handing on of humanness most precisely. The two terminologies are not necessarily exclusive; each represents a different mode of consideration and thus a different aspect of reality. But the language has in each case the totality in mind; it is hard to deny that deeper problems show up than just the words:

This article first appeared as "Der Mensch zwischen Reproduktion und Schöpfung. Theologische Fragen zum Ursprung menschlichen Lebens," in *Internationale katholische Zeitschrift Communio* no. 1 (1989). English publication in *Communio: International Catholic Review* 16, no. 2 (Summer, 1989): 197-211. It was originally an address given by Cardinal Ratzinger in connection with the 900th anniversary celebration of the University of Bologna (30 April 1988), and, with slight modifications, on the occasion of the conferral of an honorary doctorate on Cardinal Ratzinger at the University of Lublin (23 October 1988).

two differing views of mankind can be heard, two differing ways of explaining reality altogether.

Let us attempt first to understand the new language in its inner scientific origins, in order then to touch carefully upon the more far-reaching problems. The word "reproduction" means the process of originating a new human being through biological knowledge of the properties of living organisms, which can, in contradistinction to artifacts, "reproduce" themselves. J. Monod, e.g., speaks of three determining characteristics of a living thing: its proper teleonomy, autonomous morphogenesis, and invariant reproduction.[1] There is a special emphasis on the invariance: the distinctive genetic code is "reproduced" unchanged each time; each new individual is an exact repetition of the same "message."[2] So "reproduction" expresses on the one hand the genetic identity – the individual "reproduces" anew only the same thing – while on the other hand the word refers to the mechanical way in which this imitation occurs. This process can be exactly described. J. Léjeune has formulated the essentials of human "reproduction" as follows: "Children are always united with their parents by a material bond, the long DNA molecule, on which the complete genetic information can be found in an unchangeable miniature language. In the head of a spermatozoon is the master DNA in twenty-three parts. . . . As soon as the twenty-three chromosomes of the father, which are introduced in the spermatozoon, are united with the twenty-three of the mother, which are carried in the ovum, all the information is collected which is necessary and sufficient to determine the genetic constitution of the new human being."[3]

We could also say, in rough shorthand, that the "reproduction" of the human species occurs through the uniting of two information strings. The accuracy of the description is undoubted, but is it also complete? Two questions force themselves upon us immediately: Is the being thus reproduced merely another individual, another copy of the species of man, or is it more: a person, that is, a being which, on the one hand

1. Jacques Monod, *Chance and Necessity: An Essay on the Natural Philosophy of Modern Biology* (New York, 1971), 13.

2. Ibid., 14f., and especially chapter 6, "Invariance and Perturbations," 99-117.

3. J. Léjeune, "Intervention au Synode des Evèques," printed in *Résurrection,* Nouvelle Série 14 (1988): 15-21, at 16. Cf. also the informative article of A. Lizotte, "Réflexions philosophiques sur l'âme et la personne de l'embryon," *Anthropotes* 3, no. 2 (1987): 155-195.

represents invariantly the species man, and on the other is something new, one of a kind, not reproducible, with a uniqueness that goes beyond the simple individuation of its common type? If the latter, whence the uniqueness? And the second question is related to this: How do the two information strings come together? This apparently too simple question has become today the locus of the real decision, on which not only theories about man split, but where praxis becomes the incarnation of theories and gives them their whole pointedness. The answer seems, as we said, to be at first the most obvious thing in the world: the two complementary strings of information come together in the union of man and woman, through their "becoming one flesh," as the Bible has it. The biological process of "reproduction" is enveloped in a personal process of the body-soul self-giving of two human beings.

Since the biochemical part of this totality, so to speak, has been successfully isolated in the laboratory, another question arises: How necessary is the connection between the biological and the personal? Is it essential to the event as such, should and must it be so, or have we here a case of what Hegel calls a trick of nature, which uses human beings' attraction to one another as it uses the wind or the bees as a means to transport seed in the plant world? Can one claim that an isolated cell process is the only really important element in this union, and can one accordingly replace the natural process with other rationally directed methods? Various counter questions arise here: Can one designate the coming together of man and woman as a mere natural process, whereby the psychic turning to each other of the two would be also merely a trick of nature which deceives them, so that they are not acting as persons but merely as individuals within a species? Or must we say exactly the opposite? Must we not say that in the love of two people and the spiritual freedom from which it comes, a new dimension of reality comes into being which corresponds to it, that the child too is not simply a repetition of invariant information, but a person, in the newness and freedom of an I, forming a new center in the world? And is not one blind who would deny this newness and reduce it all to the mechanical, even while in order to do so he must invent a "trick of nature" to account for it, which is an irrational and cruel myth?

A further question arises in this context from an observation: obviously one can isolate the biochemical process in a laboratory today, and thus bring the two information strings together. The connection to the psychic-personal event thus cannot be defined with the kind of "necessity" that is valid in the physical sphere. But the question is whether there is not another kind of necessity than just the purely physical. Even if the personal and the biological are separable, is there not a deeper kind of inseparability, a higher kind of necessity for the union of the two? Has one not in reality denied humanity if one acknowledges only the necessity of physical laws, and denies the ethical necessity which bears the obligation of freedom? In other words, if I consider solely the "reproduction" as real, and everything beyond that which leads to the notion of "procreation" as inexact and scientifically irrelevant verbiage, have I not then denied the human being as human? But then who is having the discussion with whom, and what can be said of the reasonableness of the laboratory or of science itself?

From these considerations we can fashion the question we want to take up precisely: How is it that the origin of a new human being is more than "reproduction"? What is this *more?* The question has acquired a new urgency, as already indicated, from the fact that it is possible to "reproduce" a human being in a laboratory without any personal self-giving, without any union of man and woman. Today one can in practice separate the natural, personal event of the union of man and woman from the purely biological process. Against this practical separability, in the conviction of the morality grounded in Scripture and mediated by the Church, stands an ethical inseparability.[4] On both sides decisions of principle come into play: the activity in the laboratory does not follow from purely mechanical premises, but is the result of a basic view of the world and of man. Therefore, before we proceed with arguments, a twofold historical review will be helpful. First we will attempt to lay out the philosophical background of the idea of artificial "reproduction" of man, and then we will look at the biblical witness regarding our question.

4. Cf. *On the Inviolability of Human Life. On Ethical Questions of Biomedicine,* Instruction for the Congregation for the Doctrine of the Faith, published with a commentary by R. Spaemann (Freiburg, 1987). From the extensive literature on the question, note: M. Schooyans, *Maîtrise de la vie, domination des hommes* (Paris/Namur, 1986); R. Löw, *Leben aus dem Labor. Gentechnologie und Verantwortung: Biologie und Moral* (Munich, 1985); D. Tettamanzi, *Bambini fabbricati. Fertilizzazione in vitro, embryo transfer* (Casale Monferrato, 1985); R. Flöhl, ed., *Genforschung: Fluch oder Segen? Interdisziplinäre Stellungnahmen* (Munich, 1985).

2. A Dialogue with History

a. "Homunculus" in the History of Thought

The thought of being able to "make" a human being most likely had its first form in Jewish Kabbalism with the idea of the Golem.[5] At the basis of this notion lies the idea recorded in the Book of Jezira (c. A.D. 500) that numbers have creative power. Through the proper recitation of all possible creative combinations of letters the *homunculus,* or Golem, will come into being. Already in the thirteenth century the notion of the death of God arises in conjunction with this: the *homunculus* when he finally appears will tear away the first letter, aleph, from the word *emeth* (truth). Thus there will be on his forehead, instead of the inscription "God is Truth" the new motto, "God is Dead." This new saying is explained with a comparison that ends, in brief, "When you, like God, can make men, people will say, 'There is no God in the world but this one.'" Making is brought into conjunction with power. Power belongs to those who can produce human beings, and with such power, they have done away with God; he no longer appears upon the human horizon.[6] The question remains whether the newly powerful, who have found the key to the language of creation and can combine its building blocks themselves, will remember that their activity is only possible because the numbers and letters which they know how to combine already exist.

The best known variation of the *homunculus* idea is in the second part of Goethe's *Faust.* Wagner, the fanatical scientist and disciple of the great Dr. Faust, succeeds with the masterpiece in Faust's absence. So the "Father" of this new art is not the all-questioning spirit reaching out toward greatness, but rather the positivist of knowing and making, as one might well characterize Wagner. Nonetheless the little test-tube man recognizes Mephistopheles immediately as his cousin. Thus Goethe establishes an inner relationship between the artificial, self-made world of positivism and the spirit of negation. For Wagner and his kind of rationalism this is, of course, the moment of greatest triumph.

5. Cf. K. Schubert, "Golem," in *Lexikon für Theologie und Kirche* IV, 1046 (bibliogr.).

6. Cf. G. Thielicke, *Der evangelische Glaube. Grundzüge der Dogmatik* I (Tübingen, 1968), 328-331; G. Scholem, *On the Kabbalah and Its Symbolism* (New York, 1965).

God forbid! As formerly begetting was the custom,
We declare it as an empty farce.
. . . .
If still the beast himself therein delight,
Still man must, with his so much greater gifts,
In future have a more exalted source.

And a little later:

So 'tis our wish in future chance to scorn,
And so a brain which ought to think aright,
Will also in the future thinkers fashion.
. . . .
What do we wish? What does the world want more?
The mystery lies open to the day.

Goethe exhibits clearly in these verses two driving forces in the search for the artificial production of man, and wants thereby to criticize a form of natural science which he rejects, as something he would consider "Wagnerian." First there is the desire to unveil mysteries, to see through the world and reduce it to a flat rationalism, which attempts to prove itself through its capacity to make something. Besides this, Goethe also sees operative here a despising of "nature" and its mysterious higher reasonableness, in favor of a calculating, goal-determined rationalism. The symbol for the narrowness, falsity, and inferiority of this kind of reason and its creations is the glass; the *homunculus* lives *in vitro:*

Here a peculiarity of things:
The universe suffices nature not,
What's artificial needs a closed-in space.

Goethe's prognosis is that the glass, the wall of the artificial, will eventually smash against reality. Since the *homunculus* is artificial even though taken from nature, he will slip out of the hands of his maker; he stands in tension between an anxious concern for his protective glass ("The taste of glass and flame are not alike") and an impatience to split the glass in search of real becoming. Goethe sees a conciliatory ending: the *homunculus* returns in flame to the elements, in a Hymn to the Universe in its creative power, to "Eros who began all." The flame in which he disappears becomes a fiery wonder. But even though Goethe both here and at the end of Faust's road replaces judgment with reconciliation, the fiery smashing of the glass is still a judgment on the arrogance of a making that puts itself in the place of becoming, and that, after a journey full of contradictions, must end in fire and smoke.

On the very threshold of the realization of the world he depicts, Aldous Huxley wrote his dystopia *Brave New World* in 1932.[7] In this definitively and fully scientific world it is clear that men should now only be generated in laboratories. Man has now emancipated himself from his nature; he wants no longer to be a natural thing. Each individual will, as needed, be purposefully concocted in the laboratory according to the task he will be assigned. Sexuality has by far nothing to do with propagation; the very memory of it is felt as an insult to planned man. Instead, it has become part of the anesthetizing by which life is made endurable, a positivistic hedge around human consciousness by which man is protected and the questions arising from the depth of his being are eliminated. And so naturally sexuality may no longer have anything to do with personal commitment, with fidelity and love – that would lead man back to the same old sphere of personal existence. In this world there is no more pain, no anxiety, only rationality and enjoyment; everything is planned for everyone. But the question remains, who are the bearers of this planning intelligence? They are named the World Controllers; and thus the rule of reason simultaneously makes its basic lunacy apparent.

Huxley had written his book, as he remarked in 1946, as a skeptical aesthete, who saw mankind living between the alternatives of "insanity" and "lunacy," of scientific utopia and barbarian superstition.[8] In the Foreword of 1946 and again in *Brave New World Revisited* he makes it clear that his work is to be understood as a brief for freedom, as a challenge to mankind to seek out the narrow space between insanity and lunacy: existence in freedom.[9] Huxley is understandably more precise and cogent in his critique than in the more generalizing positive im-

7. A. Huxley, *Brave New World* and *Brave New World Revisited* (London, 1984).

8. "Pyrrhonic aesthete" in the Foreword of 1946, 6; "insanity . . . and lunacy" (ibid.).

9. Ibid. See especially the Foreword and the chapter, "Education for Freedom," 361-373.

ages that he develops. On one thing he is certainly clear: the world of rational planning, of the scientifically directed "reproduction" of mankind, is not a world of freedom. The fact that it reduces the origin of human beings to reproduction is, on the contrary, an expression of the denial of personal freedom: reproduction is a montage of necessities; its world is the reality pictured in the Kabbalah, a combination of letters and numbers. Whoever knows the code has power over the universe. Is it a coincidence that up to now there is no positive poetic vision of a future in which mankind will be produced *in vitro?* Or is there in such an enterprise an inner denial and ultimate elimination of that dimension of humanity which poetry brings to light?

b. The Origin of Mankind According to the Bible

After this glance at the best-known historical sketch of reproduction ideology, let us turn to that work which is the decisive source for the idea of human procreation, the Bible. Here too there can of course be no question of an exhaustive analysis, but merely a first glance at some of its characteristic statements on our subject. We may restrict ourselves in this essentially to the first chapters of Genesis, where the biblical picture of mankind and of creation is established. A first, essential point is formulated very precisely in the Genesis homilies of St. Gregory of Nyssa:

> But man, how is he created? God does not say "Let there be man!" . . . The creation of man is higher than all. "The Lord took. . . ." He wishes to form our own bodies with his own hands.[10]

We shall have to return to this text when we are no longer speaking of the first man, but of every man: it will become apparent that what the Bible shows in the person of the first man is its conviction about every man. Parallel to the picture of man's coming from the hands of God, which form him from the earth, is the statement in the later, so-called priestly document, "Let us make man after our image and likeness" (Gn 1:26). In both cases the aim is to present man in a specific way as

10. Gregory of Nyssa, *Second Homily on Genesis 1:26, PG* 44: 277ff.

God's creation, to have him appear not merely as one specimen in a class of beings, but as a new being in each case, in whom more appears than reproduction: a new beginning, which reaches beyond all present combinations of information, one who presupposes another – *the* other – and thus teaches us to think "God." Even more important is the fact that in the creative act itself he created them man and woman. Unlike with the animals and plants, where the charge to be fruitful and multiply is simply imposed, fruitfulness is here expressly bound up with being a man and a woman. The emphasis of the text on God's being Creator does not make human orientation to one another superfluous, but rather gives it its unique quality: indeed, because God is engaged in this action, man cannot configure the "transporting" of the chromosomes at will; the mode of such creation must be worthy of God. According to the Bible, there is only one such worthy mode: the becoming one of husband and wife, who "become one flesh."

We have touched upon two important formulations of biblical language here, about which we must think more closely. The description of Paradise ends with a saying that seems to be a prophetic oracle about the being of mankind: "Therefore a man leaves father and mother and cleaves to his wife, and they become one flesh" (Gn 2:24). What is the meaning of "they become one flesh"? There has been much argument about this. Some say it means sexual intercourse, others that it refers to the child in which the two are joined into one flesh. We cannot be certain, but probably Delitzsch comes closest when he says that it expresses "psychic unity, all-embracing personal community."[11] In any case such a profound unity of man and wife is looked upon as characteristic of mankind, and as the locus in which the Creator's mandate to man is fulfilled, because it corresponds to the call of his being in freedom.

Another term of biblical anthropology points in the same direction: the sexual union of man and woman is referred to with the verb "to know." The beginning of the history of human begetting reads "Adam knew his wife Eve" (Gn 4:1). It may be correct that one cannot read too much philosophy into this way of speaking. To begin with, we have here simply a case of what Gerhard von Rad rightly calls a "modesty of speech," which reverentially covers the inmost human together-

11. Claus Westermann, *Genesis,* I, Chapters 1-11 (Neukirchen, 1974), 318. [The English edition is a condensation – Trans.]

ness with mystery.[12] But then it is important that the Hebrew word *yada'* means "to know" also in the sense of experiencing, of being acquainted with. Claus Westermann believes he can go a step further when he says *yada'* means "not really knowing and understanding in the sense of objective knowing, as to know *something* or understand *something*, but the knowing in an encounter." The use of the word for the sexual act then shows "that here the corporal relationship of man and woman is thought of not primarily as physiological, but primarily personal."[13] There appears again an inseparability of all the dimensions of being human, which precisely in their being combined comprise the specialness of this being "man," which is falsified when one begins to isolate individual parts.

How does the Bible concretely represent the becoming of man? I would like to present only three places which provide us with a good, clear answer. "Thy hands have made and fashioned me," says the petitioner to his God (Ps 119:73). "Thou didst form my inmost parts, thou didst knit me together in my mother's womb. . . . My frame was not hidden from thee, when I was being made in secret, intricately wrought in the depths of the earth" (Ps 139:13, 15). "Thy hands fashioned me and made me. . . . Remember that thou hast made me of clay. . . . Didst thou not pour me out like milk and curdle me like cheese?" (Job 10:8-10). Something important shows up in these texts. For one thing, the biblical writer knows very well that man is "knit together" in the mother's womb, that there, he is "curdled like cheese." But the mother's womb is also identified with the depths of the earth, and so each biblical worshiper can say of himself, "Your hands have fashioned me, like clay you have formed me." The picture that describes the origin of Adam is valid for each human being in the same way. Each human is Adam, a new beginning; Adam is each human being. The physiological event is more than a physiological event. Each human is more than a new combination of information; the origin of each human being is a creation. Its wonder is that it happens not next to but precisely *in* the processes of a living being and its "invariant reproduction."

12. Gerhard von Rad, *Genesis. A Commentary* (Philadelphia, 1961), 100.

13. Westermann, *Genesis,* 393. Valuable clarifications can be found in the extensive article "jada" by J. Bergmann and G. J. Botterweck in *Theologisches Wörterbuch zum Alten Testament,* ed. Botterweck and Ringgren, vol. 3 (1982), 479-512.

Let us add a last, puzzling word to round out the picture. At the very first birth of a human being, according to the biblical narrative, Eve breaks out into a joyous cry, "I have gotten a man with the help of the Lord" (Gn 4:1). The word "gotten" here is rare and much debated, but one could say with good grounds that it is rare because it has a unique content to express. The word means, as in other ancient Near Eastern languages, "creation through begetting or birth."[14] In other words, the joyous cry expresses the entire pride, the whole happiness of the woman become a mother; but it also expresses the knowledge that each human begetting and birth stands under a special presence of God, is a self-transcending of man, in which there is more than he has and is: through the human action of begetting and birth, there occurs creation.

3. The Unique Element in Human Origin

The current importance of this biblical statement is obvious. Certainly the question forces itself upon men of today, for whom the positivistic hemming in of thought seems a kind of obligation of honesty: Must God really be involved here? Is not that a mythologizing, which explains nothing, and impedes human freedom in dealing with the data of nature? Is not nature thus made taboo, and conversely, spirit made natural, insofar as its freedom of movement is tied to a law of nature as a supposed expression of the will of God?

Whoever enters into such a dispute must be clear on one thing: what is said about God and about man as a person, as a new beginning, cannot be taken as the same kind of positively verifiable knowledge as that which can be ascertained about the mechanics of reproduction using scientific instruments. The statements about God and man intend precisely to point toward this, that man denies himself, and so denies incontrovertible reality, if he refuses to go beyond the laboratory in his thinking. So one can best "prove" the correctness of the biblical synthesis by making apparent the impasse that results from its denial. Goethe predicted that the glass world of the *homunculus,* the one who reduces himself to reproduction, will someday necessarily shatter against reality. In the ecological crisis of today something of the tinkle of glass can be

14. Westermann, *Genesis,* 395.

heard. Marx had already been able to call with enthusiasm for the battle of man for the subjugation of nature. "Battle against Nature" and "Freeing of Mankind" are for him almost synonyms.[15] Today this freeing of man begins to be alarming. The use of nature turns into using it up, and the notion that technical understanding will bring about the reasonable assembling of unreasonable reality has long proven itself to be a romantic myth. The inner reasonableness of creation is greater than that of man the maker, who does not possess it as pure reason anyway, but as an interest group with all the short-sightedness of a party-determined goal, which pays the bill of today with the life of tomorrow.

And here we touch upon deeper levels of the impasse. The notion that an ethics coming to us from the nature of things is in reality but a myth replaces the idea of freedom with an assemblage of necessity. But this is in reality the denial of any freedom. The reduction of reality that is bound up with such a viewpoint means first and foremost the denial of man as man. Of course the danger arises here that the glass of the *homunculus* will not only strike its inhabitant, but will fall upon all of mankind and destroy it too. The logical connection, and that is what we are concerned with here, is unavoidable. It seems harmless to remove the taboo from the personal union of man and woman as a mythic divinization of nature. It seems to be progress to isolate the biological cellular process and to imitate it in the laboratory. It is then logical to consider human becoming as mere reproduction, and it is unavoidable to consider all that goes beyond reproduction as a mythical illusion. Demythologized man is only a combination of information, and so one can, guided by evolution, go in search of new combinations. The freedom which emancipates man and his research from ethics thus presupposes at its inception the denial of freedom. What remains is the power of the "World Controllers Council," a technical rationality which itself stands only in service to necessity, but wants to replace the accidental occurrences of its combinations with the logic of planning.[16] Here Huxley is simply correct. This rationality and its freedom is a contradic-

15. R. Spaemann refers to this in the commentary in *On the Inviolability of Human Life,* 81.

16. Current positions under discussion concerning dealings with humans can be seen, e.g. in S. Z. Leiman, "Therapeutic Homicide," *Journal of Medicine and Philosophy* 8 (1983): 257-267; see also R. Löw, "Die moralische Dimension von Organtransplantationen," *Scheidewege* 17 (1987/88): 16-48.

tion in itself, an absurd arrogance. The impasse of reproduction logic is man; it is on him that the glass shatters, and proves itself the shell of the artificial. "Nature," for which the faith of the Church demands respect in the begetting of a human being, is therefore not a falsely sacralized biological or physiological process; this "nature" is rather the dignity of the person itself, or of the Three Persons who are involved. This dignity reveals itself also precisely in bodiliness; to this bodiliness must correspond that logic of self-giving which stands written into creation and into the hearts of men, in accordance with the great statement of St. Thomas Aquinas, "Love is by its nature the primary gift, from which all other gifts follow of themselves."[17] Such considerations make clear where God's creative activity can enter into what seems merely a physiological, natural process: the natural process is borne and made possible by the personal action of love, in which human beings give to one another nothing less than themselves. This giving is the inner *locus* where God's giving, where creative love, is at work as a new beginning.

The alternative before which we stand today can now be formulated very precisely: On the one hand, one can regard only the mechanical, nature's laws, as real, and consider all that is personal, all love and self-giving, as mere appearance, which, though psychologically useful, is ultimately unreal and untenable. I find for this position no other designation than the denial of humanity. If one follows out this logic, then of course the notion of God becomes just mythological talk with no real content. On the other hand, according to the other alternative, things are just the opposite: One can consider the personal as the really real, the stronger and higher form of reality, which does not reduce the biological and mechanical to mere appearance, but draws them into itself and thus opens them up to a new dimension. Then not only does the notion of God retain sense and meaning, but the notion of nature appears in a new light; nature is then not just a fortuitously functioning rational order of letters and numbers, but carries within it a moral message, which precedes it and which appeals to mankind to find answers within it. The nature of things is such that the rightness of the one or the other basic decision cannot be decided in the laboratory. In the dispute about man only man can decide whether to accept or to deny himself.

Is it still necessary to defend this vision of reality against the charge

17. *Summa Theologiae* I, q. 38, a. 2, response.

that it is inimical to science and progress? I think it has become adequately apparent that a view of mankind that does not permit the reduction of man's origin to reproduction, but understands it instead as creation, in no way denies or hinders freedom, for only when there is such a thing as a person, and when it is the central locus of all human reality, is there such a thing as freedom at all. Bracketing out man, bracketing out ethics, does not increase freedom but rather tears it from its roots. Therefore the notion of God is not in opposition to human freedom, but is rather its presupposition and basis. We no longer say enough about man, about his dignity and his rights, if we treat speech about God as unscientific and banish it from our language of thought into the sphere of the subjective and the edifying. Language about God belongs in language about man, and it therefore also belongs in the university. It is no accident that the phenomenon of the university arose where each day the verse rang out: "In the beginning was the *Logos*" – meaning reason, the intelligent word. The *Logos* brought forth *logos,* and gave it space. Only under the presupposition of the foundational, original and internal intelligibility of the world, and its origin in intelligence, could human intelligence engage in questioning the intelligibility of the world in detail and as a whole. But where intelligibility is accepted only in the details, while in the whole and as a foundation it is denied, the university dissolves into juxtaposed individual disciplines. It follows very quickly from this that reason, intelligence, is valid only for partial areas of our existence, but that reality as a whole is unreasonable. The consequences of this for the entire life and activity of mankind are evident. Thus it is a false impasse if, in the name of progress and freedom, one declares the law of power, of success, of ability to make, the only law of science, and then wishes in the name of this law to fend off a supposed tendency by man to make nature taboo. In place of such false alternatives a new synthesis of science and wisdom must step forward, in which questions about details do not suppress the view of the whole, and the concern for the whole does not undo carefulness about details. This new synthesis is the great intellectual challenge that stands before us today. It will decide whether there will be a human future, a future worthy of man, or whether we are heading for chaos and the self-destruction of man and of creation.

Translated by Thomas A. Caldwell, S.J.

Jesus Christ Today

1. Preliminary Consideration: Today, Yesterday, and Eternity

"Jesus Christ is the same, yesterday, today, and forever" (Heb 13:8). This was the profession of those who had known him on earth and who had seen the Risen One. This means that we can only correctly recognize Jesus Christ today when we understand him as one with the Christ of "yesterday" and when we see in the Christ of yesterday and today the eternal Christ. An encounter with Christ always requires the three dimensions of time and a stepping beyond time into that which is its origin and its future. When we set out to find the true Jesus, we must be prepared for this broad span. Ordinarily we will meet him at first in the present: in the way he shows himself in the present, in the way people see him and understand him, in the way they live for or against him, in the way his words and his deeds take effect today. But if all that is not to remain second-hand knowledge, but is rather to become an actual encounter, we must go back and ask: "Where does all this come from? Who was he really, back then when he lived a human life?" We will have to listen to the sources which testify to that beginning, and thereby correct our present age when it loses its way in its own ideals. This humble submission to the word of the sources, this preparedness to have our dreams torn from us and to bow to reality, is a basic prerequi-

---

This article first appeared as "Jesus Christus heute," in *Internationale katholische Zeitschrift Communio* 17, no. 1 (Spring 1990).

site for a true encounter. An encounter demands the asceticism of truth, that humility of listening and seeing which leads to authentic perception of truth.

But there is another danger here, which has gradually taken on quite dramatic forms in modern theology. Modern theology begins in the Enlightenment with a turning to the Christ of yesterday. Luther had already complained that the Church had subjected Scripture to herself and thus belonged not at all to yesterday, to that unrepeatable historical "once," but mirrored only her own present, and thus missed the true Christ, preaching only the Christ of today, without his essential and foundational past, thus even making herself Christ. The Enlightenment then laid hold of this thought systematically and radically: only the Christ of yesterday, or of history, is the true Christ at all; all else is later fantasy. Christ is only what he *was*.[1] The search for the historical Jesus clearly locks Christ into the past; it denies him today and eternity.

I need not describe here how the search for the historical Jesus gradually pushed aside the Pauline and the Johannine Christ, and finally had to deny also the Jesus of the Synoptics, in order to picture behind him, ever farther behind, the Jesus who really was, who then became all the more fictitious the more authentic he was supposed to become through this strict concentration on the past. Whoever wants to see only the Christ of yesterday will not find him; and whoever wants to have him only today will likewise not encounter him.

From the very beginning it is proper to him that he was, he is, and he will come. As the living one, he was always already the one who is to come. The message of his coming and remaining belongs essentially to the image of himself: this claim on all the dimensions of time rests again upon the claim that he understood his earthly life as a going forth from the Father and a simultaneous remaining with him, thus bringing eternity into relation with time. If we deny ourselves an existence which allows itself to span these dimensions, we cannot understand him. Whoever grasps time merely as an unrecallable disappearing moment and lives accordingly, turns away in principle from what

1. Cf. the penetrating analysis of the question in H. Schlier, "Wer ist Jesus?" in *Der Geist und die Kirche. Exegetische Aufsätze und Vorträge,* ed. V. Kubina and K. Lehmann (Freiburg, 1980), 20-32.

the figure of Jesus constitutes and what it proclaims. Knowledge is always a way. Whoever denies the possibility of such an extended existence has in reality thereby denied himself access to the sources which invite us to this journey of Being, which becomes a journey to recognition. Augustine has phrased this thought with incomparable beauty, "Come you also to Christ. . . . Think not of long journeying. . . . One arrives at him, the omnipresent one, through love, not by sea-faring. And yet, since on this journey too the floods and storms of manifold temptations come aplenty, believe in the crucified one, that your faith be strong enough to mount the wood. Then you shall not founder."[2]

Let us summarize our thoughts up to this point. The first encounter with Jesus Christ takes place in today; in fact one can only encounter him because he truly has a today. But in order for me to come close to the whole Christ and not to some coincidentally perceived part, I must listen to the Christ of Scripture. If at the same time I listen carefully, and do not, because of some dogmatizing world-view, cut off essential parts of his self-revelation, I see him open to the future, and see him coming toward us from eternity, which encompasses past, present, and future at once. Precisely wherever such holistic understanding has been sought out and lived, there Christ has always become completely "today," for only that which possesses roots in yesterday and the power of growth for tomorrow and for all time has true power over today and in today, and stands in contact with eternity. Thus have the great epochs of the history of the faith each brought forth their own image of Christ, as they were able to see him anew from their own today, and thus recognized "Christ yesterday, today, and forever."

In the early days of Christianity, the "Christ of today" was primarily seen in the image of the shepherd who carries the lost sheep, mankind, on his shoulder.[3] Whoever looked on this image knew, "I myself am this sheep. I had sought to grasp more for my life, run after this and that promise, until I was caught in a pathless tangle and found no way out. But he has taken me on his shoulders, and in carrying me has himself become my way." In the next period there followed the image of the

2. Augustine, Sermon 131.2, PL 28, 730.

3. Cf. F. van der Meer, *Christus. Der Menschensohn in der abendländischen Plastik* (Freiburg, 1980), 21. Also *Die Ursprünge christlicher Kunst* (Freiburg, 1982), 88, 152ff. (*Early Christian Art* [London, 1967]). Also informative is F. Gerke, *Christus in der spätantiken Plastik* (Mainz, 1948).

pantocrator, which soon shifted to an attempt to depict the "historical Jesus" as he truly was upon earth. But this was accompanied by the conviction that, in the man Jesus, God himself appears, that Jesus is the image of God and allows us to see through the visible to the invisible, so that looking upon this image becomes a way for man to proceed beyond the boundary which without Christ would be impassible. In Romanesque times, the Latin Middle Ages depicted the triumphant Christ on the cross, with the cross as a throne. Just as the Eastern Church icon wants to show the invisible in the visible, so would the Romanesque crucifix make the Resurrection visible, and thus make our own cross transparent to the promise that is concealed in it. In Gothic art, the human Jesus Christ comes forward powerfully; the cross is depicted more and more in its unmitigated horror, but the God who suffers so unspeakably, who suffers as we do but more, without the light of the approaching triumph, becomes the great consoler and the assurance of our salvation. Finally, in the image of the Pietà, Christ appears only as a dead man on the lap of his mother for whom nothing remains but sorrow; God seems dead. Only from afar comes the consoling word: in the evening sadness, but joy comes in the morning (Ps 30:5) – the knowledge that there is an Easter. The teaching of these images of a "Christ today" remains valid because it is composed of all viewpoints, knowing also Christ yesterday, tomorrow, and in eternity.[4]

I have spent so much time on these considerations because they give the methodology for our theme. From considerations of the experiences and hardships of our time, contemporary theology has proposed fascinating images of Christ today: Christ the Liberator, the new Moses in a new Exodus; Christ the poor among the poor, as he shows himself in the beatitudes; Christ the completely loving one, whose being is being for others, who in the word "for" expresses his deepest reality. Each of these images brings forth something essential to the image of Jesus; each of them presupposes basic questions: what is freedom, and where does one find the road that leads not just anywhere but to true freedom, to the real "Promised Land" of human existence? What is the blessedness of poverty, and what must we do that others and we ourselves arrive at it? How does Christ's "being-for" reach us, and where does it lead us? On all these questions there is today a lively de-

4. On this whole matter, see the development in van der Meer, *Christus.*

bate, which will be fruitful if we do not try to solve it only out of the present, but also keep our gaze on the Christ of yesterday and of eternity. Within the limits of a single article it is impossible to enter into this debate, even though as background it gives the leading perspectives. Starting with our methodological considerations, I would like to choose a different route: to take our current question and way of thinking and connect them to a biblical theme, and thus draw it into our consideration of the tension of Yesterday-Today-Eternity. I am thinking of the fundamental saying of the Johannine Christ, "I am the way and the truth and the life" (Jn 14:6). The idea of the *way* is clearly connected with the Exodus. *Life* has become a key word of our time in view of the threats of a "civilization" of death, which is in truth the loss of all civilization and culture; the motif "being-for" is obvious here. On the other hand, *truth* is not a favorite notion of our time; it is associated with intolerance, and is thus perceived more as threat than promise. But precisely for this reason it is important that we ask about it, and allow ourselves to be questioned about it from the perspective of Christ.

2. Christ the Way — Exodus and Liberation

Jesus Christ today — the first image in which we can see him in this our time is that of the *Way*, which from the history of Israel we call the Exodus: as the way out into the open. Here is expressed a consciousness of not living in freedom, of not being where we really belong. True, the new Exodus theology has been developed in connection with situations of political and economic oppression. The specific form of government of this or that country is of less importance in this than the basic form of our contemporary world, which is built not on mutual solidarity but on a system of profit and power, which produces and requires dependence. Curiously, people of the dominant nations are not at all satisfied with their own type of freedom and power. They too feel themselves dependent on anonymous structures which leave them breathless, and this even where the form of government assures the greatest possible freedom. Paradoxically, the cry for a new exodus into a land of true freedom is loudest among those who possess more and have more freedom of movement than had even been imagined before now. We are not in the place we should be, and we do not live in the way we would like. Where is this way? How can one travel it? We find ourselves in the position of the disciples to whom Jesus says, "You know the way where I am going." Thomas replies, "Lord, we do not know where you are going; how can we know the way?" (Jn 14:4-5).

There is only one place in the gospels where the word "exodus" occurs: it is in the Lukan account of the Transfiguration. There it says that during his prayer Jesus' countenance was altered and his raiment became dazzling white. Two men, Moses and Elijah, appeared in their glory and spoke with him about the *exodus* he was to accomplish in Jerusalem. At first glance, the word "exodus" here means simply departure, death. Moses and Elijah, the two great sufferers for the sake of God, speak of Jesus' passover, of the exodus of his cross. They are the two privileged witnesses of Jesus because they have preceded him along the route of the passion. Both are valid interpreters of the exodus: Moses, the leader of the exodus of Israel from Egypt; Elijah, who lived in that moment of Israel's history when his people had, though still in the land of promise, reverted to Egypt in their mode of existence. Forgetful of God, they were living under a tyrannical existence, like that of the time before the exodus. The word of Sinai, the instructions of the covenant, which were the inner goal of the exodus, had been cast off as manacles, in order to achieve a self-made freedom, which then showed itself as the strongest tyranny. So Elijah must symbolically return to Sinai, retrace Israel's wandering, to bring anew from the mountain of God the fruit of the exodus. In this way, in Elijah the true nature of the exodus history can be seen: the exodus is not a matter of a geographical or a political way. One cannot trace this way on either a geographical or a political map. An exodus which does not lead to covenant and does not find its "land" in living according to the covenant is no true exodus.[5]

In this connection, two observations on the biblical text are important. While Luke introduces his narrative with the more approximate dating "about eight days after these sayings," Matthew and Mark offer a precise date for the Transfiguration: six days after Peter's confession and the accompanying promise of primacy. H. Gese explains the Old Testament background of this dating: "After six days of cloud cover,

5. This subject is treated more completely in J. Ratzinger, *Kirche, Ökumene und Politik* (Einsiedeln, 1987), 235-40 (*Church, Ecumenism, and Politics: New Endeavors in Ecclesiology* [San Francisco: Ignatius Press, 2008]).

Moses climbed Mount Sinai and entered into the divine light" (Ex 24:16).[6] Moses was accompanied by the high priest Aaron and the two priests Nadab and Abihu (Ex 24:1), just as Jesus is accompanied by Peter, John, and James. And as Moses' face became shining through the encounter, "so Jesus changed in unearthly light." In the ancient Sinai event God revealed himself with the formula "I am YHWH," which introduces the decalogue. Here the cry is, "This is my beloved son; listen to him." Jesus is the living Torah, the covenant in person, in whom law turns to gift. The chronology of Matthew conceals another level, too. J. M. van Cangh and M. van Esbroeck have made clear how with this dating the two experiences – Peter's confession, with the promise of the primacy, and the Transfiguration – fit into the Jewish festal calendar, and thus their meaning is grasped more exactly. Peter's confession falls on Yom Kippur, the Day of Atonement, which is followed by five feast days leading to the Feast of Booths, where the offer of three tents at the Transfiguration rings through.[7] Here we need not go into the entire breadth of the sayings which thus appears both for the two experiences and for their inner relationship. Let us hold onto what is essential for us: in the background for the one experience is the mystery of atonement, for the other the Feast of Booths, which is a thanksgiving for the land and a commemoration of the homelessness of the wanderers. The exodus of Israel and the exodus of Jesus touch: all the feasts and all the ways of Israel lead up to the passover of Jesus Christ.

We can say, then, that the "departure" of Jesus in Jerusalem is the real and definitive exodus, in which Christ treads the path into freedom and becomes himself the way to freedom for mankind. Let us add that for Luke the entire public life of Jesus is depicted as a going up to Jerusalem, and so the life of Jesus as a whole is an exodus in which he is like Moses and Israel. To grasp all the dimensions of this way, we must also look at the Resurrection; the Epistle to the Hebrews describes the exodus of Jesus as not ending in Jerusalem: "He has opened for us a new and living way through the curtain, that is, through his flesh" (Heb 10:20). His exodus leads beyond all things created, to the "tent not

6. H. Gese, *Zur biblischen Theologie. Alttestamentliche Vorträge* (Munich, 1977), 81.

7. J.-M. Van Cangh and M. van Esbroeck, "La primauté de Pierre (Mt. 16:16-19) et son context judaique," *Revue théologique de Louvain* 11 (1980): 310-324, esp. 310f. Valuable insights on the Transfiguration pericope are also to be found in P. H. Kolvenbach, *Der österliche Weg. Exerzitien zur Lebenserneuerung* (Freiburg, 1988), 220-227.

made by human hands" (9:11), into contact with the living God. The promised land to which he comes and to which he leads us is the act of sitting "at the right hand of God" (cf. Mk 12:36; Acts 2:33; Rom 8:34, etc.). There lives in every human the thirst for freedom and liberation; at each step reached along this way we are also conscious that it is only a step, and that nothing which has been reached fulfills our desire. The thirst for freedom is the voice of the image of God within us; it is the thirst "to sit at God's right hand," to be "like God." A liberator who wishes to deserve the name must open the door to this, and all empirical forms of freedom must be measured against this.

But how does this come about? What does an exodus really mean? Mankind has stood and still stands here before two ways. There is the voice of the serpent which says, "Step out of that dependence which is your own fault; make yourself God, and toss away him who can never be anything but a limit for you." It is no wonder that a part of mankind on hearing the message of Christ identified him with the serpent and wished to understand him as a liberator from the ancient God.[8] But that is not his own way. What does his way look like? There are two sayings of Jesus in which he refers the promise of sitting at the right hand of God to mankind. In the image of the Last Judgment, he speaks of the sheep, which the king, the Son of Man, places on the right and to whom he will give the kingdom. They are the ones who gave him to eat when he was hungry, to drink when he was thirsty, who took him in when he was without shelter, visited him when he was sick or in prison. They did all these things to him in doing them for "the least" (Mt 25:31-40). In the second text the sons of Zebedee ask to sit at the right and left hand of Jesus in his glory. They are told that the seating precedence is tied to the will of the Father, and it demands as a condition that they drink the chalice which he shall drink, and receive the baptism with which he will be baptized (Mk 10:35-40).

We must remember these two hints when we turn back to the related texts of Peter's confession and the Transfiguration. The two expe-

8. With great insight J. Magné has recently described this "gnostic" interpretation of Jesus and attempted to update it in his two works, *Logique des dogmes* and *Logique des sacrements,* published by the author (Paris, 1989). An interpretation of Christianity along the same lines is that of Ernst Bloch, *Atheismus in Christentum* (Suhrkamp, 1968), e.g., 11ff. (*Atheism in Christianity* [New York, 1972]). Related to this, see L. Weimer, *Das Verständnis von Religion und Offenbarung bei Bloch* (Munich Dissertation, 1971).

riences are tied together by the prediction of death and resurrection, that is, by Jesus' own speaking of his exodus, which Peter resists, since he entertained a completely different idea of exodus. He is told brusquely, "Get thee behind me, Satan" (Mt 16:23). Peter takes on the role of the tempter the moment he propounds an exodus without the cross, an exodus that does not lead to the Resurrection but to an earthly utopia. "Get thee behind me" – Jesus sets this attempt to limit the exodus to an empirical goal against the demand to follow him. The existential correspondent to the idea of the liberating way is this following as the way to freedom, to liberation.

We must of course not construe the notion of following as the core of New Testament exodus too narrowly. A correct understanding of the following of Christ depends on a correct understanding of the figure of Jesus Christ. This following cannot be narrowed down to morality. It is a christological category, and only then does it flow over into a moral charge. And so "following" says too little if one thinks too narrowly of Jesus himself. One who sees Jesus only as a pioneer for a freer religion, for a more open morality, or for a better political structure, must reduce the following to the acceptance of specific programmatic ideas. The result of this is that one then ascribes to Jesus the beginnings of a program which one has oneself further developed and whose use can then be interpreted as joining oneself to him. Such a following through participating in a program is as arbitrary as it is insufficient, for the empirical situations then and now are all too different; what one thinks to be able to take over from Jesus does not extend beyond quite general intentions. Recourse to such a diminution of the notion of following, and thus of the message of exodus, often rests on a logic that at first seems enlightening: Jesus was, it is true, God and man, but *we* are only human; *we* cannot follow him in his being God, but only as humans. In such an explanation we think all too little of mankind, of our freedom, and fall completely away from the logic of the New Testament and its bold statement, "Be imitators of God" (Eph 5:1).

No, the call to following concerns not just some human program, or the human virtues of Jesus, but his *entire* way, "through the curtain" (Heb 10:20). What is essential and new about the way of Jesus Christ is that he opens *this* way for us, for only thus do we come into freedom. The meaning of "following" is to enter into communion with God, and thus it is bound up with the Paschal mystery.[9] Thus the summons to following which comes after Peter's confession says: "If anyone will come after me, let him deny himself and take up his cross, and so follow me" (Mk 8:34). That is not just a bit of moralizing, which sees life primarily from the negative side, nor is it masochism for those who dislike themselves. One does not come near the true meaning of the saying if one twists it as a stern morality for heroic temperaments who decide for martyrdom. The call of Jesus is only to be understood from the great Easter context of the entire exodus, which "goes through the curtain." It is from this goal that the fundamental human wisdom gets its meaning: only the one who loses self finds self; only the one who gives life receives it (Mk 8:35).

It is for this reason that following is validly defined in those elements we found earlier formulated in Jesus' words: baptism, chalice, life. The Church Fathers had this whole idea of following clearly in view. Rather than a multitude of texts, I would like to cite just one from St. Basil:

> The plan of God and of our Redeemer consists in a calling back from banishment and a return from the alienation that came about as a result of disobedience. . . . For the completeness of life, the following of Christ is necessary, not only the meekness, humility, and endurance in his *lifetime,* but also in his *death.* . . . How do we achieve a similarity to his death? . . . What is the profit in this imitation? First it is needful that the form of our earlier life be broken through. But that is impossible unless one is born again, according to the word of the Lord (cf. Jn 3:3). For being born again is . . . the beginning of a second life. But to begin the second, one must put an end to the first. Just as for those in the stadium making the turn there is a stopping point which separates the two opposite directions, so also there is necessarily a death for a turn of life, which puts an end to the life that went before and provides a beginning for the one that follows.[10]

9. This interpretation, taken for granted by the Fathers, can be found in brief in one of the unsurpassable statements of Augustine: *Ascendit Christus in caelum: sequamur eum.* Sermon 304.4, PL 38, 1397. Still important in this connection is R. Peterson, "Zeuge der Wahrheit," in his *Theologische Traktate* (Munich, 1951), 165-224.

10. Basil, "On the Holy Spirit" XV, 35, *Sources chrétiennes* 17 bis, ed. B. Pruche, O.P. (Paris, 1968), 364ff. (PG 32: 128C-129B).

To put it straightforwardly, Christian exodus involves a conversion which accepts the promise of Christ in its entire breadth, and is prepared to lose one's self, and life itself, therein. To this conversion belong therefore the overcoming of self-reliance and the entrusting of one's self to the mystery, to the sacrament in the community of the Church, where God as the agent enters my life and frees it from its isolation. To this conversion belongs, with faith, that losing of self in love which is resurrection because it is a dying. It is a cross contained in an Easter, which for all that is not necessarily less painful. Augustine expressed this in his inimitable way in connection with the words of the Psalm, "pierce my flesh with the nails of thy fear" (Ps 119:120). "Nails are the commandments of justice: with these the fear of the Lord nails each one fast, and crucifies us as acceptable offerings to him."[11] Thus eternal life is continually made present in this life, and throws light on an exodus in a world which is in itself anything but a "promised land." And so Christ becomes a way, he himself, not his word. And so he becomes truly "today."

3. Christ the Truth — Truth, Freedom, and Poverty

Let us now attempt at least a short glance at the other two terms that belong with *way: truth* and *life*. Our era looks at Christ's avowal, "I am the truth," with much the same skepticism as Pilate, with the same arrogant and resigned question: What is truth? The man of today recognizes himself not in Christ, but in the fifth trope of Diogenes Laertius: "There is no truth. For the same thing seems just to one, unjust to another, good to one, evil to another. So let our slogan be: Withholding of judgment on the truth."[12] Skepticism seems to us to be a demand of tolerance, and thus true wisdom. But we should not forget in this that truth and freedom are inseparable. "No longer do I call you servants," says the Lord, "for the servant does not know what his master is doing; but I have called you friends, for all that I have heard from my Father I have made known to you" (Jn 15:15). Ignorance is dependence, slavery:

11. Sermon 205, 1, PL 38: 1039.

12. 9.83 and 84. Cited from R.-P. Martin, *Pontius Pilatus. Römer, Ritter, Richter* (Munich-Zurich, 1989), 96.

he who does not know, remains a slave. It is only when understanding arises, when we begin to grasp what is essential, that we begin to be free. A freedom from which the truth has been removed is a lie. Christ the truth: this means God has transformed us from unknowing slaves into friends, in that he has allowed us to become partakers with him of his self-knowledge. The image of being a friend of Christ is precious to us, especially today; but his friendship consists in this, that he has drawn us into his trust, and the realm of trust is truth.

Of course when we talk today of knowledge as liberating us from the slavery of ignorance, we usually do not think of God, but of mastery, the knowledge of dealing with art, with things, with people. God remains out of the picture; for questions of getting along he seems unimportant. First one must know how to assert oneself; once that is secured, one wants room for speculation. In this shrinking of the question of knowledge lies not only the problem of our modern idea of truth and freedom, but *the* problem of our time altogether, for it presumes that for the shaping of things human and the fashioning of our lives it is indifferent whether or not there is a God. God seems to lie outside the functioning relationships of our lives and our society, the well-known *Deus otiosus* (superfluous God) of the history of religions.[13] A God who is insignificant for human life is no God at all, since he is powerless and unreal. But if the world does not come from God, and is not influenced by him even in the smallest things, then it does not come out of freedom, and freedom is thus not a power in it; it is merely a conglomerate of necessary mechanisms, and any freedom is only appearance. And so from another angle, we once more come up against the notion that freedom and truth are inseparable. If we can know nothing of God, and he cares to know nothing of us, we are not free beings in a creation opening toward freedom, but parts in a system of necessities, in whom the call for freedom, however, will not be quenched. The question about God is simultaneous and one with the question about freedom and about truth.

Basically we have arrived again at that point where Arius and the Church once split, the question of what is distinctively Christian, and

13. Helpful is A. Brunner, *Die Religion* (Freiburg, 1956), 67-80. Cf. also A. Dammann, *Die Religion Afrikas* (Stuttgart, 1963), 33; G. van der Leeuw, *Phänomenologie der Religion* (Tübingen, 1956), 180ff. (*Religion in Essence and Manifestation* [Princeton, N.J., 1986]).

of the human capacity for reaching truth. The real kernel of Arius's heresy consists in holding fast to that notion of the absolute transcendence of God which he acquired from the philosophy of late antiquity. This God cannot communicate himself; he is too great, man is too small; there is no meeting of the two. "The God of Arius remains locked up in his impenetrable solitariness; he is incapable of imparting his own life fully to the Son. Out of care for the transcendence of God, Arius makes of the one and exalted God a prisoner of his own greatness."[14] So the world is not God's creation; this God cannot operate outwardly, he is closed up in himself, just as, consequently, the world is closed in on itself. The world proclaims no Creator, and God cannot proclaim himself. Man does not become a "friend"; there is no bridge of trust. In a world estranged from God we remain without truth, and thus remain slaves.

Here a saying of the Johannine Christ is of great importance: "He who sees me, sees the Father" (Jn 14:9). Christoph Schönborn has shown penetratingly how in the battle over the image of Christ a deeper wrestling with the divine capability of man, that is, his capacity for truth and freedom, was being mirrored. What does he see, who sees the man Jesus? What can an image that represents this man Jesus show? According to one view, we see there only a man, nothing more, since God cannot be captured in a likeness. His divinity lies in his "person," which as such cannot be "delineated" nor brought into a picture. The exact opposite view has managed to prevail as orthodox in the Church, that is, as the proper explanation of Holy Scripture: He who sees Christ, truly sees the Father; in the visible is seen the invisible, the invisible one. The visible figure of Christ is not to be understood as static, one-dimensional, belonging only to the world of the senses, for the senses themselves are for movement and starting points beyond themselves. The one who looks upon the figure of Christ enters into his exodus, of which the Church Fathers speak expressly in connection with the experience of Mount Tabor. He is led along the Easter road of going beyond, and learns in the visible to see more than the visible.[15]

A first high point in this understanding was reached in the work of Cyril of Alexandria, after great beginnings by Athanasius and Gregory

14. Christoph Schönborn, *Die Christus-Ikone* (Schaffhausen, 1984), 20.

15. Ibid., esp. 30-54.

of Nyssa. Cyril does not deny that the Incarnation is at first a veiling, a hiding, of the glory of the Word. "The incomparable beauty of the divinity makes the humanity of Christ appear simply as 'extreme ugliness.' But this extreme degradation shows the greatness of the love whence it springs. The surrender to the formlessness of his death makes the love of the Father visible. . . . The crucified one is 'the image of the invisible God' (Col 1:15)."[16] Thus the humanity of Christ appears as "the image of the love of the Father made visible, the human translation of the eternal sonship."[17] Maximus the Confessor brought this line of theology to its peak, sketching a Christology that looks like one great interpretation of the saying, "He who sees me, sees the Father." In the exodus of Christ's love, that is, in the passage from opposition to community to which the cross of obedience leads, true redemption, or liberation, occurs. This exodus leads out of the slavery of *philautia,* of self-decay and self-isolation, into the love of God. "In Christ human nature has become capable of being like the love of God. . . . Love is the image of God."[18] Therefore he who sees Christ, the crucified one, sees the Father, and the entire trinitarian mystery. For we must add, when one sees the Father in Christ, then in him the veil of the temple is truly rent, and the interior of God is laid bare. For then the one and only God is visible not as a monad, but as Trinity. Then man truly becomes a friend, initiated into the innermost mystery of God. He is no longer a slave in a dark world, he knows the heart of the truth. But this truth is a way; it is the fatal, yet precisely — in the losing-of self — life-giving adventure of love that alone is freedom.

In the years between the World Wars and the decade preceding the council, great theologians like Karl Rahner and J. A. Jungmann spoke of a factual monophysitism of the faithful, of monophysitism as the danger to the Church in their time.[19] I do not venture to make that

16. Ibid., 96.

17. Ibid., 97.

18. Ibid., 134.

19. J. A. Jungmann, *Die Frohbotschaft und unsere Glaubensverkündigung* (Regensburg, 1936), 76ff., 100, n. 2. An abridged English translation appeared in *The Good News Yesterday and Today* (New York and Chicago, 1962). What Jungmann formulates here for dogmatic and pastoral uses in the present, he had already laid the groundwork for in his pioneering historical work, *Die Stellung Christi im liturgischen Gebet* (Münster, 1925; reprinted 1962), esp. 51f. and 200ff. For an English translation, see *The Place of Christ in Liturgical*

judgment, though one would be hard put to contradict some of their arguments. Whatever the case, today we stand before the exact opposite danger, the danger of a new Arianism, or milder, at least a well-marked new Nestorianism, reflected by an inner logic in a new flood of images. Now Maximus the Confessor is anything but a monophysite; we have him to thank in great part for overcoming that last form of monophysitism, monothelitism. For him it is essential that precisely in the *man* Jesus, we truly see the Father. His entire theology of Mt. Olivet and the Cross, the exodus of mankind in a new Moses, would otherwise lose its meaning. But Maximus is also thus the decisive overcoming of Nestorianism, which cuts us off from the mystery of the Trinity and again makes the wall of transcendence practically impenetrable. If we remain on this side of that wall, we are slaves, not friends.[20]

I would like to add a second remark. In calling Christ the "way," the thought of freedom and liberation forces itself on us. Now it is clear that truth and freedom are inseparably bound together. On the other hand, it seems far-fetched, if not senseless, to tie in the idea of the poor Christ with the motif of truth; and yet there is a profound relationship. Truth has been discredited in history because it has been offered from a position of domination and made an excuse for force and oppression. Plato had already seen the danger that comes when one sees truth as a possession and thus as power for domination. Out of respect for the greatness of truth, he coupled his acknowledgment of it with self-irony, as an expression "of his own inadequacy, from which not skepti-

---

Prayer (New York, 1965). Both books were formative for a whole generation of scholars and pastors. Cf. the much respected contribution of Karl Rahner, "Chalkedon. Ende oder Anfang?" in A. Grillmeier and H. Bacht, *Das Konzil von Chalkedon III* (Würzburg, 1954), 9ff. Formative importance in this connection also belongs to the publications of F. X. Arnold, e.g., his contribution in the same volume, "Das gott-menschliche Prinzip der Seelsorge und die Geschichte der christlichen Frömmigkeit," 287-340. Arnold calls especially upon Karl Adam, *Christus unser Bruder* (Regensburg, 1934), where the great Tübingen theologian formulated critiques similar to Jungmann's. See esp. 300f. (Eng., *Christ Our Brother* [New York, 1931]).

20. Cf. in this connection the penetrating analysis of the foundations of Christology by Maximus in Schönborn, *Die Christus-Ikone,* 107-138. Also F. Heinzer, *Gottes Sohn als Mensch. Die Struktur des Menschseins Christi bei Maximus Confessor* (Fribourg, Switzerland, 1980); F. Heinzer, Christoph Schönborn, eds., *Maximus Confessor. Actes du Symposium sur Maxime le Confesseur* (Fribourg, 1982).

cism but highest caution" resulted.[21] Thus did the eighty-year-old Romano Guardini summarize Plato's understanding of truth, and thereby characterize his own way, which was always marked both with a passionate dedication to truth and his own self-effacement. The paradox of Plato between truth and irony seems to me to be an approach to the paradox of divine truth, which shines forth in the crucified one precisely as poverty and helplessness: *he* is the image of God, because he is the shining forth of love, and therefore the cross is his "glory." William of St. Thierry, in his *Treatise on Love,* dramatically expressed this divine paradox, that the truth of the trinitarian God, the highest glory, shines forth in the ultimate poverty of the crucified.

> As now the "Image of God," God the Son, saw how angels and men who were created after him, that is, according to the image of God (without being themselves the image of God), were destroyed by a disordered grasping after the image, he said to himself: "Alas, only misery awakens no envy. . . . So I will present myself to mankind as the despised man and as the last of all, . . . that they may burn with ambition to imitate me in humility, through which they may then reach glory."[22]

The truth, the real truth, has made itself tolerable to man, has become a *way,* in that it has appeared and now appears in the poverty of the powerless. Not the rich carouser, but the despised Lazarus outside the door represents the mystery of God, the Son.[23] In Christ, poverty has become the genuine sign, the inner "power," of truth. Nothing else has opened his way into the hearts of men so much as this, the truth of his poverty. The humility of God is the door to truth in the world; there is no other. It is only in this way that truth can become a way. What Paul says at the end of his letter to the Galatians, after all argumentation, holds firm: his last argument consists not in words, but in

21. Romano Guardini, *Stationen und Rückblicke* (Würzburg, 1965), 50 (in his acceptance speech, "Wahrheit und Ironie" on the occasion of his eightieth birthday).

22. William of St. Thierry, *De natura et dignitate amoris,* 40. Cited according to the German translation of Hans Urs von Balthasar, *Der Spiegel des Glaubens* (Einsiedeln, 1981), 170.

23. The christological meaning of the Lazarus parable is penetratingly brought out in P. H. Kolvenbach, *Der österliche Weg* (Herder, 1988), 136.

the stigmata of Christ, which he bears in his own body.[24] In any dispute about true Christianity, about the right faith and the right way, the community of the Cross is the last and determinative measure.

4. Christ the Life — Pre-existence and Love

Our closing reflection must take up at least briefly the third word of Jesus' self-proclamation: Jesus the life. The fanatical eagerness for life which we meet on all continents today has sprouted an anti-culture of death, which is becoming more and more the physiognomy of our time. The unleashing of sexual desires, drugs, and the traffic in arms have become an unholy triad, whose deadly net stretches ever more oppressively over the continents. Abortion, suicide, and collective violence are the concrete way in which the syndicate of death works. AIDS has become a portrait of the inner sickness of our culture. There is no longer an immune system for the soul. Positivistic intelligence offers the soul's organism no ethical immune power; it is the ruin of the soul's immune system, and thus the defenseless surrender to the lying promises of death, which appear in the guise of more life. Medical research is at full tilt in search of a vaccine against the disintegration of the body's immunizing powers, and that is its obligation. It will, nevertheless, merely displace the arena of destruction, and not hold back the victorious campaign of the anti-culture of death, unless at the same time it is recognized that bodily immune sickness is an outcry of misused human nature, an image which represents the real sickness, the defenselessness of souls in an intellectual climate that annuls the real values of being human, that is, the values of God and the soul.

If we Christians in this situation just stand by and offer appeasing words, we are totally superfluous. In order to satisfy the claim to be modern or post-modern, it is not enough to submit oneself to one's own standards and to demonstrate that one can take part in society by so doing. This false kind of progressive Christianity would be only ridiculous, if it were not so dismal and dangerous. It accelerates the spiral of death, instead of setting against it the healing power of life. The Marxist analysis, with which some still wish to show the way out of the

24. H. Schlier, *Der Brief an die Galater* (Göttingen, 1962), 179-185.

contradictions of our time, is an absurd anachronism in the face of the kind of dominion of money and desires, which are the unifying bond in the devilish trinity of sex, drugs, and collective violence. If there is not a basic healing of souls, these structural analyses are nothing but a pure superstition, which then furthers the destruction of the inner immune powers because it strives to replace the powers of ethos with the technical and the mechanical or structural.

In this situation the realism of the Christian must be found anew: Jesus Christ must be found in today; we must grasp anew what it means to say, "I am the way, the truth, and the life." For this it would be proper to offer an exact analysis of the sickness, but that is impossible here. Let us be satisfied with the fundamental question: Why do people flee to drugs? In general terms we can say they do it because the life that is offered them is too insipid, too scanty, too empty. After all the pleasures, after all the liberations and hopes that one has pinned on these, there remains a "much-too-little." To endure and accept life as hardship becomes insufferable. Life itself should be an inexhaustibly giving, unbounded joy. Two other things are also in play: for one, the desire for completeness, for infinity, which contrasts with the limitations of our life; for another, the wish simply to have all this without pain, without effort. Life should give to us, without our self-giving. Thus we could also say that the reality of the whole process is the denial of love, which leads to the flight into lies. But behind this is a false view of God, that is, the denial of God and the worship of an idol. For God is understood in the way of the rich man: he could yield nothing to Lazarus because he wanted to be a god himself, and for that reason even the much that he had was always too little. Thus, God is understood in the manner of Arius, for whom God can have no external relationships because he is only entirely himself. Man desires to be such a god, one to whom everything comes and who gives nothing. And therefore the true God is the real enemy, the competition for a man so inwardly blind. Here is the real core of his sickness, for then he is settled in the lie and turned aside from love, which even in the Trinity is a boundless, unconditional self-giving. Thus it is that the crucified Christ – Lazarus – is the true picture of the trinitarian God. In him, this trinitarian being, the whole of love and the whole of self-giving, is seen undimmed.[25]

25. Cf. Kolvenbach, *Der österliche Weg*, 133-142.

Now perhaps we can begin to understand the meaning of a saying of Jesus from his high-priestly prayer, one which at first might seem a completely unreal expression of a special religious world: "This is eternal life, that they know you, the only true God, and Jesus Christ, whom you have sent" (Jn 17:3). Today we are generally unable to see any longer that the matter of God is something of the greatest reality, that it is the real key to our deepest needs. And this points out the seriousness of the sickness of our civilization. In fact there will be no healing if God is not again recognized as the foundation of our entire existence. Only in union with God is human life truly life. Without him, it remains within the threshold of self and destroys itself. This redemptive union with God is only possible in him whom he has sent, through whom he is God-with-us. We cannot "construct" this union. Christ is the life because he brings us into this union with God. Only here do we find the fountain of living water.

"He who thirsts, let him come to me and drink," says Christ on the last great day of the Feast of Booths (Jn 7:37). The feast commemorates the thirst of Israel in the scorching heat of the waterless desert, which appears as a kingdom of death with no escape. But Christ announces himself as the rock from which flows an inexhaustible fountain of fresh water: in death he becomes the fountain of life.[26] Let him who thirsts come: Has not our world, with all its capabilities and power, become a desert where we can no longer find the fountain of life? Let him who thirsts come: he is even today the inexhaustible fountain of living water. We must only come and drink, that the saying may apply to us: "He who believes in me, as the scripture has said, 'Out of his heart shall flow rivers of living water'" (Jn 7:38). One cannot simply "take" or receive life, the real life. Rather, it draws us into its own dynamic of Christ who is the life. To drink of the living water of the rock means consenting to the saving mystery of the water and the blood. Here is the radical opposite of that desire which drives one to drugs. It is the consent to love and the entering into truth. And yes, that is life.

Translated by Thomas Caldwell, S.J.

26. Cf. the fine interpretation of this text in Kolvenbach, *Der österliche Weg,* 176ff.; it also contains important insights on the notion of "life." For historical background on the text and patristic exegesis, cf. R. Schnackenburg, *Das Johannesevangelium. II Teil* (Freiburg, 1871), 211-218 (*The Gospel According to St. John* [New York, 1980]).

Concerning the Notion of Person in Theology

The concept of person, as well as the idea that stands behind this concept, is a product of Christian theology. In other words, it grew in the first place out of the interplay between human thought and the data of Christian faith and so entered intellectual history. The concept of the person is thus, to speak with Gilson, one of the contributions to human thought made possible and provided by Christian faith. It did not simply grow out of mere human philosophizing, but out of the interplay between philosophy and the antecedent given of faith, especially Scripture. More specifically, the concept of person arose from two questions that have from the very beginning urged themselves upon Christian thought as central: namely, the question, "What is God?" (i.e., the God whom we encounter in Scripture); and, "Who is Christ?" In order to answer these fundamental questions that arose as soon as faith began to reflect, Christian thought made use of the philosophically insignificant or entirely unused concept "prosopon" = "persona." It thereby gave to this word a new meaning and opened up a new dimension of human thought. Although this thought has distanced it-

---

This article appeared in *Communio* 17, no. 3 (Fall 1990). The article is a translation of the chapter, "Zum Personenverständnis in der Theologie," in Joseph Ratzinger, *Dogma und Verkündigung* (Munich: Erich Wewel Verlag, 1973).

AUTHOR'S NOTE: This article reproduces a lecture given at a congress on the understanding of the person in educational theory and related disciplines. The form of the lecture was preserved with slight modifications. This origin explains the sketchiness and preliminary nature of the text.

self far from its origin and developed beyond it, it nevertheless lives, in a hidden way, from this origin. In my judgment one cannot, therefore, know what "person" most truly means without fathoming this origin.

For this reason please forgive me because, although I was asked to talk as a systematic theologian about the dogmatic concept of the person, I will not present the latest ideas of modern theologians. Instead, I will attempt to go back to the origin, to the source and ground from which the idea of "person" was born and without which it could not exist. The outline flows from what was said above. We will simply take a closer look at the two origins of the concept of person, its origin in the question of God, and its origin in the question of Christ.

1. The Concept of Person in the Doctrine of God

a. The Origin of the Concept of Person

The first figure we meet is that of the great Western theologian Tertullian. Tertullian shaped Latin into a theological language and, with the almost incredible sureness of a genius, he knew how to develop a theological terminology that remained unsurpassable in later centuries, because already on the first attempt it gave form permanently to valid formulae of Christian thought. Thus it was Tertullian who gave to the West its formula for expressing the Christian idea of God. God is *"una substantia — tres personae,"* one being in three persons.[1] It was here that the word "person" entered intellectual history for the first time with its full weight.

It took centuries for this statement to be intellectually penetrated and digested, until it was no longer a mere statement, but truly a means of reaching into the mystery, teaching us, not, of course, to comprehend it, but somehow to grasp it. When we realize that Tertullian was able to coin the phrase while its intellectual penetration was still in its infancy, the question arises, How could he find this word with almost somnambulant sureness? Until recently, this was a puzzle. Carl Andresen, historian of dogma at Göttingen, has been able to solve this puzzle so that

1. The final formula of the West was *una essential — tres personae;* Tertullian had said, *una substantia — tres personae,* Augustine *una essential — tres substantiae.*

the origin of the concept of person, its true source and ground, is somewhat clear to us today.[2] The answer to the question of the origin of the concept "person" is that it originated in "prosopographic exegesis." What does this mean? In the background stands the word *prosopon,* which is the Greek equivalent of *persona.* Prosopographic exegesis is a form of interpretation developed already by the literary scholars of antiquity. The ancient scholars noticed that, in order to give dramatic life to events, the great poets of antiquity did not simply narrate these events but allowed persons to make their appearance and to speak. For example, they placed words in the mouths of divine figures and the drama progresses through these words. In other words, the poet creates the artistic device of roles through which the action can be depicted in dialogue. The literary scholar uncovers these roles; he shows that the persons have been created as "roles" in order to give dramatic life to events (in fact, the word *prosopon,* later translated by "persona," originally means simply "role," the mask of the actor). Prosopographic exegesis is thus an interpretation that brings to light this artistic device by making it clear that the author has created dramatic roles, dialogical roles, in order to give life to his poem or narrative.

In their reading of Scripture, the Christian writers came upon something quite similar. They found that here too, events progress in dialogue. They found, above all, the peculiar fact that God speaks in the plural or speaks with himself (e.g., "Let *us* make man in our image and likeness," or God's statement in Genesis 3, "Adam has become like one of *us,*" or Psalm 110, "The Lord said to my Lord," which the Greek Fathers take to be a conversation between God and his Son). The Fathers approach this fact, namely, that God is introduced in the plural as speaking with himself, by means of prosopographic exegesis, which thereby takes on a new meaning. Justin, who wrote in the first half of the second century (d. 165), already says, "The sacred writer introduces different *prosopa,* different roles." However, now the word no longer really means "roles," because it takes on a completely new reality in terms of faith in the Word of God. The roles introduced by the sacred writer are realities, they are dialogical realities. The word *prosopon* =

2. C. Andresen, "Zur Entstehung und Geschichte des trinitarischen Personenbegriffs," *Zeitschrift für die neutestamentliche Wissenschaft und die Kunde der älteren Kirche* 52 (1961): 1-38. The patristic texts cited below are taken from Andresen's article.

"role" is thus at the transitional point where it gives birth to the idea of person. I will cite merely one text by Justin to clarify this process. "When you hear that the prophets make statements as if a person were speaking *(hos apo prosopou),* then do not suppose that they were spoken immediately by those filled with the spirit (i.e., the prophets), but rather by the *Logos* who moves them."[3] Justin thus says that the dialogical roles introduced by the prophets are not mere literary devices. The "role" truly exists; it is the *prosopon,* the face, the person of the Logos who truly speaks here and *joins* in dialogue with the prophet. It is quite clear here how the data of Christian faith transform and renew a pre-given ancient schema used in interpreting texts. The literary artistic device of letting roles appear to enliven the narrative with their dialogue reveals to the theologians *the one* who plays the true role here, the *Logos,* the *prosopon,* the person of the Word which is no longer merely role, but person.

About fifty years later, when Tertullian wrote his works, he was able to go back to an extensive tradition of such Christian prosopographic exegesis in which the word *prosopon* = *persona* had already found its full claim to reality. Two examples must suffice. In *Adversus Praxean,* Tertullian writes, "How can a person who stands by himself say, 'Let us make man in our image and likeness,' when he ought to have said, 'Let *me* make man in my image and likeness,' as someone who is single and alone for himself. If he were only one and single, then God deceived and tricked also in what follows when he says, 'Behold, Adam has become like one of us,' which he said in the plural. But he did not stand alone, because there stood with him the Son, his Word, and a third person, the Spirit in the Word. This is why he spoke in the plural, 'Let *us* make' and *'our'* and *'us.'*"[4] One sees how the phenomenon of *intra*-divine dialogue gives birth here to the idea of the person who is person in an authentic sense. Tertullian similarly says in his interpretation of "The Lord said to my Lord" (Ps 110:1), "Take note how even the Spirit as the third person speaks of the Father and of the Son, 'The Lord said to my Lord, sit at my right hand until I put your enemies at your feet.' Likewise through Isaiah, 'The Lord says these words to my Lord Christ.' . . . In these few texts the distinction within the Trinity is clearly set before our eyes. For him-

3. Text cited by Andresen, ibid., 12.

4. *Adv. Prax.* 12, 1-3; Corpus Christianorum II, 1172f.; Andresen, 10-11.

self exists the one who speaks, namely, the Spirit; further the Father *to* whom he speaks, and finally the Son *of* whom he speaks."[5]

I do not wish to enter into the historical details of these texts. I will merely summarize what results from them for the issue of the idea "person." First, the concept "person" grew out of reading the Bible. Secondly, it grew out of the idea of dialogue, more specifically, it grew as an explanation of the phenomenon of the God who speaks dialogically. The Bible with its phenomenon of the God who speaks, the God who is *in* dialogue, stimulated the concept "person." The particular interpretations of Scripture texts offered by the Fathers are certainly accidental and outdated. But their exegetical direction as a whole captures the spiritual direction of the Bible inasmuch as the fundamental phenomenon into which we are placed by the Bible is the God who speaks and the human person who is addressed, the phenomenon of the partnership of the human person who is called by God to love in the word. However, the core of what "person" can truly mean comes thereby to light. To summarize we can say: The idea of person expresses in its origin the idea of dialogue and the idea of God as the dialogical being. It refers to God as the being that lives in the word and consists of the word as "I" and "you" and "we." In the light of this knowledge of God, the true nature of humanity became clear in a new way.

b. Person as Relation

The first stage of the struggle for the Christian concept of God has been sketched above. I want to add a brief look at the second main

5. *Adv. Prax.* 11, 7-10; Corpus Christianorum II, 1172. In my judgment it would be important to investigate the rabbinic antecedents of this prosopographic exegesis. Interesting relevant material is found in E. Sjöberg, "Geist im Judentum," *Theologische Wörterbuch zum Neuen Testament* 6, 385ff. Sjöberg shows that in rabbinic literature the Holy Spirit is often depicted in personal categories: he speaks, cries, admonishes, mourns, weeps, rejoices, consoles, etc. He is also portrayed as speaking to God. Sjöberg notes on this "that the stylistic device of personification and dramatization is typical for rabbinic literature" and "that the personal reaction of the Spirit is always tied to words of Sacred Scripture" (386). A closer analysis of the texts could perhaps show that the patristic elaboration of the concept of person does not take its point of departure from the literary criticism of antiquity, but from this rabbinic exegesis.

stage, in which the concept of "person" reached its full maturity.[6] About two hundred years later, at the turn of the fifth century, Christian theology reached the point of being able to express in articulated concepts what is meant in the thesis: God is a being in three persons. In this context, theologians argued, person must be understood as *relation*. According to Augustine and late patristic theology, the three persons that exist in God are in their nature relations. They are, therefore, not substances that stand next to each other, but they are real existing relations, and nothing besides. I believe this idea of the late patristic period is very important. In God, person means relation. Relation, being related, is not something superadded to the person, but it *is* the person itself. In its nature, the person exists only *as* relation. Put more concretely, the first person does not generate in the sense that the act of generating a Son is added to the already complete person, but the person *is* the deed of generating, of giving itself, of streaming itself forth. The person is identical with this act of self-donation.

One could thus define the first person as self-donation in fruitful knowledge and love; it is not the one who gives himself, in whom the act of self-donation is found, but it is this self-donation, pure reality of act. An idea that appeared again in our century in modern physics is here anticipated: that there is pure act-being. We know that in our century the attempt has been made to reduce matter to a wave, to a pure act of streaming. What may be a questionable idea in the context of physics was asserted by theology in the fourth and fifth century about the persons in God, namely, that they are nothing but the act of relativity or relationality toward each other. In God, person is the pure relativity of being turned toward the other; it does not lie on the level of substance — the substance is *one* — but on the level of dialogical reality, of relationality toward the other. In this matter Augustine could attempt, at least in outline, to show the interplay between threeness and unity by saying, for example: *in Deo nihil secundum accidens dicitur, sed secundum substantiam aut secundum relationem* (in God there is nothing accidental, but only substance and relation). Relation is here recognized as a third specific fundamental category between substance and accident, the two great categorical forms of thought in antiquity. Again we encoun-

6. For the historical background of the following discussion, see A. Grillmeier, "Person II," *Lexicon für Theologie und Kirche* 8.290-292 with bibliography.

ter the Christian newness of the personalistic idea in all its sharpness and clarity. The contribution offered by faith to human thought becomes especially clear and palpable here. It was faith that gave birth to this idea of pure act, of pure relativity, which does *not* lie on the level of substance and does not touch or divide substance; and it was faith that thereby brought the personal phenomenon into view.

We stand here at the point in which the speculative penetration of Scripture, the assimilation of faith by humanity's own thought, seems to have reached its highest point; and yet we can notice with astonishment that the way back into Scripture opens precisely here. For Scripture has clearly brought out precisely *this* phenomenon of pure relativity as the nature of the person. The clearest case is Johannine theology. In Johannine theology we find, for example, the formula, "The Son cannot do anything of himself" (5:19). However, the same Christ who says this says, "I and the Father are one" (10:30). This means, precisely because he has nothing of himself alone, because he does not place himself as a delimited substance next to the Father, but exists *in* total relativity toward him, and constitutes nothing but relativity toward him that does not delimit a precinct of what is merely and properly its own – precisely because of this they are one. This structure is in turn transferred – and here we have the transition to anthropology – to the disciples when Christ says, "Without me you can do nothing" (15:5). At the same time he prays "that they may be one as we are one" (17:11). It is thus part of the existence even of the disciples that man does not posit the reservation of what is merely and properly his own, does not strive to form the substance of the closed self, but enters into pure relativity toward the other and toward God. It is in this way that he truly comes to himself and into the fullness of his own, because he enters into unity with the one to whom he is related.

I believe a profound illumination of God as well as man occurs here, the decisive illumination of what person must mean in terms of Scripture: *not* a substance that closes itself in itself, but the phenomenon of complete relativity, which is, of course, realized in its entirety only in the one who is God, but which indicates the direction of all personal being. The point is thus reached here at which – as we shall see below – there is a transition from the doctrine of God into Christology and into anthropology.

One could go much further in following out this line of the idea of relation and of relativity in John, and in showing that it is *the* dominant theme of his theology, at any rate of his Christology. I want to mention only two examples. John picks up the theology of mission found in the Synoptics and in the Judaism of antiquity in which the idea is already formulated that the emissary, inasmuch as he is an emissary, is not important in himself, but stands for the sender and is one with the sender. John extends this Jewish idea of mission, which is at first a merely functional idea, by depicting Christ as *the* emissary who is in his entire nature "the one sent." The Jewish principle, "The emissary of a person is like that person," now takes on a completely new and deepened significance, because Jesus has absolutely nothing besides being the emissary, but is in his nature "the one sent." He is like the one who sent him precisely because he stands in complete relativity of existence toward the one who sent him. The content of the Johannine concept "the one sent" could be described as the absorption of being in "being from someone and toward someone." The content of Jesus' existence is "being from someone and toward someone," the absolute openness of existence without any reservation of what is merely and properly one's own. And again the idea is extended to Christian existence of which it is said, "As the Father has sent me, so I am sending you" (20:21). The other example is the doctrine of the *Logos,* the concept of the *Word* which is applied to Jesus. Once again, John picks up a schema of theological thought that was extremely widespread in the Greek and Jewish world. Of course, he thereby adopts a whole series of contents that are already developed therein and he applies them to Christ. However, there was a new element he introduced into the concept of the *Logos.* In important respects, what was decisive for him was not so much the idea of an eternal rationality – as among the Greeks, or whatever other speculation there may have been; what was decisive was much rather the relativity of existence that lies in the concept of the *Logos.*

For again, the point is that a word is essentially from someone else and toward someone else; word is existence that is completely path and openness. Some texts express this idea differently and clarify it, for instance when Christ says: "*My* teaching is *not* my teaching" (7:16). Augustine offers a marvelous commentary on this text by asking: Is this not a contradiction? It is either my teaching or not. He finds an answer in the statement, Christ's doctrine is he himself, and he himself is not his own, because his "I" exists entirely from the "you." He goes on to say, "*Quid tam tuum quam tu, quid tam non tuum quam tu* – what belongs to you as much as your 'I,' and what belongs to you as little as your 'I'?" Your "I" is on the one hand what is most your own and at the same time what you have least of yourself; it is most of all not your own, because it is only from the "you" that it can exist as an "I" in the first place.

Let us summarize: in God there are three persons – which implies, according to the interpretation offered by theology, that persons are relations, pure relatedness. Although this is in the first place only a statement about the Trinity, it is at the same time the fundamental statement about what is at stake in the concept of person. It opens the concept of person into the human spirit and provides its foundation and origin.

One final remark on this point: As already indicated, Augustine explicitly transposed this theological affirmation into anthropology by attempting to understand the human person as an image of the Trinity in terms of this idea of God. Unfortunately, however, he committed a decisive mistake here to which we will come back later. In his interpretation, he projected the divine persons into the interior life of the human person and affirmed that intra-psychic processes correspond to these persons. The person as a whole, by contrast, corresponds to the divine substance. As a result, the trinitarian concept of person was no longer transferred to the human person in all its immediate impact. However, at present we can merely hint at this point; it will become clearer below.

2. The Concept of Person in Christology

The second origin of the concept of person lies in Christology. In order to find its way through difficult problems, theology again used the word *persona* and thus gave the human mind a new task. Theology answered the riddle, "Who and what is this Christ?" by means of the formula, "He has two natures and one person, a divine and a human nature, but only a divine person." Here again the word *persona* is introduced. One must say that this statement suffered from tremendous misunderstandings in Western thought. These misunderstandings must be removed first, in order to approach the authentic meaning of the christological concept of person. The first misunderstanding is to take the statement, "Christ has only one person, namely, a divine person," as a subtraction from the wholeness of Jesus' humanity. This misunderstanding has occurred *de facto* and is still occurring. All too easily one thinks as follows: Person is the authentic and true apex of human existence. It is missing in Jesus. Therefore the entirety of human reality is not present in him. The assumption that some defect is present here was the point of departure of various distortions and aberrations, for example in the theology of the saints and of the Mother of God. In reality, this formula does *not* mean that anything is lacking in the humanity of the man Jesus. That nothing is lacking in his humanity was fought through inch by inch in the history of dogma, for the attempt was made again and again to show where something is missing. Arianism and Apollinarianism first thought Christ had no human *soul;* monophysitism denied him his human *nature.* After these fundamental errors had been rejected, weaker forms of the same tendency made their appearance. The monothelites asserted that although Christ had everything, he had at least no human will, the heart of personal existence. After this view had been rejected too, monergism appeared. Although Christ had a human will, he did not have the actualization of this will; the actualization comes from God. These are all attempts at locating the concept of person at some place in the psychic inventory. One after another was rejected in order to make one point clear: this is not how the statement is meant; nothing is missing; no subtraction from humanity whatever is permitted or given. I believe that if one follows this struggle in which human reality had to be brought in, as it were, and affirmed for Jesus, one sees what tremendous effort and intellectual transformation lay behind the working out of this concept of person, which was quite foreign in its inner disposition to the Greek and the Latin mind. It is not conceived in substantialist, but, as we shall soon see, in existential terms. In this light, Boethius's concept of person, which prevailed in Western philosophy, must be criticized as entirely insufficient. Remaining on the level of the Greek mind, Boethius defined "person" as *naturae rationalis individua substantia,* as the individual substance of a rational nature. One sees that the concept of person stands entirely on the level of substance. This cannot clarify anything about the Trinity or about Christology; it is an affirmation that remains on the level of the Greek mind which thinks in substantialist terms.

By contrast, at the beginning of the Middle Ages, Richard of St. Victor found a concept of the person derived from within Christianity when he defined person as *spiritualis naturae incommunicabilis existentia,* as the incommunicably proper existence of spiritual nature. This definition correctly sees that in its theological meaning "person" does not lie on the level of essence, but of existence. Richard thereby gave the impetus for a philosophy of existence which had, as such, not been made the subject of philosophy at all in antiquity. In antiquity philosophy was limited entirely to the level of essence. Scholastic theology developed categories of existence out of this contribution given by Christian faith to the human mind. Its defect was that it limited these categories to Christology and to the doctrine of the Trinity and did not make them fruitful in the whole extent of spiritual reality. This seems to me also the limit of St. Thomas in the matter, namely, that within theology he operates, with Richard of St. Victor, on the level of existence, but treats the whole thing as a theological exception, as it were. In philosophy, however, he remains faithful to the different approach of pre-Christian philosophy. The contribution of Christian faith to the whole of human thought is not realized; it remains at first detached from it as a theological exception, although it is precisely the *meaning* of this new element to call into question the *whole* of human thought and to set it on a new course.

This brings us to the second misunderstanding that has not allowed the effects of Christology to work themselves out fully. The second great misunderstanding is to see Christ as the simply unique ontological exception which must be treated as such. This exception is an object of highly interesting ontological speculation, but it must remain separate in its box as an exception to the rule and must not be permitted to mix with the rest of human thought. I believe it is useful here to remind ourselves of a methodological insight developed by Teilhard de Chardin in a completely different field. He raises the question of the nature of life, "Is it only an accident, on a tiny planet in the midst of the great cosmos, or is it symptomatic for the direction of reality as a whole?" He uses the discovery of radium as an example to address this question: "How should one understand the new element? As an anomaly, an aberrant form of matter? . . . As a curiosity or as the beginning for a new physics?" Modern physics, Teilhard continues, "would not have come to be if physicists had insisted on understanding radioactivity as an anomaly."[7] Something methodologically decisive for all human thinking becomes visible here. The seeming exception is in reality very often the symptom that shows us the insufficiency of our previous schema of order, which helps us to break open this schema and to conquer a new realm of reality. The exception shows us that we have built our closets too small, as it were, and that we must break them open and go on in order to see the whole.

This is the meaning of Christology from its origin: what is disclosed in Christ, whom faith certainly presents as unique, is not only a speculative exception; what is disclosed in truth is what the riddle of the human person really intends. Scripture expresses this point by calling Christ the last Adam or "the second Adam." It thereby characterizes him as the true fulfillment of the idea of the human person, in which the direction of meaning of this being comes fully to light for the first time. If it is true, however, that Christ is not the ontological exception, if from his exceptional position he is, on the contrary, the fulfillment of the entire human being, then the christological concept of person is an indication for theology of how person is to be understood as such. In fact, this concept of person, or simply the dimension that has become visible here, has always acted as a spark in intellectual history and it has propelled development, even when it had long come to a standstill in theology.

After these two fundamental misunderstandings have been rejected, the question remains, What does the formula mean positively, "Christ has two natures in one person"? I must admit right away that a theological response has not yet completely matured. In the great struggles of the first six centuries, theology worked out what the person is not, but it did not clarify with the same definiteness what the word means positively. For this reason I can only provide some hints that point out the direction in which reflection should probably continue.[8]

7. Quoted from Cl. Tresmontant, *Einführung in das Denken Teilhard de Chardins* (Munich, 1961), 41f.

8. On what follows, see the instructive contribution of B. Welte, *"Homoousios hemin,"* in A. Grillmeier and H. Bacht, *Das Konzil von Chalcedon,* vol. 3 (Würzburg, 1954), 51-80; H. Conrad-Martius, *Das Sein* (Munich, 1957). For the patristic period, special mention should be made of Maximus the Confessor, by whom the positive clarification of the christological concept of person was pushed furthest; cf. H. U. von Balthasar, *Kosmische Liturgie: Das Weltbild Maximus' des Bekenners,* 2nd ed. (Einsiedeln, 1961), 232-253 (*Cos-*

I believe two points can be made: (a) It is the nature of spirit to put itself in relation, the capacity to see itself and the other. Hedwig Conrad-Martius speaks of the retroscendence of the spirit: the spirit is not merely there; it goes back upon itself, as it were; it knows about itself; it constitutes a doubled existence which not only *is,* but *knows* about itself, *has* itself. The difference between matter and spirit would, accordingly, consist in this, that matter is what is *"das auf sich Geworfene"* (that which is thrown upon itself), while the spirit is *"das sich selbst Entwerfende"* (that which throws itself forth, guides itself or designs itself) which is not only there, but is itself in transcending itself, in looking toward the other and in looking back upon itself.[9] However this may be in detail – we need not investigate it here – openness, relatedness to the whole, lies in the essence of the spirit. And precisely in this, namely, that it not only *is,* but reaches beyond itself, it comes to itself. In transcending itself it *has* itself; by being with the other it first becomes itself, it comes to itself. Expressed differently again: being with the other is its form of being with itself. One is reminded of a fundamental theological axiom that is applicable here in a peculiar manner, namely Christ's saying, "Only the one who loses himself can find himself" (cf. Mt 10:39). This fundamental law of human existence, which Mt 10:39 understands in the context of salvation, objectively characterizes the nature of the spirit that comes to itself and actualizes its own fullness only by going away from itself, by going to what is other than itself.

We must go one step further. The spirit is that being which is able to think about, not only itself and being in general, but the wholly other, the transcendent God. This is perhaps the mark that truly distinguishes the human spirit from other forms of consciousness found in animals, namely, that the human spirit can reflect on the wholly other, the concept of God. We may accordingly say: The other through which the spirit comes to itself is finally that wholly other for which we use the stammering word "God." If this is true, then what was said above can be further clarified in the horizon of faith and we may say: If the human person is all the more with itself, and is itself, the more it is

---

mic Liturgy: The Universe According to Maximus the Confessor [San Francisco: Ignatius Press/Communio Books, 2003]).

9. H. Conrad-Martius, *Das Sein,* 133.

able to reach beyond itself, the more it is with the other, then the person is all the more itself the more it is with the wholly other, with God.

In other words, the spirit comes to itself in the other; it becomes completely itself the more it is with the other, with God. And again, formulated the other way around, because this idea seems important to me: relativity toward the other constitutes the human person. The human person is the event or being of relativity. The more the person's relativity aims totally and directly at its final goal, at transcendence, the more the person is itself.

(b) In this light we may venture a second approach: According to the testimony of faith, in Christ there are two natures and one person, that of the *Logos.* This means, however, that in him, being with the other is realized radically. Relativity toward the other is always the pregiven foundation to all consciousness as that which carries his existence. But such total being-with-the-other does not cancel his being-with-himself, but brings it fully to itself. Of course, one will admit that the chosen terminology, *una persona — duae naturae,* remains accidental and is not without problems. But the decisive thing that emerges from it for the concept of the person and for the understanding of human beings is, in my judgment, still completely clear. In Christ, in the man who is completely with God, human existence is not canceled, but comes to its highest possibility, which consists in transcending itself into the absolute and in the integration of its own relativity into the absoluteness of divine love.

As a consequence, a dynamic definition of the human person flows from Christ, the new Adam. Christ is the directional arrow, as it were, that indicates what being human tends toward, although, as long as history is still on the way, this goal is never fully reached. At the same time it is clear that such a definition of being human manifests the historicity of the human person. If person is the relativity toward the eternal, then this relativity implies "being on the way" in the manner of human history.

(c) In closing, a third idea. In my judgment Christology has a further significance for the understanding of the concept of "person" in its theological sense. It adds the idea of "we" to the idea of "I" and "you." Christ, whom Scripture calls the final Adam, that is, the definitive human being, appears in the testimonies of faith as the all-encompassing space in which the "we" of human beings gathers on the way to the Father. He is not only an example that is followed, but he is the integrating space in which the "we" of human beings gathers itself toward the "you" of God. Something emerges here that has not been sufficiently seen in modern philosophy, not even in Christian philosophy. In Christianity there is not simply a dialogical principle in the modern sense of a pure "I-thou" relationship, neither on the part of the human person that has its place in the historical "we" that bears it; nor is there such a mere dialogical principle on God's part who is, in turn, no simple "I," but the "we" of Father, Son, and Spirit. On *both* sides there is neither the pure "I," nor the pure "you," but on both sides the "I" is integrated into the greater "we." Precisely this final point, namely, that not even God can be seen as the pure and simple "I" toward which the human person tends, is a fundamental aspect of the theological concept of the person. It explicitly negates the divine monarchy in the sense of antiquity. It expressly refuses to define God as the pure *monarchia* and numerical unity.[10] The Christian concept of God has as a matter of principle given the same dignity to multiplicity as to unity. While antiquity considered multiplicity the corruption of unity, Christian faith, which is a Trinitarian faith, considers multiplicity as belonging to unity with the same dignity.[11]

This trinitarian "we," the fact that even God exists only as a "we," prepares at the same time the space of the human "we." The Christian's relation to God is not simply, as Ferdinand Ebner claims somewhat one-sidedly, "I and Thou," but, as the liturgy prays for us every day, *"per Christum in Spiritu Sancto ad Patrem"* (through Christ in the Holy Spirit to the Father). Christ, the one, is here the "we" into which Love, namely the Holy Spirit, gathers us and which means simultaneously being bound to each other and being directed toward the common "you" of the one Father.

The bracketing from Christian piety of the reality of the "we" that emerges in the three-fold formula "through Christ in the Holy Spirit to the Father," and that binds us into the "we" of God and into the "we" of our fellow human beings, happened as a consequence of the anthro-

10. Cf. E. Peterson, "Der Monotheismus als politisches Problem," in *Theologische Traktate* (Munich, 1951), 45-147.

11. Cf. J. Ratzinger, *Einführung in das Christentum,* 11th ed. (Munich, 1970), 92, 139f. (*Introduction to Christianity* [San Francisco: Ignatius Press/Communio Books, 2004]).

pological turn in Augustine's doctrine of the Trinity and was one of the most momentous developments of the Western Church. In fundamental ways it influenced both the concept of the Church and the understanding of the person, which was now pushed off into the individualistically narrowed "I and you" that finally loses the "you" in this narrowing. It was indeed a result of Augustine's doctrine of the Trinity that the persons of God were closed wholly into God's interior. Toward the outside, God became a simple "I," and the whole dimension of "we" lost its place in theology.[12] The individualized "I" and "you" narrow themselves more and more until finally, for example in Kant's transcendental philosophy, the "you" is no longer found. In Feuerbach (and thus in a place where one would least suspect it) this leveling of "I" and "you" into a single transcendental consciousness gave way to the breakthrough to personal reality. It thus gave the impetus to reflect more deeply on the origin of our own being, which faith recognizes as once and for all disclosed in the word of Jesus the Christ.

Translated by Michael Waldstein

12. On Augustine's doctrine of the Trinity up to 391, see O. Du Roy, *L'intelligence de la foi en la Trinité selon St. Augustin* (Paris, 1966); for the further development, see M. Schmaus, *Die psychologische Trinitätslehre des heiligen Augustinus,* 2nd ed. (Münster, 1967). Today, of course, I would not judge as harshly as I did in the lecture above, because for Augustine the "psychological doctrine of the Trinity" remains an attempt to understand that is balanced by the factors of the tradition. The turn brought about by Thomas through the separation of the doctrine of the one God and the theological doctrine of the Trinity was more incisive. It led Thomas to consider the formula, "God is one person" legitimate, although it had been considered heretical in the early Church (*Summa theologiae* III, q. 3, a. 3 ad 1). On the subject of the "we," see H. Mühlen, *Der Heilige Geist als Person,* 2nd ed. (Münster, 1967).

The Meaning of Sunday

1. The Question

It is the year 304. In a place in northern Africa, at the height of the persecution ordered by Diocletian, some Roman officials surprise a group of about fifty Christians during the Sunday celebration of the Eucharist, and they arrest them.

The minutes of the raid and of the subsequent interrogation have been conserved. The proconsul says to the presbyter Saturninus: "You have acted in opposition to the orders of the Emperors and the Caesars in assembling all those people here together." At this point the Christian editor adds that the reply of the presbyter was the fruit of the inspiration of the Holy Spirit. He chimes out: "Without any apprehension we have celebrated all that which pertains to the Lord." "All that which pertains to the Lord" – this is the way I translate the Latin word *dominicus* (*Dominica dies,* the Lord's day). Because of its wealth of meaning, it is not easy to render this word in any modern language. In the first place, in fact, it indicates the *day* of the Lord, but it also refers at the same time to that which constitutes its subject matter: to the sacrament of the Lord, to his Resurrection and to his presence in the eucharistic event.

But let us return to the minutes. The proconsul is insistent with

---

This article first appeared as "Was feiern wir am Sonntag?" in *Internationale katholische Zeitschrift Communio* 3 (1982). Published in *Communio* 21, no. 1 (Spring 1994).

his questions; and here is the response, at once serene and stately, of the priest: "We did it because all that pertains to the Lord cannot be neglected." Here the consciousness that the Lord is on a plane more elevated than that of other divinities and powers is unequivocally expressed. Such a consciousness gives assurance to this priest (as he himself affirms) exactly at the moment in which the total material instability of the small Christian community at the mercy of its own jailors is fully manifested.

In a certain sense, the response given by Emeritus, the owner of the home at which the festive eucharistic celebration took place, makes an even greater impression. Asked why he would have given permission for an assembly forbidden by law to occur in his own house, he answers in the first place that, in truth, the assembled were his brothers; he, therefore, could not put them out the door. The proconsul is not satisfied and presses on. And thus, in the second response, that which properly constitutes the basis and motivation of their activity comes to light. "You ought to have forbidden their entry," the proconsul objects to him. "I could not," repeats Emeritus, who continues: *"Quoniam sine dominico non possumus"* ("because without the day of the Lord, without the Mystery of the Lord, we simply could not be"). To the will of the Caesars is opposed a clear and resolute "it is not possible" of Christian conscience.[1] This is placed in continuity with the "We cannot keep still" – the obligation of Christian proclamation – with which Peter and John had responded to the order given them by the Sanhedrin not to preach anymore (Acts 4:20).

"Without the day of the Lord we cannot live." This is not a labored obedience to an ecclesiastical prescription considered as some external precept, but is instead the expression of an interior duty and, at the same time, of a personal decision. It refers to that which has become the supporting nucleus of one's existence, of one's entire being, and it documents what has become so important as to need to be fulfilled even in the case of danger of death, imparting as it does a real assurance and internal freedom. To those who so expressed themselves, it

1. The texts of the Fathers concerning the issue of the Sabbath and the "day of the Lord" are found in the volume by W. Rordorf, *Sabbat und Sonntag in der Alten Kirchen* (Zurich, 1972) (*Traditio christiana,* II). The above cited minutes are in the *Acta ss. Saturini et aliorum,* col. 109, p. 176.

would have seemed manifestly absurd to guarantee survival and external tranquility for themselves at the price of the renunciation of this vital ground. They did not think of a casuistry nor of a pondering of what would be better to do — whether to fulfill a festal precept or a civil one, whether to respect an ecclesiastical prescription or to take into account the sentence incumbent on a capital conviction that might have led one to deem liturgical service as of lesser importance and thus able to be not followed. For them it was not a question of a choice between one precept and another, but rather of a choice between all that gave meaning and consistency to life and a life devoid of meaning. From this, the expression of Ignatius of Antioch becomes understandable: "We live in conformity with what we celebrate on the day of the Lord to whom our life is entirely consecrated. How could we live without him?"[2]

When one is confronted with the pallor and routine of the Sunday praxis of Christians in our old Europe, similar testimonies to those at the dawn of the history of the Church can readily give rise to nostalgic considerations. These also show that the "crisis of Sunday" is not an original phenomenon and exclusive to our generation. It has its beginnings from the moment in which, from the *internal* duty of Sunday — the "without celebrating the day of the Lord we cannot live" — an external canonical precept ensued, a formal "duty," which then, as happens to all duties that come "from without," is continually reduced until all that remains is a constraint to participate for a half hour at increasingly extraneous ritual practices. The question if and why it may be possible for us to exonerate ourselves of all this becomes, in the last analysis, more important than the question of why we normally should fulfill the duty. In the end, nothing else matters than freeing ourselves from it without any need for justification.

Since the meaning of Sunday has so gradually faded away and has been reduced to something merely superficial and external, it is now time for us to ask ourselves, even among believers, whether in our time the "day of the Lord" is, in actuality, still a really meaningful problem, and whether in our world, which has been freed from continuing threats of war and from so many social problems, there may be — even

2. Ignatius of Antioch, *Ad Magnesios,* 9:1, 2; in W. Rordorf, *Sabbat und Sonntag,* 134, no. 78.

for Christians, even above all for Christians – far more important questions. Tacitly, sometimes we ourselves end up by asking ourselves whether the aim of worship has not been simply a perpetrating of our "corporation," justifying, so to speak, our particular "profession."

In the background one finds a more profound question: whether it may not be above all an "idea" of God on whose realization the world depends. On the other hand, by nostalgically lingering in a comparison between the past and the present, we do not render justice either to the witness of the martyrs or to the reality of today. Notwithstanding all necessary self-criticism, we must not forget that even today there are many, many Christians who would from the bottom of their hearts conscientiously respond: "Without the Lord we can do nothing; it is not licit to neglect all that pertains to the Lord." And, to the contrary, we know that already at the time of the New Testament (Heb 10:25) the "poor attendance" in the temple on the part of believers had to be lamented. This rebuke will subsequently reverberate from the lips of the Fathers of the Church.

As a whole, it seems to me that in the frenzy of contemporary "consumption" of free time, in the avoidance of everydayness, and in the search for what is "totally new," the truly characteristic operating mechanism, even if it is misunderstood and for the most part unacknowledged, consists of a nostalgia for what the martyrs called *dominicus* – that is, the necessity to encounter that which reveals existence, the search for what Christians have experienced and still experience in the "day of the Lord." Our problem is how we can show this to people who are searching for it, and how we ourselves can rediscover it. Before indicating solutions or practical norms, which without a doubt are urgent and necessary, we must, above all, recover anew a deep understanding of all that is the "day of the Lord."

2. The Theology of the "Day of the Lord"

Let us begin with the most elementary aspect. In the first place, Sunday is a determinate day of the week. According to the Judaic numeration adopted precisely by Christians, it is the first day. We immediately must take into account the blunt fact that it can appear positivist and external. Why can we not celebrate on Fridays in the country of Islam, on

Saturdays where the majority is Jewish, and elsewhere on still another day? Why can't everyone choose the festal day that is most adequate for one's work and lifestyle? In other words, how is it that we have arrived at precisely this day as "festive"? Is it merely the question of a convention that we are able to rest and feast together? Or is something else at stake?

In the background, behind Sunday, the first day, another chronological formula of the New Testament also stands out, which is also found in the Church's profession of faith: "He arose on the third day, in accordance with the Scriptures" (1 Cor 15:4). In the most ancient ecclesiastical tradition, the accent was placed on the third day, maintaining thereby the memory of the discovery of the empty tomb and of the first apparitions of the risen Lord.[3] At the same time – and for this reason one adds "in accordance with the Scriptures" – it must be remembered that the third day was the day prefigured by Scripture, hence by the Old Testament itself, for this fundamental event of world history. More accurately, it is not an event of world history, but one of going beyond world history and overcoming the destiny of death of mortals and of the emerging and flowering of new life in time.

Through the connotation of the "third day," the concrete date is immediately interpreted in reference to its meaning. In the Old Testament descriptions of the sealing of the covenant on Mt. Sinai, the third day is always the day of theophany, that is, the day on which God shows and reveals himself.[4] Consequently, the indication of the "third day" serves to characterize the Resurrection of Jesus as the event that signals the definitive execution of the covenant as the real and definitive entry of God into history, which allows one to "touch him by the hand" in the living reality of our world – a "God at arm's length," as one would say today. The Resurrection means that God conserves his power over history and in history, that he has not abandoned it to natural laws. It means that he has not become impotent in the realm of matter and of materially determined life. All this means that the principle which all

3. Cf. J. Blank, *Paulus und Jesus* (Munich, 1968), 154ff.

4. Cf. especially Ex 19:11, 16. I have tried to describe the context of the phenomenon in an analytical way in my small study entitled *Der Gott Jesu Christi* (Munich, 1976), 76-84 (*The God of Jesus Christ* [San Francisco: Ignatius Press, 2008]). See also J. Ratzinger, *Suchen was droben ist* (Freiburg, 1985), 40ff. (*Seek That Which Is Above,* 2nd ed. [San Francisco: Ignatius Press, 2008]).

laws obey, the universal law of transience and death, is not yet the last word of the world and does not have the last power over it. The Ultimate is, and remains, he who is also the First.

In the world, "theophany" is made real: the formula of the "third day" affirms this. And it has taken place in such a way that God himself has reinstated justice not only for the living or for an unknown future generation, but justice for death, justice for him who died for the dead and for all. The theophany thus came about in this way: that one returned from death or, better, has victoriously thwarted the condition of death. It is realized because the body also was assumed into eternity – that it too was able to be clothed in eternity and in God. Jesus is not in some way dead in God, as one says today with an apparent pity, while despairing over the reality of the effective power of God and of the reality of the Resurrection of Christ. Behind this formula there is, in fact, the fear of unduly adhering to the language of the natural sciences in case the body, flesh, and bones of Christ were assumed into the generative potency of God, whereby one would think that he had imprinted the seal of his creative energy on the fabric of time and history.

Things being such, the disposition to receive salvation would be disavowed by matter. And, thus, it would be contested even by man, who is precisely the mutual compenetration of spirit and matter. I believe that several theories, which at first sight emphatically underscore the totality of man and, therefore, speak of a "total death" and of an "entirely new" corporal life, are nothing but poorly disguised dualisms that imagine the existence of an entirely unknown matter in order to wipe out the real, true, and proper, the concrete reality considered by theology – that is, the sphere of the word and action of God. But the Resurrection means that God says his "yes" to the *whole of reality* and that he *can* do this. In the Resurrection, God brings the approval of creation, already confirmed on the seventh day, to conclusion. Man's sin has been to try to make God a liar by declaring that his creation is by no means a good since it is precisely destined for death. The Resurrection means that God, by crossing through the labyrinth of sin and having power also over evil, definitively says: "It is something good." God pronounces his definitive approval and positive judgment of creation, assuming it to himself and thus transfiguring it beyond the transitory to the level of that which has perennial value.

At this juncture the link between Sunday and the Eucharist is proclaimed. The Resurrection is thus not an ordinary event on a level with others, one fact followed by others, which then slides little by little into the past. The Resurrection is instead the beginning of a present that does not know an end. Often, we live fully extraneously to this present. We distance ourselves all the more from it insofar as we are attached to all that is ephemeral and immediately disappears. And so do we distance ourselves from all that is made evident on the Cross and in the Resurrection as that which is properly present in midst of all that is transitory: the love that in the act of losing itself finds itself. *This love* remains present. The Eucharist is the living and actual presence of the Risen One who permanently communicates himself in the event of the Passion and, thus, is our life. The Eucharist itself is, therefore, the "day of the Lord": *dominicus,* as the martyrs of North Africa said in one word.

At the same time, it is here that the correlation between the Christian Sunday and faith in creation is revealed. The third day after the death of Jesus is precisely the first day of the week, the day of creation on which God said: "Let there be light!" Wherever faith in the Resurrection conserves the concreteness and integrity documented in the New Testament, Sunday and the meaning of Sunday can never be reduced to a merely historical dimension and be circumscribed by the event of the Christian community and its Easter. Here the world and matter are at issue; it is a question of creation and the "first day." At one time, Christians also called it the "eighth day," the day of the restoration of creation in its totality. The Old and New Testaments do not allow us to separate them, even less for an understanding of the meaning of Sunday. Creation and faith do not admit of mutual separation, and certainly not of anything at the center of the Christian message.[5]

For many and diverse reasons, one frequently encounters a kind of "fear of contagion" in contemporary theology in regard to the theme of

5. For the symbolism dear to patristics for the first, third, seventh, and eighth days, cf. J. Danielou, *Liturgie und Bibel* (Munich, 1963), 225-305 (*The Bible and the Liturgy* [Notre Dame: University of Notre Dame Press, 2002]). K. H. Schwarte, *Die Vorgeschichte der augustinischen Weltaltlehre* (Bonn, 1966), helps in understanding the patristic view of the link between creation and the history of salvation. See also H. Auf der Maur, *Feiern im Rhythmus der Zeit* I (Regensburg, 1983) (Gottesdienst der Kirche. Handbuch der Liturgiewissenschaft, Teil 5), for concise information. Also for interesting indications, see W. Rordorf, "Le dimanche – source et plenitude du temps liturgique chrétien," *Cristianesimo nella storia* 5 (1984): 1-9.

creation. This fact, however, leads to a yielding and impoverishment of the faith and to a sliding into the most diverse forms of ideology. It leads to a loss of reference to the reality of the faith itself and to the loss of the world, as if "abandoned by God." This tack is deadly both for the faith and for the world. When we no longer speak of "creation," but of the "environment," the world and man lose their placement in the whole; they lack the ground under their feet. It is this cry of creation, unjustly reduced to "environment," which ought to bring to our attention again that creatures, in effect, yearn for the appearance of the children of God.

3. The Sabbath and Sunday

a. The Problem

It is now the moment to ask ourselves about the relation that obtains between the "Sabbath" and "Sunday." It is a question of a controversy that does not find a univocal response in the New Testament. Only little by little in the course of the fourth and at the beginning of the fifth century of the Christian era is a solution found that subsequently is held to be universally valid. This solution is now fiercely contested once again. According to the unanimous testimony of the synoptic tradition, Jesus himself repeatedly entered into conflict with the Judaic practice of the Sabbath then in force. He combated it as a misunderstanding of the law of God. Paul made this his orientation; his battle for freedom from the law was also a fight against the constrictions of the Judaic festive calendar, including the obligations regarding the Sabbath. An echo of this fight is heard even in the text of Ignatius of Antioch that I have referred to: "he who has come to enjoy the newness of life and Christian hope beyond the orientation of the past is no longer a 'man of the Sabbath,' but rather lives in the law of the 'day of the Lord.'" The rhythms of the Sabbath and of "living in the law of the 'day of the Lord'" are thus counterposed as two fundamentally different ways of life: the one is a "prisoner" of a determinate *habitus* of behavior; the other relies instead on the future and on hope.

Nevertheless, this antithesis did not hinder the fact that, in many of the communities of the Church in the first centuries, the Sabbath retained its importance in common practice. There is much evidence in favor of the thesis according to which the first Christian community conserved the Sabbath and did not interpret the rejection by Jesus of the norm concerning the Sabbath as a negation of principle. It is certain that Judeo-Christianity conserved the feast of the Sabbath. At the same time, the Sabbath was still afforded a place in much of Christianity of pagan origin. Only in this way can we explain why in the fourth century — and thus after the peace of Constantine — we encounter the celebration of both days among Christians.

Texts from the so-named *Apostolic Constitutions,* from which I would like to draw attention to only two examples here, serve as a characteristic proof of this. One passage exhorts us: "Unite the Sabbath and Sunday in the gladness of the feast day because the first confesses creation, the second the Resurrection!"[6] A little further we read: "I Peter and I Paul make the order: the servant must work five days; he must, however, arrange time on the Sabbath and on the day of the Lord in order to receive catechetical instruction on the faith of the Church. The Sabbath, in fact, has its foundation in creation, the day of the Lord in the Resurrection."[7] Perhaps the same author, who speaks here under the pseudonym of "I Peter and I Paul," appears in the guise of St. Ignatius of Antioch and offers an expanded version of the Letter to the Christians of Magnesia, from which comes our inscription. It is his interest here to mitigate the decisive opposition to the "Sabbathizers." Hiding thus under the name of the great Bishop of Antioch, he is able to write:

> We do not, then, continue to observe the Sabbath in the manner of the Jews, and we do not suffer from inertia and inactivity because "he who does not work does not eat" (2 Thess 3:10). . . . Rather each of you maintains the practice of the Sabbath in its spiritual sense. One delights in the study of the law of God and not in the care of the body. You admire the creation of God and do not take food which is already old and do not consume inebriating drink nor follow accustomed pathways, nor enjoy dancing or other noisy and chaotic bustle![8]

6. *Apostolic Constitutions,* VII: 23, 3; in Rordorf, *Sabbat und Sonntag,* 100, no. 58. The Apostolic Constitutions are datable to the fourth century; cf. H. Rahner, in *Lexicon für Theologie und Kirche* I, col. 759.

7. *Apostolic Constitutions,* VII: 33, 1; in Rordorf, *Sabbat und Sonntag.*

8. Ps. Ignatius, *Ad Magnesios,* 9; in Rordorf, *Sabbat und Sonntag,* 102, no. 59.

Here is a manifest attempt to reconcile the Pauline polemic against Judaism with a synthesis from the two traditions, which was formed by common practice. At the same time, we see that the model of the "work week," of five days, effectively recalls the quite ancient tradition to mind.

In this text, it is also clearly possible to recognize how the subject matter of the Sabbath and that of Sunday do not mutually exclude one another but have, in fact, "become brothers" – to use the well-known expression of Gregory of Nyssa.[9] There is obviously no longer any reason to justify the absolute separation of such a spiritual subject matter that is intimately related and to distribute it into two different days. It can also be abridged into one day alone, in which case the day of Jesus Christ must necessarily have precedence. At once, we find the third, first, and eighth days as the expression of the newness of Christianity and, at the same time, as the Christian synthesis of the whole of created reality.[10]

The fact that the "Sabbath" is a moment already listed in the Decalogue was also a decisive point in the working out of this synthesis. Now, even for Paul – and notwithstanding all his polemic against the law – there is no doubt that the Decalogue is entirely valid as a more detailed formulation of the dual commandment of love, and that through it Christians guard the Law and the Prophets in their entirety and their authentic depth.[11] On the other hand, it has also become clear that the Decalogue must be reread in the light of the Christ-event and must be understood in the Holy Spirit. All of this has made it pos-

9. Gregory of Nyssa, *Adversus eos qui castigationes aegre ferunt,* PG 46: 309B-C, in Rordorf, *Sabbat und Sonntag,* 92-93, no. 52: "What impedes you from looking at the day of the Lord with a limpid eye, you who have not even considered the Sabbath as worthy of honor? Do you not know that these days are familiar among themselves, as children of the same mother [*adelphai*]?"

10. In this regard, cf. the beautiful formulation with which an anonymous homily (attributed to Athanasius), which is probably of the end of the fourth century, synthesizes the patristic contribution to the discussion regarding the relation between the Sabbath and Sunday and makes it precise in resolute terms: "*. . . metetheke de o kurios ten tou sabbatou emeran eis kuriaken*" (". . . the Lord has assumed and transfigured the Sabbath in the 'today' of his day"). Cf. Rordorf, *Sabbat und Sonntag,* 110-111, no. 64.

11. Cf. H. Gese, *Zur biblischen Theologie* (Munich, 1977), 54-84, for important considerations on the genuine Old Testament meaning of the Sabbath and on its acceptance by Jesus. Cf. also Rordorf, *Sabbat und Sonntag,* 12f.

sible to drop the Sabbath as a festivity and to inscribe its subject matter into the "day of the Lord." From this has arisen a deeper sense of freedom for the meaning and physiognomy of the Sabbath, thus overcoming the casuistry opposed by Jesus and Paul. At the same time, the necessity of perceiving the real subject matter of the Sabbath and observing it in full has also been placed into relief.

b. The Theology of the Sabbath

The question concerning the specific and real subject matter of the "Sabbath" must similarly be posed by us with a certain urgency. In order to respond adequately, one should carefully explain the fundamental texts of the Old Testament that speak of it, thus not only the account of creation (Gn 2:1ff.), but also the passages taken from Exodus (in particular 20:8-11; 31:12-17) and from Deuteronomy (especially 5:12; 12:9), in which the precepts of the Law are formulated, as well as the prophetic tradition (e.g., Ezek 20:12). Here, obviously, I cannot resolve everything. I would like only to attempt in brief to shed light on three essential moments of the whole question.

(1) The "Sabbath" in the Account of Creation In the first place, the fact that the "Sabbath" pertains to the account of creation is fundamental. We could, in fact, say that the canon of the "week" as a period of time articulated in "seven days" was chosen for the account of creation precisely as a function and reason for the "Sabbath." When the account of creation results in the "Sabbath," which proves to be a sign of the covenant, it clearly shows that "creation" and "covenant" are in mutual relation from the very beginning and so define themselves – and that the Creator could not but be the sole and same God. In addition, it attests to the fact that the world is not a neutral container in which people then come into being by chance, but rather that it is, a priori, creation and, therefore, the "place" prefigured for the covenant. Conversely, it is seen that the covenant also enjoys its own proper foundation only if one refers to the measure of creation. Accordingly, a pure "religion of history," a pure "salvation history" without metaphysics, is inconceivable just as a religiosity "without a world" is. Otherwise one could be satisfied with individual luck, with a "private" interior salvation, or with taking refuge in an amiably inviting and active community.

The "Sabbath" thus, above all, encourages reverence and gratitude before the Creator and his creation. If it is true that the creation narration in some way also prefigures the structure and organization of worship, this at any rate means that worship, both in its configuration and in its subject matter, is necessarily also in relation with creation. It means that God has full dominion over created reality and that we can and must ask him for it. On the other hand, this also means that, by availing ourselves of created things, it is not permissible for us to forget this peculiar property right of God: things are not entrusted to us for domination and purely arbitrary possession, but rather for a possession that is service according to the measure of him who is the true Lord to whom all things belong. Whenever the Sabbath and Sunday receive their due honor, creation also enjoys a corresponding esteem.

(2) The "Sabbath," the Day of the "Freedom of God" All this refers to a second aspect. The Sabbath is the day of the freedom of God and is the day of man's participation in the freedom of God. The consciousness of Israel's liberation from slavery in Egypt is a part of the nucleus that founds and justifies the Sabbath, but it is much more than simple memory. The Sabbath is not only a remembrance of the past, but is also an active exercise of freedom. From this fundamental core of meaning, the need for a pause in ordinary work practice, both on the part of men and animals and on the part of the master and the slave, is derived.

The legislation of Israel concerning the jubilee year shows that it concerns more than a question of mere regularization of free time. In the jubilee year, all patrimonial rights and property relations are brought back to their source once again, and all the forms of subordination among men that have been erected over time come to an end.[12]

In this way, the feast of the "great Sabbath" of the jubilee year shows the aim of the "Sabbath" that recurs every week: the anticipation

12. Cf. T. Maertens, *Heidnisch-jüdische Wurzeln christlicher Feste* (Mainz, 1965), 114-117 and 150-159. In considering the passage from the Old to the New Testament, Maertens places in relief – unilaterally, to tell the truth – the moment of "spiritualization." He does not, however, grasp very clearly that Christian "spiritualization" is the Incarnation, that it is Christic concentration.

of a society without domination, the anticipation of the future city. There is no longer a servant or a master of the Sabbath, but only the freedom of the sons of God and the profound breathing of peace by the whole of creation. For a sociologist or politician, all of this is nothing but a utopian vision of a world that will never be realizable, a moment concretely accomplished on the day of the Sabbath, a moment of fraternal freedom and of the equality of every creature. Because of this, the Sabbath is also the mainstay of social legislation. If on the first or seventh day all forms of social subjugation are canceled, if with the recurrence of the cycle of seven days all social structures are put under examination, this means that these structures are always related to the freedom of all and to the communal property of things. In point of fact, the book of Chronicles teaches us that Israel's exile was able to happen precisely because Israel transgressed the jubilee law, the great rule of the Sabbath – and with that the fundamental law of creation and the Creator. From its point of view, all other sins seem secondary in respect to this fundamental infidelity, namely, the confining of oneself to a world of human activity that is believed to be self-sufficient and that thus denies the sovereignty of God.[13]

(3) The "Eschatological" Dimension of the "Sabbath" Here, then, is the third essential factor of the theology of the Sabbath – its eschatological dimension. It is the anticipation of messianic time. It is not only the thought or desire of it, but it is messianic time in word and deed. Living according to the coordinates of messianic expectation, the doors of the world are opened wide from the inside to the advent, to the "today," of the Messiah. In this way, we begin to have confidence in the way of living the "end of time" and in the reality that lies beyond the consummation of the world. Irenaeus would say: we become family members in the life of God, as in his human existence he has been made family to us.

The cultural, social, and eschatological dimensions thus mutually permeate one another. Worship, which has its roots in biblical faith, is not an imitation of cosmic processes in miniature. This is the fundamental form of worship in natural religions. Biblical worship is rather an imitation of God himself and, accordingly, is a preparatory exercise

13. Cf. 2 Chron 36:21.

for the future world. Only in this way can one correctly understand the particularity of the biblical account of creation. Pagan accounts of creation, on the basis of which the biblical narrative is partially constructed, all end without exception on one point: at the bottom line, they are nothing other than a justification of a cultural praxis in which worship fully revolves around the logic of *do et des*. The gods create man in order to have themselves maintained by the latter; man has need of the gods because they guarantee the cosmic order of events. In a certain sense, as I have already said, the biblical account of creation also has to be understood as nothing other than a prefiguration and justification of cultural praxis. Nevertheless, here worship means the freedom of man through participation in the freedom of God and, consequently, means the freedom of creation itself as assumed in the freedom of the children of God.

c. The Christian Synthesis

When we consider in this light the debate over the Sabbath which had Jesus himself as a protagonist, or also the Pauline polemic against the observance of the Sabbath, we see quite clearly that in both cases what was disputed was not the specific and peculiar subject matter of the Sabbath. Something else was rather at stake, namely, its essential meaning as a feast of freedom from a practice that marred it, rendering it a day of "un-freedom."

If Jesus, therefore, did not wish to abolish the Sabbath in the subject matter that is proper to it, but rather wished to redeem and conserve it in its true value, I think I can say that when Christian theology wishes to separate the Sabbath from Sunday it does not go in the right direction. In his fundamental research concerning the "Sabbath" and "Sunday," Willy Rordorf sustains the thesis according to which their conjoining is due to the Constantinian turning point. In this way, however, a negative judgment on this synthesis is already pronounced. He maintains that until now, with few exceptions, the Christian Churches have remained aground on the shoals of this post-Constantinian option, adding: "One must, then, ask whether today it may be a good thing to be freed from the ancient and traditional certainties of the Constantinian era, and whether the Churches may also have the courage to be freed from the chains of the synthesis of the 'Sabbath' and 'Sunday.'"[14]

Several recent stands on the Catholic side sound even more radical. Thus, for example, L. Brandolini affirms both that the institution of Sunday represents a choice in strong opposition to the Hebraic Sabbath and that, starting with the fourth century, an opposite movement is observed that would lead to a progressive "Sabbathization" of Sunday and, accordingly, to a naturalistic, legalistic, and individualistic reduction of the Christian understanding of worship.[15] For these reasons, a reform would be difficult today. The Church would seem even more at a standstill than in the medieval ages and, notwithstanding all the efforts at renewal at the Second Vatican Council, would appear barely capable of change.[16]

In such considerations, it is of grave importance that the Christian Sunday not be tied to governmental recognition of this day as a day of rest from work. In no case can it be compared to a social and political phenomenon, which by its very nature can be so only in a very precise and determined social context. In this sense, the struggle for a real understanding of the core meaning of Sunday, independent of the inconstancy of external circumstances, is justified. Wherever, however, one deduces from this blunt datum the total opposition between the spiritual matter of the "Sabbath" and "Sunday," one falls into a grave misunderstanding of both the Old and New Testaments. The spiritualization of the Old Testament, which pertains to the essence of the New, is at the same time an always new incarnation. It is not a retreat or estrangement from society and creation, but rather a new and more profound mode of their mutual penetration. The question of the exact determination of the relation between the Old and New Testaments is also seen to be fundamental here, just as it is for all the chief themes of theology.[17]

Today, theology often oscillates between a Marcionism that would free itself from the burden of the Old Testament and retreat into the pure intimacy of Christian interiority, on the one hand, and a return –

14. Rordorf, *Sabbat und Sonntag*, 20.

15. L. Brandolini, "Domenica," in *Nuovo dizionario di liturgia*, ed. D. Sartore and M. Triacca (Rome, 1984), cols. 377-395 (especially cols. 385f.).

16. Ibid., col. 379; cf. also col. 386.

17. Cf. in this regard what the instruction of the Congregation for the Doctrine of the Faith (X, nn. 14-16) says about the inversion of Christian symbology.

beyond the turning point of the New Testament – to an exclusively political and social interpretation of the biblical heritage, on the other. Only the synthesis of the two Testaments, worked out by the Church in the first centuries of the Christian era, corresponds to the essential marks of the New Testament proclamation, and it alone is capable of conferring to Christianity its unique historical efficacy. By separating the fact of creaturehood and of the social dimension as found in the Old Testament – in this case in the phenomenon of the "Sabbath" – Christianity is reduced to a game of society, and the liturgy to entertainment. From this one gets the impression, among other things, that both Christianity and the liturgy are already out of style insofar as they present themselves in up-to-date garments and in step with the times. With a similar loss of reference to reality, with a loss of the world, the starting point of the Christian doctrine of freedom is also lost. This also distorts the Christian understanding of worship, which discerns its essential archetype in the weekly structure of the creation narrative and which, in turn, achieves its dramatically meaningful wealth only through Christ's Pasch. But Christ's Pasch does not eliminate the outlook of the creation narrative. It rather makes it concrete. Christian worship is an anticipation of the freedom of communion in which man imitates God and is transformed "according to his image and likeness." This freedom can be experienced until now because creation has been willed from the beginning to be predestined to this ultimate fullness.

4. Implications for Ecclesial Praxis

In conclusion, we can now decisively pose the questions regarding the implications for praxis of all that has been said so far. In this regard, we must never lose sight of the fact that an attentive consideration of theological truths is already of itself something eminently "practical." In his autobiographical annotations, Romano Guardini movingly expressed how he came to realize that, ultimately, the most urgent, most immediate, and most concrete task placed before his generation was how to make the evidence of the truth resplendent.[18] On the basis of such a

18. R. Guardini, *Berichte über mein Leben. Autobiographische Aufzeichnung* (Dusseldorf, 1984), 109-113 and 114. Cf. especially 109: "The more I was preaching, the less the immedi-

frame of mind, in the years during which he lived in Berlin, he became a protagonist in a heated dispute in which he was opposed by leading personalities of the time, like Professor Münch, the then-president of the association of university professors, and Professor Sonnenschein, an authoritative spiritual guide of Berlin students. Today, looking back at this controversy, we have to recognize that each of them perceived real and urgent pastoral needs and offered indispensable contributions to pastoral life because of them. But in the meantime, a half century later, it is possible to reconcile what was then an open attack. At the same time, we must also recognize – without any partisanship – that Guardini's impassioned and disinterested solicitude to see to it that the truth return to the debate floor at a time dominated by lies had profound and lasting effects. Furthermore, its eminently practical value was, in time, to be fully appreciated – even in the resolutions adopted by Vatican II. We also could act with a greater and more far-sighted effectiveness if we would, above all, not count on our own strengths, but on the intrinsic power of the truth, which is something we ought to learn to discern and to communicate more eloquently.

On the basis of the theological outcomes arrived at thus far, I would like now to offer briefly two considerations among a number of quite topical questions.

a. Sunday Liturgical Service in the Absence of a Priest

In drawing conclusions from the above reflections, two principles emerge that must guide our way of acting in ordinary pastoral practice. First, the priority of sacrament with respect to any psychologism is at stake. It is a question of the primacy of the Church as a mystery over

ate efficacy of what I was expounding mattered to me. Right from the very beginning onward, at first just instinctively, then later more consciously, all that I wanted was to bring the truth to light. The truth is such a power, however, only once it does not pretend to have any immediate effect." An affirmation quoted later (110) is also moving: "Here (on the occasion of the evening conferences in the Canisius Church of Charlottenburg), I experienced in a heightened way all that I was saying above about the power of the truth. Rarely have I realized, as on these evenings, how profoundly true and fertile is the Christian message for living. At times it was as if the truth were physically present between us."

any sort of associational thinking. Second, on the basis of the hierarchical distinction of different levels, local churches must search for an adequate solution to their varying situations, keeping in mind that their specific task is the salvation of people *(salus animarum).* In focusing on the obligation, their constraints and freedom can be outlined.

Let us analyze both principles more closely. In mission countries, in the diaspora, and in situations of overt persecution, there is nothing new about the fact that it might be impossible to participate at the celebration of the Eucharist on Sundays and that one might have to attempt to adjust with the Church that does celebrate the day of the Lord to whatever degree possible. Now, with the decrease of priestly vocations, a phenomenon of similar proportions seems at hand, one to which we have yet to grow accustomed.

Many times, unfortunately, in the search for a just solution, ideologies of a collectivist cast are proposed that impede rather than respond to the real needs. For example, it is said that every church that in the past has had a pastor or, at any rate, a regular Sunday liturgical service, should also be a place of festive gathering for the local community in the future. Only in this way can the church be preserved as the center of civic association. Only in this fashion can the community remain alive precisely as a community. The fact that the community may come together to listen to and celebrate the Word of God thus becomes more important than availing oneself of the possibility – itself a given – of participating in the celebration of the Eucharist at a neighboring or nearby church.

There is much that is reasonable and also well-intentioned in this argumentation. But the fundamental faith criteria for judgment are done away with. The experience of mutual proximity and solicitude for the texture of relationships found in the most elemental of life communities counts more, in this way of thinking, than the grace of the sacrament. Without a doubt, the feeling for community life is more immediately experienced and readily understood than the reality of the sacrament. What is evident here is the yielding of the objectivity of the sacrament to the subjectivity of individual experience, of what is properly theological to what is a purely sociological and psychological field. But the consequences of such an overestimation of communal experience over sacramentality are serious: now the community does not celebrate anything but itself. The Church becomes the vehicle for social ends. Beyond this, it ends up playing a romantic game of "jolly good fellows" that in today's society, which is both dynamic and in continual transformation, is definitely something anachronistic. Certainly, a person who is well-intentioned and of an optimistic temperament at the outset feels gratified by the fact that he is participating in the liturgy in "his" own church, that he is one of its "protagonists." But it should not take long for him to realize that all that remains is *only* that which he himself can do, that he does not receive anything from on high, but can put forth only himself. Thus, everything that constitutes the Foundation and the All is no longer indispensable. Sunday divine liturgy, in this way, no longer surpasses or transcends in principle that which man normally and ordinarily does. He does not reach any other plane of existence, but is himself the one real plane of existence. And thus the possibility is lost that one encounters in him that unconditional "you must" of which the Church has always made mention.

As a consequence, then, such an appraisal also extends to the concrete celebration of the liturgy. When the Church, in fact, purportedly holds that the act of gathering is more important than the Eucharist, then the Eucharist itself is, in truth, nothing other than a "gathering." The leveling of the two would not otherwise be possible. The reality of the Church is now reduced to a manmade product, and here we find the sad outlook of Durkheim confirmed, according to which religion and worship are nothing but, in general, forms of social stabilization through processes of self-identification. But once we become conscious of this, this same social stabilization no longer works because it can work only when one thinks that something else is at stake in it. Anyone who directly strives for a community of persons finds that, instead, he really severs the foundations for it. All that which initially seems so pious and illuminating is in actuality an inversion of the deepest roots of the hierarchy and the order of value, in which after a time the contrary of what was desired is obtained. Only when the sacrament conserves its unconditional character and its absolute primacy over all social ends and over all spiritually "edifying" intentions does it also create community and "edify" man. Only a psychologically less overburdened liturgical service somewhat unadorned and uniform (from the point of view of individual subjectivity) is – if it is licit to speak in strictly functionalistic language – in the end also "socially" more efficacious than the self-enlightenment of a psychologically and socially successful community. At this point, we must indeed ask the fundamental question whether something happens here that does not depend on ourselves or whether even we are exactly ourselves, and so it suffices just to plan and build community. When one does not assign the highest "duty" to the sacrament, the freedom that then takes hold of us becomes insipid because it is devoid of its subject matter.

The situation is totally different when it is really a question of necessity. If we think of a liturgical event without the presence of a priest, we are not, to speak the truth, locked into what is only human. This action rather becomes a common initiative through which the effort is made together to achieve, at least in part, all that which the "day of the Lord," Sunday in the life of the Church, means. With such a way of acting, we remain steadfast in the ordinary duty and wishes of the Church and, in this way, of the Lord himself.

The decisive question is: Where is the boundary line between one's own obstinacy and real necessity? Of course, it is not possible to show this boundary clearly in the abstract, since there will always be fluctuations in the particulars. It must be determined in particular situations by the pastoral tack of those involved and in agreement with the bishop. There are rules that can lend a hand. That it is not licit for a priest to celebrate more than three times on a Sunday is not a positive decree of canon law, but corresponds to the limits of what is really feasible. This is a regulation that concerns the celebrant; in reference to the faithful, the problem has to be posed as to the reasonableness of liturgical forms and of the suitability of the place and time of the liturgy. For this, it should not be necessary to repeat unnecessarily prefabricated surveys, but rather opportunities should be allowed for conscientious decision-making in the face of different situations and their demands. The essential point is that the burdens be equitably shared and that the Church not celebrate herself but the Lord whom she receives in the Eucharist and to whom she draws near in those situations in which communities without priests stretch out *toward his grace.*

b. The Christian Sunday in the "Weekend" Society

In my opinion, there is a much more realistic, and contrary, problem at hand. What are we to do in regard to the fact that members of our communities hurriedly leave their homes on Friday and Saturday evenings and return again when the last Sunday liturgy is already long over? How can we reconcile Sunday with the "weekend" society? How can we once again relate free time with that larger freedom to which the "day of the Lord" wishes to introduce us?

I think that in this regard we must, even more than we have done to date, make an effort at real planning and imagination, on the one hand, in regard to all that concerns the vitality of pastoral care and the mutual openness of communities toward one another. On the other hand, such planning and imagination are needed in respect to the ways that will enable parochial communities – that "no man's land" which the liturgy is in a certain sense – to become a spiritual "homeland" for those who frequent them, thus intercepting and blocking the tendency toward escape which is characteristic of industrial society and proposing a different end for it. I am, in fact, of the opinion that all these "gateways" of which we are witnesses certainly aim at amusement, relaxation, encounter, and liberation from the slavery of everyday life. I believe also, however, that a more profound exigency lies behind these desires, fully justified in themselves: namely, a nostalgia for a true "at-home-ness" in brotherly communion and for an experience of real "requital"; a nostalgia, therefore, for all that is "totally other" in respect to all the saturation caused by the endless supply of goods of every type.

Sunday liturgy ought to offer a response to this need. It will enjoy no success whatsoever if it tries to enter into competition with show business. A pastor is not a showman, and the liturgy is not a variety show. If one takes it so badly, then the liturgy will be something like a recreational circle. I do not want to exclude that it could happen, but only, and not necessarily, as an eventual consequence of encounters and relations on the level of human relationships due to communitarian participation at the liturgy. The liturgy must be something more. The fact that something unique happens here that cannot be found elsewhere must be of primary importance. It must be made clear that a dimension of existence is opened up here to which everyone secretly aspires, namely, the presence of that which cannot be made by man's own hand – a theophany – a revelation of mystery, and in it the benevolent gaze of God who governs being with his power and who alone is capable of making it "good." This fact can be grasped and appropriated by us even though we live in the midst of tensions and sufferings of every type.[19]

Put otherwise, we must find the right balance between ritualism, in which the liturgical event is officiated only by the priest in a way that is incomprehensible to most people and devoid of links with life, and the obsession to render everything easy and readily at hand, which in fact reduces everything to a merely human effort and which robs it of what is "specific" about Catholicism and about the objectivity of the mystery. It is through the community of believers who, by believing, understand more than what is sensed that the liturgy must have its own force of diffusion that can also become an appeal to conversion and a motive for hope for non-believers who in some sense do not yet understand. Insofar as it is an *opus Dei,* it must be the place where every *opera hominum* ceases and is surmounted, and thus reveals that new freedom for which we anxiously search in vain in the immoderate consumption of goods of evasion and in the uncontrolled abandon to different passions.

In such fashion, the liturgy, in conformity with the essential meaning of Sunday, ought once again to become the "place" of that freedom which is much more than "free time" or "freedom of movement." It is precisely this authentic freedom that has been the focus of this investigation.

Translated by Fr. Robert Slesinski

19. For this reason, the variously diffused theory, according to which one can celebrate the liturgy only with a priest one knows and only in a community which knows itself, is erroneous. In this process, the liturgy is entirely reduced to a purely social ritual. The most imposing and significant feature of the Catholic faith is, instead, the fact that no believer is estranged from another. Where there is faith, a believer finds himself at home. A paradigmatic example of this overestimation of psychological and sociological matters (gathering, communal activity, mutual knowledge) in regard to what is specifically theological is offered in Brandolini's article, "Domenica."

God in Pope John Paul II's Crossing the Threshold of Hope

This is the sort of book that one finishes without putting down, even though, or precisely because, page after page it involves the reader in a demanding reflection. *Crossing the Threshold of Hope* is first of all a very personal work of the pope, which contains a good deal of autobiographical passages and is also marked by the experiences of a pontificate that already spans sixteen years. Among these passages there are, for example, touching accounts of the synagogue in Wadowice and of the town's primary school, where a fourth of Karol Wojtyla's schoolmates were Jews. One of them was Jerzy Kluger, to whom the pope is still bound by close friendship. The reader realizes how the question of Jewish-Christian relations was part of his life from very early on and how various experiences and encounters with his fellow men formed the thought, the theology, and the piety of the future pope. For example, the author recalls the prayer to the Holy Spirit that his father gives to the young Karol to recite every day. What this meant for the future prayer and life of the pope may be guessed from the following sentence: "I understood for the first time the meaning of Christ's words to the Samaritan woman about the true worshippers of God . . ." (142). We perceive how much the Marian element entered into the spiritual world of the future pope, how Fatima became a decisive reality for him. We see how, in the horrors of the War and in the subsequent confronta-

This article first appeared as "God in Pope John Paul II's *Crossing the Threshold of Hope*," in *Communio* 22 (Spring 1995).

tion with Marxist ideology, his vocation took shape; we are introduced to the impassioned inquiry concerning the image of man which took place among Catholic thinkers in Krakow and Lublin.

I said that this is a very personal book, but at the same time it is a dialogue of faith with the questions which modern man poses to Christianity. Vittorio Messori deserves our gratitude for having incorporated thirty-five interludes – if I may so call them – in which with great respect, but also with great ease and candor, he formulates the doubts and reproaches that contemporary man brings forward regarding the Church and its message. Among them is the question of the existence of God and of the figure of Christ. This, in turn, gives rise to the problem of the multiplicity of religions and of Christianity's claim to uniqueness. Messori asks the question: why is it all so complicated? And the disturbing question: isn't the number of Christians steadily decreasing? If so, does Christianity have a future? Or else: is only Rome right? The question of women and the question of eternal life also appear. Near the end there is another very practical consideration: what is the use of believing?

Of all of these topics I would like to take up here just one, which happens to be the basis of all the rest, in order to describe it more closely, though I cannot exhaust the wealth of the answers given in this book. Everything which I am about to say can only be an invitation to read the book itself.

The topic I would like to probe in greater depth is the question of God. It is obvious when reading the book that for the pope this is the most personal of all matters, the power that gives shape to his very life, but that at the same time it is also the most universal concern, which touches every man. Putting it in other terms, we could say that for him God is not only an intellectual problem, but the foundation of life, indeed, the reality that precedes and sustains every thought. This pope's faith in God has assuredly found its most important expression in the motto which on the inaugural day of his ministry he proclaimed to the people gathered in St. Peter's Square and to the people of the whole world: "Be not afraid!" This phrase sums up in just a few words the significance that God has for this man – what it means to believe in God. He recounts that at that moment, 22 October 1978, he himself did not yet guess the full import of these words, that he did not yet know to what degree they captured the essence of his pontificate: "Their meaning came more from the Holy Spirit . . . than from the man who spoke them" (219).

In the past the critics of religion formulated the thesis that fear had created God and the gods. Today we are experiencing the opposite: the elimination of God has generated the fear which lurks beneath the surface of modern existence. The man of today is afraid that God might really exist and that he is dangerous. He is afraid of himself and of the terrible possibilities he carries within him. He is afraid of the dark and unforeseeable side of a world that he no longer attributes to a loving reason but to the play of chance and to the victory of the strongest. The fear of what men can do to themselves and to the world, the fear of the absence of meaning, of the emptiness of human life, the fear of the future, of overpopulation, of war, of disease and disasters has taken profound hold of the men of today. Under the thin veneer of optimism and faith in progress this fear is increasingly the dominant mood. "Be not afraid": with these words the pope desires to renew in us that certainty which dwells in the depths of the human soul: "Someone exists who holds in his hands the destiny of this passing world; Someone who holds the keys to death and the netherworld (cf. Rev 1:18); Someone who is the Alpha and the Omega of human history (cf. Rev 22:13) . . . and this Someone is Love (cf. 1 Jn 4:8, 16)" (222). Here the question of God meets the question of man and the question of redemption, and this three-way connection is characteristic of the thought of Karol Wojtyla. He who knows God, the true God, the living God who loves men, is redeemed, set free from fear and kept safe in loving confidence.

This knowledge of God, in which God is no longer merely thought, but is also experienced, ripens in that dialogue with God which we call prayer. "Prayer is a search for God, but it is also a revelation of God," says the pope (25): to pray is not just to talk, but also to listen. The pope puts it like this: "The 'Thou' is more important because our prayer begins with God" (16). This act of leaving the circle of our own words and our own desires, this drawing back of the I, this self-abandonment to the mysterious presence which awaits us – this more than anything constitutes prayer. The pope thus also responds to the question of Oriental forms of prayer, which he examines at full length elsewhere in the book (84ff.). Christian prayer has a mystical dimension, but it does not end with the disappearance of the I; rather, it ignites the flame of love, which goes beyond the boundaries of the I and at the same time radically renews it in the encounter with the other. Christian prayer therefore signifies entering together into the universality of God; not an exit from being into nothingness, but a new ingress into the world, this time from the liberating perspective of God. The Holy Father speaks of the geography of his prayer (23), of the "solicitude for all the Churches" (cf. 2 Cor 11:28) which he bears in the heart of God, so that in prayer he can visit them all, and what is far off draws near and becomes present.

God in Karol Wojtyla is not only thought but also experienced. The pope expressly opposes the limitation of the concept of experience that occurred in Empiricism; he points out that the form of experience elaborated in the natural sciences is not the only kind, but that there are also other forms which are no less real and important: moral experience, human experience, religious experience (34). But this experience is, of course, also reflected upon and verified in its rational content. The presentation of the reasonability of faith is an essential element of this book. The pope engages here in a dialogue with the history of Western thought, which, with its wide perspectives, reveals the breadth and depth of his philosophical formation. Of course, I can give only a very general idea of this dialogue here. The central core of Wojtyla's philosophy lies in the fact that he does not accept the separation of thought and existence that typifies the modern era. Descartes, says the pope, severed thinking from existing and identified this isolated thought with reason itself: I think, therefore I am. But it is not thought that determines existence, but existence that determines thought (38).

Beginning with Descartes' fundamental approach, there developed that "absolutization of subjective conscience" (51) which not only limited the perception of reality in general, but also resulted in a reduced concept of God. God, who for St. Thomas, an heir of the biblical tradition, is subsistent being (which led Gilson to speak of St. Thomas's philosophy of existence), is now nothing but absolute thought. In the cultural climate that arose from this initial premise, the idea of God increasingly finds itself on the fringe, or better, a God who is sheer thought is already *ipso facto* relegated to the fringe. In this way God was gradually expelled from reality: Deism permits God to remain in existence, but he no longer has anything to say in the world. He has thus become for man a marginal hypothesis which he may or may not accept: whether or not he does no longer makes much difference.

The fact that God no longer appears to many to be attainable by reason is the fault not of an irrationality of the faith, but of the narrowing of our reason. This narrowing must be overcome. Reason must once again return to its integrity; if it does so, it will also once more see God.

In his book the pope describes two ways to this recovery of integrity. He recounts that, faced with Marxism, the Catholic thinkers of Poland had turned their attention above all to problems of natural philosophy, because it was in this quarter that they expected the real attack of Marxist thought. The pope sums up the outcome of the philosophical debate of the day in these words: "The visible world, in and of itself, cannot offer a scientific basis for an atheistic interpretation of reality. Instead, honest reflection does find sufficient elements in the world to arrive at the knowledge of God" (198). Nevertheless, in his reminiscences of these post-war discussions, he confides that to his surprise it was not the philosophy of nature but the question of man – anthropology – that turned out to be the true arena of the contest with Marxism. And it is precisely anthropology that was and is the great passion of the pope as a thinker and as a pastor. Anthropology was decisive in overcoming the atheist interpretation in favor of faith in God. In the dispute about man the atheist answer proves to be deficient. The great personalist philosophers of our century – Buber, Rosenzweig, Levinas, to whom the pope adds the names of the Lublin School – appear as that turning point of thought which leads beyond Descartes and on the basis of anthropology gives us new eyes for God. The entire philosophical thought of Karol Wojtyla revolves around man, and concern for man also occupies the center of his teaching as the supreme shepherd of Christianity. But the pope's anthropology is theological, because it is soteriological: the question of man is the question of his redemption, and if this latter problem is taken seriously, the question of man becomes a focusing on God and a new thinking in the light of God. In this sense, God is the key to this personality and to his work.

Three times in the pope's book we find a citation from the Gospel of John (5:17): "My Father is always at work, and I too am at work." After the act of creation, God did not recede into the past; after the Big Bang he did not remove himself from the reality of this world. God is not a God of the past, but a God of the present and of the future. The pope translates the content of this verse from St. John into his, into our language: "Christ is forever young" (113). The pope's love for the young is closely connected with his image of God. He tells of how the "discovery of the fundamental importance of youth" was the decisive experience of his first years as a priest (120).

And he explains how during the years of his pontificate he has felt guided and challenged by the young. Youth – as he teaches us – is the time of "personalization," the time in which man must develop a concrete way "to go about living his life" (121). But both aspects, personalization and the development of a life plan, mean, in the final analysis, to learn love. The task of the priest, of the educator is, therefore, "to teach them love." "As a young priest I learned to love human love," writes the pope (123). Here the image of God and the image of man come once more into contact and penetrate each other: the God who is at work is a God who loves. He works because he loves. Because he loves, he cannot withdraw from the scene; because he loves, he desires to be near. He draws so close that men pull away in fright and want to keep him at a distance: not like this, O God! God himself becomes a man and now remains so forever. To learn to love means to learn to know God. Because the world is in the hands of the God who is at work, of the love which is always present, to all of us it is said: "Be not afraid!"

Translated by Adrian J. Walker

Truth and Freedom

1. The Question

In the mind of contemporary man, freedom appears to a large extent as the absolutely highest good, to which all other goods are subordinate. Court decisions consistently accord artistic freedom and freedom of opinion primacy over every other moral value. Values which compete with freedom, or which might necessitate its restriction, seem to be fetters or "taboos," that is, relics of archaic prohibitions and fears. Political policy must show that it contributes to the advancement of freedom in order to be accepted. Even religion can make its voice heard only by presenting itself as a liberating force for man and for humanity. In the scale of values on which man depends for a humane existence, freedom appears as the basic value and as the fundamental human right. In contrast, we are inclined to react with suspicion to the concept of truth: we recall that the term "truth" has already been claimed for many opinions and systems, and that the assertion of truth has often been a means of suppressing freedom. In addition, natural science has nourished skepticism with regard to everything which cannot be explained or proved by its exact methods: all such things seem in the end to be a mere subjective assignment of value which cannot pretend to be universally binding. The modern attitude toward truth is summed up

---

This article first appeared as "Freiheit und Wahrheit" in *Internationale katholische Zeitschrift Communio* 6 (1995). Published in *Communio* 23, no. 1 (Spring 1996).

most succinctly in Pilate's question, "What is truth?" Anyone who maintains that he is serving the truth by his life, speech, and action must prepare himself to be classified as a dreamer or as a fanatic. For "the world beyond is closed to our gaze"; this sentence from Goethe's *Faust* characterizes our common sensibility today.

Doubtless, the prospect of an all too self-assured passion for the truth suggests reasons enough to ask cautiously, "What is truth?" But there is just as much reason to pose the question, "What is freedom?" What do we actually mean when we extol freedom and place it at the pinnacle of our scale of values? I believe that the content which people generally associate with the demand for freedom is very aptly explained in the words of a certain passage of Karl Marx in which he expresses his own dream of freedom. The state of the future Communist society will make it possible, he says, "to do one thing today and another tomorrow; to hunt in the morning, fish in the afternoon, breed cattle in the evening and criticize after dinner, just as I please. . . ."[1] This is exactly the sense in which average opinion spontaneously understands freedom: as the right and the opportunity to do just what we wish and not to have to do anything which we do not wish to do. Expressed in other terms: freedom would mean that our own will is the sole norm of our action and that the will not only can desire anything but also has the chance to carry out its desire. At this point, however, questions begin to arise: how free is the will after all? And how reasonable is it? Is an unreasonable will truly a free will? Is an unreasonable freedom truly freedom? Is it really a good? In order to prevent the tyranny of reason must we not complete the definition of freedom as the capacity to will and to do what we will by placing it in the context of reason, of the totality of man? And will not the interplay between reason and will also involve the search for the common reason shared by all men and thus for the compatibility of liberties? It is obvious that the question of truth is implicit in the question of the reasonableness of the will and of the will's link with reason.

It is not merely abstract philosophical considerations, but the quite concrete situation of our society, which compels us to ask such questions. In this situation, the demand for freedom remains undiminished, yet doubts about all the forms of struggle for liberation move-

1. K. Marx and F. Engels, *Werke*, 39 vols. (Berlin, 1961-1971), 3:33.

ments and the systems of freedom which have existed until now are coming more and more dramatically to the fore. Let us not forget that Marxism began its career as the one great political force of our century with the claim that it would usher in a new world of freedom and of human liberation. It was precisely Marxism's assurance that it knew the scientifically guaranteed way to freedom, and that it would create a new world, which drew many of the boldest minds of our epoch to it. Eventually, Marxism even came to be seen as the power by which the Christian doctrine of redemption could finally be transformed into a realistic praxis of liberation – as the power whereby the kingdom of God could be concretely realized as the true kingdom of man. The collapse of "real socialism" in the nations of Eastern Europe has not entirely extirpated such hopes, which quietly survive here and there while searching for a new face. The political and economic collapse was not matched by any real intellectual defeat, and in that sense the question posed by Marxism is still far from being resolved. Nevertheless, the fact that the Marxist system did not function as had been promised is plain for all to see. No one can still seriously deny that this ostensible liberation movement was, alongside National Socialism, the greatest system of slavery in modern history. The extent of its cynical destruction of man and of the environment is rather shamefacedly kept quiet, but no one can any longer dispute it.

These developments have brought out the moral superiority of the liberal system in politics and economics. Nevertheless, this superiority is no occasion for enthusiasm. The number of those who have no part in the fruits of this freedom, indeed, who are losing every freedom altogether, is too great: unemployment is once again becoming a mass phenomenon, and the feeling of not being needed, of superfluity, tortures men no less than material poverty. Unscrupulous exploitation is spreading; organized crime takes advantage of the opportunities of the free and democratic world, and in the midst of all this we are haunted by the specter of meaninglessness. At the Salzburg University Weeks of 1995, the Polish philosopher Andrej Szizypiorski unsparingly described the dilemma of freedom that has arisen after the fall of the Berlin Wall; it is worth listening to him at length:

> It admits of no doubt that capitalism made a great step forward. And it also admits of no doubt that it has not lived up to what was

> expected of it. The cry of the huge masses whose desire has not been fulfilled is a constant refrain in capitalism. . . . The downfall of the Soviet conception of the world and of man in political and social praxis was a liberation of millions of human lives from slavery. But in the intellectual patrimony of Europe, in the light of the tradition of the last two hundred years, the anti-communist revolution also signals the end of the illusions of the Enlightenment, hence, the destruction of the intellectual conception that was at the basis of the development of early modern Europe. . . . A remarkable, hitherto unprecedented epoch of uniform development has begun. And it has suddenly become apparent – probably for the first time in history – that there is only one recipe, one way, one model, and one method of organizing the future. And men have lost their faith in the meaning of the revolutions that are occurring. They have also lost their hope that the world can be changed at all and that it is worthwhile changing it. . . . Today's lack of any alternative, however, leads people to pose completely new questions. The first question: was the West wrong after all? The second question: if the West was not right, who, then, was? Because there is no one in Europe who can doubt that Communism was not right, the third question arises: can it be that there is no such thing as right? But if this is the case, the whole intellectual inheritance of the Enlightenment is worthless. . . . Perhaps the worn-out steam engine of the Enlightenment, after two centuries of profitable, trouble-free labor has come to a standstill before our eyes and with our cooperation. And the steam is simply evaporating. If this is the way things are in fact, the prospects are gloomy.[2]

Although many questions could also be posed here in response, the realism and the logic of Szizypiorski's fundamental queries cannot be brushed aside. At the same time, his diagnosis is so dismal that we cannot stop there. Was no one right? Is there perhaps no "right" at all? Are the foundations of the European Enlightenment, upon which the historical development of freedom rests, false, or at least deficient? The question "What is freedom?" is in the end no less complicated than the question "What is truth?" The dilemma of the Enlightenment, into which we have undeniably fallen, constrains us to repose these two questions as well as to renew our search for the connection between

2. I cite Szizypiorski from the manuscript provided during the University Weeks.

them. In order to make headway, we must, therefore, reconsider the starting point of the career of freedom in modernity; the course correction that is plainly needed before paths can reemerge from the darkening landscape before us must go back to the starting points themselves and begin its work there. Of course, in the limited framework of an article I can do no more than try to highlight a few points. My purpose in this is to convey some sense of the greatness and the perils of the path of modernity and thereby to contribute to a new reflection.

2. The Problem: The History and Concept of Freedom in Modernity

There is no doubt that from the very outset freedom has been the defining theme of that epoch which we call modern. The sudden break with the old order to go off in search of new freedoms is the sole reason that justifies such a periodization. Luther's polemical writing *Von der Freiheit eines Christenmenschen (On the Freedom of a Christian)* boldly struck up this theme in resounding tones.[3] It was the cry of freedom, which made men sit up and take notice, which triggered a veritable avalanche, and which turned the writings of a monk into the occasion of a mass movement that radically transformed the face of the medieval world. At issue was the freedom of conscience vis-à-vis the authority of the Church, hence the most intimate of all human freedoms. It is not the order of the community that saves man, but his wholly personal faith in Christ. That the whole ordered system of the medieval Church ultimately ceased to count was felt to be a massive impulse of freedom. The order that was in reality meant to support and save appeared as a burden; it was no longer binding, that is, it no longer had any redemptive significance. Redemption now meant liberation, liberation from the yoke of a supra-individual order. Even if it would not be right to speak of the individualism of the Reformation, the new importance of the individual and the shift in the relation between individual conscience and authority are nonetheless among its dominant traits. However, this liberation movement was restricted to the properly religious

3. Cf. on the whole of what follows, e.g., E. Lohse, *Martin Luther* (Munich, 1981), 60f., 86ff.

sphere. Every time it was extended into a political program, as in the Peasant War and the Anabaptist movement, Luther vigorously opposed it. What came to pass in the political sphere was quite the contrary of liberation: with the creation of territorial and national churches the power of the secular authority was augmented and consolidated. In the Anglo-Saxon world the free churches subsequently broke out of this new fusion of religious and political government and thus became precursors of a new construction of history, which later took on clear features in the second phase of the modern era, the Enlightenment.

Common to the whole Enlightenment is the will to emancipation, first in the sense of Kant's *sapere aude* – dare to use your reason for yourself. Kant is urging the individual reason to break free of the bonds of authority, which must all be subjected to critical scrutiny. Only what is accessible to the eyes of reason is allowed validity. This philosophical program is by its very nature a political one as well: reason shall reign, and in the end no other authority is admitted than that of reason. Only what is accessible to reason has validity; what is not reasonable, that is, not accessible to reason, cannot be binding either. This fundamental tendency of the Enlightenment shows up, however, in diverse, even antithetical, social philosophies and political programs. It seems to me that we can distinguish two major currents. The first is the Anglo-Saxon current with its predominantly natural rights orientation and its proclivity toward constitutional democracy, which it conceives as the only realistic system of freedom. At the opposite end of the spectrum is the radical approach of Rousseau, which aims ultimately at complete autarchy. Natural rights thinking critically applies the criterion of man's innate rights both to positive law and to the concrete forms of government. These rights are held to be prior to every legal order and are considered its measure and basis. "Man is created free, and is still free, even were he born in chains," says Friedrich Schiller in this sense. Schiller is not making a statement that consoles slaves with metaphysical notions, but is offering a principle for fighters, a maxim for action. A juridical order that creates slavery is an order of injustice. From creation man has rights that must be enforced if there is to be justice. Freedom is not bestowed upon man from without. He is a bearer of rights because he is created free. Such thinking gave rise to the idea of human rights, which is the Magna Charta of the modern struggle for freedom. When nature is spoken of in this context, what is meant is not simply a system of biological processes. Rather, the point is that rights are naturally present in man himself prior to all legal constructs. In this sense, the idea of human rights is in the first place a revolutionary one: it opposes the absolutism of the state and the caprice of positive legislation. But it is also a metaphysical idea: there is an ethical and legal claim in being itself. It is not blind materiality that can then be formed in accord with pure functionality. Nature contains spirit, ethos, and dignity, and in this way is a juridical claim to our liberation as well as its measure. In principle, what we find here is very much the concept of nature in Romans 2. According to this concept, which is inspired by the Stoa and transformed by the theology of creation, the Gentiles know the law "by nature" and are thus a law unto themselves (Rom 2:14).

The element specific to the Enlightenment and to modernity in this line of thought may be seen in the notion that the juridical claim of nature vis-à-vis the existing forms of government is above all a demand that state and other institutions respect the rights of the individual. Man's nature is above all to possess rights against the community, rights that must be protected from the community: institution seems to be the polar opposite of freedom, whereas the individual appears as the bearer of freedom, whose goal is seen as his full emancipation.

This is a point of contact between the first current and the second, which is far more radical in orientation. For Rousseau, everything that owes its origin to reason and will is contrary to nature, and corrupts and contradicts it. The concept of nature is not itself shaped by the idea of a right supposedly preceding all our institutions as a law of nature. Rousseau's concept of nature is anti-metaphysical and is correlative to his dream of total, absolutely unregimented freedom.[4] Similar ideas resurface in Nietzsche, who opposes Dionysian frenzy to Apollonian order, thus conjuring up primordial antitheses in the history of religions: the order of reason, whose symbolic representation is Apollo, corrupts the free, unrestrained frenzy of nature.[5] Klages reprises the same motif with

4. Cf. D. Wyss, "Zur Psychologie und Psychopathologie der Verblending: J. J. Rousseau und M. Robespierre, die Begründer des Sozialismus," in *Jahres- und Tagungsbericht der Görres-Gesellschaft* (1992), 33-45; R. Spaemann, *Rousseau — Bürger ohne Vaterland. Von der Polis zur Natur* (Munich, 1980).

5. Cf. P. Köster, *Der sterbende Gott, Nietzsches Entwurf übermenschlicher Größ* (Meisenheim, 1972); R. Löw, *Nietzsche Sophist und Erzieher* (Weinheim, 1984).

his idea that the spirit is the adversary of the soul: the spirit is not the great new gift wherein alone freedom exists, but is corrosive of the pristine origin with its passion and freedom.[6] In a certain respect this declaration of war on the spirit is inimical to the Enlightenment, and to that extent National Socialism, with its hostility towards the Enlightenment and its worship of "blood and soil," could appeal to currents such as these. But even here the fundamental motif of the Enlightenment, the cry for freedom, is not only operative, but occurs in its most radically intensified form. In the radical politics both of the past and of the present century, various forms of such tendencies have repeatedly erupted against the democratically domesticated form of freedom. The French Revolution, which had begun with the idea of a constitutional democracy, soon cast off these fetters and set out on the path of Rousseau and of the anarchic conception of freedom; precisely by this move it became – inevitably – a bloody dictatorship.

Marxism too is a continuation of this radical line: it consistently criticized democratic freedom as a sham and promised a better, more radical freedom. Indeed, its fascination derived precisely from its promise of a grander and bolder freedom than is realized in the democracies. Two aspects of the Marxist system seem to me particularly relevant to the problem of freedom in the modern period and to the question of truth and freedom.

(1) Marxism proceeds from the principle that freedom is indivisible, hence, that it exists as such only when it is the freedom of all. Freedom is tied to equality. The existence of freedom requires before anything else the establishment of equality. This means that it is necessary to forgo freedom in order to attain the goal of total freedom. The solidarity of those struggling for the freedom of all comes before the vindication of individual liberties. The citation from Marx that served as the starting point for our reflections shows that the idea of the unbounded freedom of the individual reappears at the end of the process. For the present, however, the norm is the precedence of community, the subordination of freedom to equality, and therefore the right of the community vis-à-vis the individual.

(2) Bound up with this notion is the assumption that the freedom

6. Cf. T. Steinbüchel, *Die philosophische Grundlegung der christlichen Sittenlehre* I, 1 (Düsseldorf, 1947), 118-132.

of the individual depends upon the structure of the whole and that the struggle for freedom must be waged not primarily to secure the rights of the individual, but to change the structure of the world. However, at the question as to how this structure was supposed to look and what the rational means to bring it about were, Marxism came up short. For at bottom, even a blind man could see that none of its structures really makes possible that freedom for whose sake men were being called upon to forgo freedom. But intellectuals are blind when it comes to their intellectual constructs. For this reason they could forswear every realism and continue to fight for a system incapable of honoring its promises. They took refuge in mythology: the new structure, they claimed, would bring forth a new man — for, as a matter of fact, Marxism's promises could work only with new men who are entirely different from what they are now. If the moral character of Marxism lies in the imperative of solidarity and the idea of the indivisibility of freedom, there is an unmistakable lie in its proclamation of the new man, a lie that paralyzes even its inchoate ethics. Partial truths are correlative to a lie, and this fact undoes the whole: any lie about freedom neutralizes even the elements of truth associated with it. Freedom without truth is no freedom at all.

Let us stop at this point. We have arrived once more at the very problems that Szizypiorski formulated so drastically in Salzburg. We now know what the lie is — at least with respect to the forms in which Marxism has occurred until now. But we are still far from knowing what the truth is. Indeed, our apprehension intensifies: is there perhaps no truth at all? Can it be that there simply is no right at all? Must we content ourselves with a minimal stopgap social order? But may it be that even such an order does not work, as the latest developments in the Balkans and in so many other parts of the world show? Skepticism is growing and the grounds for it are becoming more forcible. At the same time, the will for the absolute cannot be done away with.

The feeling that democracy is not the right form of freedom is fairly common and is spreading more and more. The Marxist critique of democracy cannot simply be brushed aside: how free are elections? To what extent is the outcome manipulated by advertising, that is, by capital, by a few men who dominate public opinion? Is there not a new oligarchy who determine what is modern and progressive, what an enlightened man has to think? The cruelty of this oligarchy, its power to perform public executions, is notorious enough. Anyone who might get in its way is a foe of freedom, because, after all, the lie is interfering with the free expression of opinion. And how are decisions arrived at in representative bodies? Who could still believe that the welfare of the community as a whole truly guides the decision-making process? Who could doubt the power of special interests, whose dirty hands are exposed with increasing frequency? And in general, is the system of majority and minority really a system of freedom? And are not interest groups of every kind appreciably stronger than the proper organ of political representation, the parliament? In this tangled power play, the problem of ungovernability arises ever more menacingly: the will of individuals to prevail over one another blocks the freedom of the whole.

There is doubtless a flirtation with authoritarian solutions and a flight from a runaway freedom. But this attitude does not yet define the mind of our century. The radical current of the Enlightenment has not lost its appeal; indeed, it is becoming even more powerful. It is precisely in the face of the limits of democracy that the cry for total freedom gets louder. Today as yesterday, indeed, increasingly so, "Law and Order" is considered the antithesis of freedom. Today as yesterday institution, tradition, and authority as such appear to be polar opposites of freedom. The anarchist trend in the longing for freedom is growing in strength because the ordered forms of communal freedom are unsatisfactory. The grand promises made at the inception of modernity have not been kept, yet their fascination is unabated. The democratically ordered form of freedom can no longer be defended merely by this or that legal reform. The question goes to the very foundations themselves: it concerns what man is and how he can live rightly both individually and collectively.

We see that the political, philosophical, and religious problem of freedom has turned out to be an indissoluble whole; whoever is looking for ways forward must keep this whole in view and cannot content himself with superficial pragmatisms. Before attempting in the last part to outline some directions which I see opening up, I would like to glance briefly at perhaps the most radical philosophy of freedom in our century, that of J. P. Sartre, inasmuch as it brings out clearly the full magnitude and seriousness of the question. Sartre regards man as condemned to freedom. In contrast to the animal, man has no "nature." The animal lives out its existence according to laws it is simply born with; it does not need to deliberate what to do with its life. But man's essence is undetermined. It is an open question. I must decide myself what I understand by "humanity," what I want to do with it, and how I want to fashion it. Man has no nature, but is sheer freedom. His life must take some direction or other, but in the end it comes to nothing. This absurd freedom is man's hell. What is unsettling about this approach is that it is a way through the separation of freedom from truth to its most radical conclusion: there is no truth at all. Freedom has no direction and no measure.[7] But this complete absence of truth, this complete absence of any moral and metaphysical bond, this absolutely anarchic freedom – which is understood as an essential quality of man – reveals itself to one who tries to live it not as the supreme enhancement of existence, but as the frustration of life, the absolute void, the definition of damnation. The isolation of a radical concept of freedom, which for Sartre was a lived experience, shows with all desirable clarity that liberation from the truth does not produce pure freedom, but abolishes it. Anarchic freedom, taken radically, does not redeem, but makes man a miscarried creature, a pointless being.

3. Truth and Freedom

a. On the Essence of Human Freedom

After this attempt to understand the origin of our problems and to get a clear view of their inner tendency, it is now time to search for answers. It has become evident that the critical point in the history of freedom in which we now find ourselves rests upon an unclarified and one-sided idea of freedom. On the one hand, the concept of freedom has been isolated and thereby falsified: freedom is a good, but only within a network of other goods together with which it forms an indissoluble totality. On the other hand, the notion itself has been narrowly restricted to the rights of individual liberty, and has thus been robbed of its human truth. I would like to illustrate the problem posed by this

7. Cf. J. Pieper, "Kreatürlichkeit und menschliche Natur. Anmerkungen zum philosophischen Ansatz von J. P. Sartre," in *Über die Schwierigkeit, heute zu glauben* (Munich, 1974), 304-321.

understanding of freedom with the help of a concrete example. At the same time this example can open the way to a more adequate view of freedom. I mean the question of abortion. In the radicalization of the individualistic tendency of the Enlightenment, abortion appears as a right of freedom: the woman must be able to take charge of herself. She must have the freedom to decide whether she will bring a child into the world or rid herself of it. She must have the power to make decisions about her own life, and no one else can – so we are told – impose from the outside any ultimately binding norm. What is at stake is the right to self-determination. But is it really the case that the woman who aborts is making a decision about her own life? Is she not deciding precisely about someone else – deciding that no freedom shall be granted to another, and that the space of freedom, which is life, must be taken from him, because it competes with her own freedom? The question we must therefore ask is this: exactly what sort of freedom has even the right to annul another's freedom as soon as it begins?

Now, let it not be said that the issue of abortion concerns a special case and is not suited to clarify the general problem of freedom. No, it is this very example that brings out the basic figure of human freedom and makes clear what is typically human about it. For what is at stake here? The being of another person is so closely interwoven with the being of this person, the mother, that for the present it can survive only by physically being with the mother, in a physical unity with her. Such unity, however, does not eliminate the otherness of this being or authorize us to dispute its distinct selfhood. However, to be oneself in this way is to be radically from and through another. Conversely, this being-with compels the being of the other – that is, the mother – to become a being-for, which contradicts her own desire to be an independent self and is thus experienced as the antithesis of her own freedom. We must now add that even once the child is born and the outer form of its being-from and -with changes, it remains just as dependent on, and at the mercy of, a being-for. One can, of course, send the child off to an institution and assign it to the care of another "for," but the anthropological figure is the same, since there is still a "from" which demands a "for." I must still accept the limits of my freedom, or rather, I must live my freedom not out of competition but in a spirit of mutual support. If we open our eyes, we see that this, in turn, is true not only of the child, but that the child in the mother's womb is simply a very graphic depiction of the essence of human existence in general. Even the adult can exist only with and from another, and is thus continually thrown back on that being-for which is the very thing he would like to shut out. Let us say it even more precisely: man quite spontaneously takes for granted the being-for of others in the form of today's network of service systems, yet if he had his way he would prefer not to be forced to participate in such a "from" and "for," but would like to become wholly independent, and to be able to do and not to do just what he pleases. The radical demand for freedom, which has proved itself more and more clearly to be the outcome of the historical course of the Enlightenment, especially of the line inaugurated by Rousseau, and which today largely shapes the public mentality, prefers to have neither a whence nor a whither, to be neither from nor for, but to be wholly at liberty. In other words, it regards what is actually the fundamental figure of human existence itself as an attack on freedom which assails it before any individual has a chance to live and act. The radical cry for freedom demands man's liberation from his very essence as man, so that he may become the "new man." In the new society, the dependencies that restrict the I and the necessity of self-giving would no longer have the right to exist.

"Ye shall be as gods." This promise is quite clearly behind modernity's radical demand for freedom. Although Ernst Topitsch believed he could safely say that, today, no reasonable man still wants to be like or equal to God. If we look more closely we must assert the exact opposite: the implicit goal of all of modernity's struggles for freedom is to be at last like a god who depends on nothing and no one, and whose own freedom is not restricted by that of another. Once we glimpse this hidden theological core of the radical will to freedom, we can also discern the fundamental error which still spreads its influence even where such radical conclusions are not directly willed or are even rejected. To be totally free, without the competing freedom of others, without a "from" and a "for" – this desire presupposes not an image of God, but an idol. The primal error of such a radicalized will to freedom lies in the idea of a divinity conceived as a pure egoism. The god thought of in this way is not a God, but an idol. Indeed, it is the image of what the Christian tradition would call the devil – the anti-God – because it harbors exactly the radical antithesis to the real God. The real God is by his very nature entirely being-for (Father), being-from (Son), and being-with (Holy Spirit). Man, for his part, is God's image precisely insofar as the "from," "with," and "for" constitute the fundamental anthropological pattern. Whenever there is an attempt to free ourselves from this pattern, we are not on our way to divinity, but to dehumanization, to the destruction of being itself through the destruction of the truth. The Jacobin variant of the idea of liberation (let us call the radicalisms of modernity by this name) is a rebellion against man's very being, a rebellion against truth, which consequently leads man – as Sartre penetratingly saw – into a self-contradictory existence which we call hell.

The foregoing has made it clear that freedom is tied to a measure, the measure of reality – to the truth. Freedom to destroy oneself or to destroy another is not freedom, but its demonic parody. Man's freedom is shared freedom, freedom in the conjoint existence of liberties which limit and thus sustain one another. Freedom must measure itself by what I am, by what we are – otherwise it annuls itself. But having said this, we are now ready to make an essential correction of the superficial image of freedom which largely dominates the present: if man's freedom can consist only in the ordered coexistence of liberties, this means that order – right[8] – is not the conceptual antithesis of freedom, but rather its condition, indeed, a constitutive element of freedom itself. Right is not an obstacle to freedom, but constitutes it. The absence of right is the absence of freedom.

b. Freedom and Responsibility

Admittedly, this insight immediately gives rise to new questions as well: which right accords with freedom? How must right be structured so as to constitute a just order of freedom? For there doubtless exists a counterfeit right, which enslaves and is therefore not right at all but a regulated form of injustice. Our criticism must not be directed at right it-

8. ["Right" renders the German "Recht." Although the term "Recht" can mean "right" in the sense of "human rights," it may also be used to mean "law," with the more or less explicit connotation of "just order," "order embodying what is right." It is in this latter sense that Ratzinger takes "Recht" both here and in the following discussion; "Recht" has been translated in this context either as "right" or (less frequently) as "just order" or a variant thereof. – Trans.]

self, inasmuch as right belongs to the essence of freedom; it must unmask counterfeit right for what it is and serve to bring to light the true right – that right which is in accord with the truth and consequently with freedom.

But how do we find this right order? This is the great question of the true history of freedom, posed at last in its proper form. As we have already done so far, let us refrain from setting to work with abstract philosophical considerations. Rather, let us try to approach an answer inductively starting from the realities of history as they are actually given. If we begin with a small community of manageable proportions, its possibilities and limits furnish some basis for finding out which order best serves the shared life of all the members, so that a common form of freedom emerges from their joint existence. But no such small community is self-contained; it has its place within larger orders that, along with other factors, determine its essence. In the age of the nation-states it was customary to assume that one's own nation was the standard unit – that its common good was also the right measure of its freedom as a community. Developments in our century have made it clear that this point of view is inadequate. Augustine had said on this score that a state that measures itself only by its common interests and not by justice itself, by true justice, is not structurally different from a well-organized robber band. After all, the robber band typically takes as its measure the good of the band independently of the good of others. Looking back at the colonial period and the ravages it bequeathed to the new world, we see today that even well-ordered and civilized states were in some respects close to the nature of robber bands because they thought only in terms of their own good and not of the good itself. Accordingly, freedom guaranteed in this way has something of the brigand's freedom. It is not true, genuinely human freedom. In the search for the right measure, the whole of humanity must be kept in mind, and again – as we see ever more clearly – the humanity not only of today, but of tomorrow as well.

The criterion of real right – right entitled to call itself true right which accords with freedom – can therefore only be the good of the whole, the good itself. On the basis of this insight, Hans Jonas has defined responsibility as the central concept of ethics.[9] This means that

9. H. Jonas, *Das Prinzip Verantwortung* (Frankfurt a.M., 1979).

in order to understand freedom properly we must always think of it in tandem with responsibility. Accordingly, the history of liberation can never occur except as a history of growth in responsibility. Increase of freedom can no longer lie simply in giving more and more latitude to individual rights – which leads to absurdity and to the destruction of those very individual freedoms themselves. Increase in freedom must be an increase in responsibility, which includes acceptance of the ever greater bonds required both by the claims of humanity's shared existence and by conformity to man's essence. If responsibility is answering to the truth of man's being, then we can say that an essential component of the history of liberation is ongoing purification for the sake of the truth. The true history of freedom consists in the purification of individuals and of institutions through this truth.

The principle of responsibility sets up a framework which needs to be filled by some content. This is the context in which we have to look at the proposal for the development of a planetary ethos, for which Hans Küng has been the preeminent and passionately committed spokesman. It is no doubt sensible, indeed, in our present situation necessary, to search for the basic elements common to the ethical traditions of the various religions and cultures. In this sense, such an endeavor is by all means important and appropriate. On the other hand, the limits of this sort of enterprise are evident; Joachim Fest, among others, has called attention to these limits in a sympathetic, but also very pessimistic analysis, whose general drift comes quite close to the skepticism of Szizypiorski.[10] For this ethical minimum distilled from the world religions lacks first of all the bindingness, the intrinsic authority, which is a prerequisite of ethics. Despite every effort to reach a clearly understandable position, it also lacks the obvious compatibility with reason which, in the opinion of the authors, could and should replace authority; it also lacks the concreteness without which ethics cannot come into its own.

One idea, which is implicit in this experiment, seems to me correct: reason must listen to the great religious traditions if it does not wish to

10. J. Fest, *Die schwierige Freiheit* (Berlin, 1993), esp. 47-81. Fest sums up his observations on Küng's "planetary ethos": "The farther the agreements – which cannot be reached without concessions – are pushed, the more elastic and consequently the more impotent the ethical norms become, to the point that the project finally amounts to a mere corroboration of that unbinding morality which is not the goal, but the problem" (80).

become deaf, dumb, and blind precisely to what is essential about human existence. There is no great philosophy that does not draw life from listening to and accepting religious tradition. Wherever this relation is cut off, philosophical thought withers and becomes a mere conceptual game.[11] The very theme of responsibility, that is, the question of anchoring freedom in the truth of the good, of man and of the world, reveals very clearly the necessity of such attentive listening. For, although the general approach of the principle of responsibility is very much to the point, it is still a question of how we are supposed to get a comprehensive view of what is good for all — good not only for today, but also for tomorrow. A twofold danger lies in wait here. On the one hand there is the risk of sliding into consequentialism, which the pope rightly criticizes in his moral encyclical (*Veritatis splendor,* 71-83). Man simply overreaches himself if he believes that he can assess the whole range of consequences resulting from his action and make them the norm of his freedom. In doing so he sacrifices the present to the future, while also failing even to construct the future. On the other hand, who decides what our responsibility enjoins? When the truth is no longer seen in the context of an intelligent appropriation of the great traditions of belief, it is replaced by consensus. But once again we must ask: whose consensus? The common answer is the consensus of those capable of rational argument. Because it is impossible to ignore the elitist arrogance of such an intellectual dictatorship, it is then said that those capable of rational argument would also have to engage in "advocacy" on behalf of those who are not. This whole line of thought can hardly inspire confidence. The fragility of consensuses and the ease with which in a certain intellectual climate partisan groups can assert their claim to be the sole rightful representatives of progress and responsibility are plain for all to see. It is all too easy here to drive out the devil with Beelzebub; it is all too easy to replace the demon of bygone intellectual systems with seven new and worse ones.

11. See the penetrating remarks on this point in J. Pieper, *Schriften zum Philosophiebegriff* III, ed. B. Wald (Hamburg, 1995), 300-323, as well as 15-70, esp. 59ff.

c. The Truth of Our Humanity

How we are to establish the right relationship between responsibility and freedom cannot be settled simply by means of a calculus of effects. We must return to the idea that man's freedom is a freedom in the coexistence of freedoms; only thus is it true, that is, in conformity with the authentic reality of man. It follows that it is by no means necessary to seek outside elements in order to correct the freedom of the individual. Otherwise, freedom and responsibility, freedom and truth, would be perpetual opposites, which they are not. Properly understood, the reality of the individual itself includes reference to the whole, to the other. Accordingly, our answer to the question above is that there is a common truth of a single humanity present in every man. The tradition has called this truth man's "nature." Basing ourselves on faith in creation, we can formulate this point even more clearly: there is one divine idea, "man," to which it is our task to answer. In this idea, freedom and community, order and concern for the future, are a single whole.

Responsibility would thus mean to live our being as an answer – as a response to what we are in truth. This one truth of man, in which freedom and the good of all are inextricably correlative, is centrally expressed in the biblical tradition in the Decalogue, which, by the way, coincides in many respects with the great ethical traditions of other religions. The Decalogue is at once the self-presentation and self-exhibition of God and the exposition of what man is, the luminous manifestation of his truth. This truth becomes visible in the mirror of God's essence, because man can be rightly understood only in relation to God. To live the Decalogue means to live our Godlikeness, to correspond to the truth of our being and thus to do the good. Said in yet another way, to live the Decalogue means to live the divinity of man, which is the very definition of freedom: the fusion of our being with the divine being and the resulting harmony of all with all (*Catechism of the Catholic Church,* 2052-2082).

In order to understand this statement aright, we must add a further remark. Every significant human word reaches into greater depths beyond what the speaker is immediately conscious of saying: in what is said there is always an excess of the unsaid, which allows the words to grow as the ages go forward. If this is true even of human speech, it must *a fortiori* be true of the word which comes out of the depths of God. The Decalogue is never simply understood once and for all. In the successive, changing situations where responsibility is exercised historically, the Decalogue appears in ever new perspectives, and ever new dimensions of its significance are opened. Man is led into the whole of the truth, truth which could by no means be borne in just one historical moment alone (cf. Jn 16:12f.). For the Christian, the exegesis of the Decalogue accomplished in the words, life, passion, and Resurrection of Christ is the decisive interpretive authority, within which a hitherto unsuspected depth opens up. Consequently, man's listening to the message of faith is not the passive registering of otherwise unknown information, but the resuscitation of our choked memory and the opening of the powers of understanding which await the light of the truth in us. Hence, such understanding is a supremely active process, in which reason's entire quest for the criteria of our responsibility truly comes into its own for the first time. Reason's quest is not stifled, but is freed from circling helplessly in impenetrable darkness and set on its way. If the Decalogue, unfolded in rational understanding, is the answer to the intrinsic requirements of our essence, then it is not the counter-pole of our freedom, but its real form. It is, in other words, the foundation of every just order of freedom and the true liberating power in human history.

4. Summary of the Results

"Perhaps the worn-out steam engine of the Enlightenment, after two centuries of profitable, trouble-free labor has come to a standstill before our eyes and with our cooperation. And the steam is simply evaporating." This is Szizypiorski's pessimistic diagnosis, which we encountered at the beginning as an invitation to reflection. Now, I would say that the operation of this machine was never trouble-free – let us think only of the two World Wars of our century and of the dictatorships which we have witnessed. But I would add that we by no means need to retire the whole inheritance of the Enlightenment as such from service and pronounce it a worn-out steam engine. What we do need, however, is a course correction on three essential points, with which I would like to sum up the yield of my reflections.

(1) An understanding of freedom that tends to regard liberation exclusively as the ever more sweeping annulment of norms and the

constant extension of individual liberties to the point of complete emancipation from all order is false. Freedom, if it is not to lead to deceit and self-destruction, must orient itself by the truth, that is, by what we really are, and must correspond to our being. Since man's essence consists in being-from, being-with, and being-for, human freedom can exist only in the ordered communion of freedoms. Right is therefore not antithetical to freedom, but is a condition, indeed, a constitutive element of freedom itself. Liberation does not lie in the gradual abolition of right and of norms, but in the purification of ourselves and of the norms so that they will make possible the humane coexistence of freedoms.

(2) A further point follows from the truth of our essential being: there will never be an absolutely ideal state of liberation within our human history, and the definitive order of freedom will never be established. Man is always under way and always finite. Szizypiorski, considering both the notorious injustice of the socialist order and all the problems of the liberal order, had posed the doubt-filled question: what if there is no right order at all? Our response must now be that, in fact, the absolutely ideal order of things, which is right in all respects, will never exist.[12] Whoever claims that it will is not telling the truth. Faith in progress is not false in every respect. What is false, however, is the myth of the liberated world of the future, in which everything will be different and good. We can erect only relative orders, which can never be and embody right except in their relative way. But we must strive precisely for this best possible approximation to what is truly right. Nothing else, no inner-historical eschatology, liberates, but it deceives and therefore enslaves. For this reason, the mythic luster attached to concepts such as change and revolution must be demythologized. Change is not a good in itself. Whether it is good or bad depends upon its concrete contents and points of reference. The opinion that the essential task in the struggle for freedom is to change the world is — I repeat — a myth. History will always have its vicissitudes. When it comes to man's ethical nature in the strict sense, things do not proceed in a straight line, but in cycles. It is our task always to struggle in the present for the relatively best constitution of man's shared existence and in so doing to preserve the good

12. Cf. *Gaudium et spes,* 78: "numquam pax pro semper acquisita est" ("peace is never acquired once and for all").

we have already achieved, to overcome existing ills, and to resist the in-breaking of the forces of destruction.

(3) We must also lay to rest once and for all the dream of the absolute autonomy and self-sufficiency of reason. Human reason needs the support of the great religious traditions of humanity. It will, of course, examine critically the individual religious traditions. The pathology of religion is the most dangerous sickness of the human mind. It exists in the religions, but it also exists precisely where religion as such is rejected and the status of an absolute is assigned to relative goods: the atheistic systems of modernity are the most terrifying examples of a religious passion alienated from its nature, which is a life-threatening sickness of the human mind. Where God is denied, freedom is not built up, but robbed of its foundation and thus distorted.[13] Where the purest and deepest religious traditions are entirely discarded, man severs himself from his truth; he lives contrary to it and becomes unfree. Even philosophical ethics cannot be unqualifiedly autonomous. It cannot renounce the idea of God or the idea of a truth of being having an ethical character.[14] If there is no truth about man, man also has no freedom. Only the truth makes us free.

Translated by Adrian J. Walker

13. Cf. J. Fest, *Die schwierige Freiheit,* 79: "None of the appeals addressed to man is able to say how he can live without a beyond, without fear of the last day, and yet time after time act against his own interests and desires." Cf. also L. Kolakowski, *Falls es keinen Gott gibt* (Munich, 1982).

14. Cf. J. Pieper, *Schriften zum Philosophiebegriff* III.

The Holy Spirit as Communio: *Concerning the Relationship of Pneumatology and Spirituality in Augustine*

The words "pneumatology" and "spirituality," which together constitute my topic, are closely tied to one another in a purely verbal sense. One is the translation of the other. This expresses a connection of fundamental significance. The Holy Spirit is recognizable in the way in which he forms human life. A life formed from faith is in turn a sign of the Holy Spirit. To speak of "Christian spirituality" means to speak about the Holy Spirit. He makes himself recognizable by gaining a new center for human life. Speaking about the Holy Spirit includes looking at him in man, to whom he has given himself.

There is a certain difficulty in speaking about the Holy Spirit, even a certain danger. He withdraws from us into mystery even more than Christ. It is quite possible that this topic has sparked only idle speculation and that human life is being based upon self-made fantasies rather than reality. This is why I hesitated to offer just my own reflections. It seems to me that three conditions must be fulfilled to speak meaningfully, reliably, and defensibly about the Holy Spirit. First, it cannot be talk based upon pure theory but must touch an experienced reality that has been interpreted and communicated in thought. But second, experience alone does not suffice. It must be tested and tried experience so that "one's own spirit" does not take the place of the

---

This article appeared in *Communio* 25, no. 2 (Summer 1998). It was originally published as "Der Heilige Geist als *communio.* Zum Verhältnis von Pneumatologie und Spiritualität bei Augustinus," in *Erfahrung und Theologie des Heiligen Geistes,* ed. C. Heitmann and H. Mühlen (Munich, 1974).

Holy Spirit. Third, in consequence, suspicion will always arise when someone speaks on his own account, "from within." Such speech contradicts the Holy Spirit's mode of being, for he is characterized precisely "by not speaking on his own" (Jn 16:13). In this respect, originality and truth can easily lead to a paradox.[1] But that means that trust is appropriate only when one does not speak on a purely private account, but from an experience of the Spirit tested in front of and standing in the context of the whole, i.e., when one submits the experience of "spirit" to the entirety of the Church. This presupposes as an axiom of Christian faith that the Church herself — when she truly exists as Church — is a creation of the Spirit.

Thus a proper treatment of my topic consists in condensing the great witnesses to the Spirit in the history of the Church into directions for life in the Spirit. Since I lack the preparatory work for this, I have settled for making comments on Augustine's doctrine of the Spirit.[2] This has the disadvantage of less relevance, but the advantage that a great witness of the tradition is speaking to us. Another advantage is its objectivity. What has survived the sieve of fifteen hundred years of history as an expression of common faith and become the starting point for life lived in the Spirit can claim a certain level of legitimacy.

Augustine himself is quite conscious of the difficulty of the matter. He also struggles with objectivity. He questions originality and trusts whatever can be objectively found in the common faith of the Church. He proceeds to try to grasp the essence of the Holy Spirit by interpreting his customary names. He does not probe the topic "pneumatology and spirituality." For him pneumatological questioning is intrinsically

1. Cf. E. M. Heufelder, *Neues Pfingsten,* 2d ed. (Meitingen-Freising, 1970), especially 51; J. Pieper, *Überlieferung* (Munich, 1970), 38ff., 97-108.

2. This limitation is not for historical purposes but only with a view to the theological question of what can be learned from Augustine today. I have consciously avoided entering into the historical discussion of Augustine's doctrine of the Trinity. On this question, see the bibliography in C. Andresen, *Bibliographia Augustiniana* (Darmstadt, 1962), 78-80, and the ongoing bibliographies of the *Revue des Études Augustiniennes.* One could also mention in this regard M. Schmaus, *Die psychologische Trinitätslehre des heiligen Augustinus,* 2d ed. (1967); A. Dahl, *Augustin und Plotin* (Lund, 1945); O. du Roy, *L'intélligence de la foi en la trinité selon St. Augustin. Genèse de sa théologie trinitaire jusqu'en* (Paris, 1966), 391; as well as the edition with commentary of *De Trinitate* in the *Bibliothèque Augustienne, Oeuvres de St. Augustin,* vol. 15 (M. Mellet, Th. Camelot, E. Hendrikx) and vol. 16 (P. Agaesse, J. Moingt), hereafter cited as *Oeuvres* vol. 15 and vol. 16.

spiritual questioning. His questions are not about things but about what is defined as light and love and therefore can be seen only by entering into their holiness and warmth.

1. The Name "Holy Spirit" as an Indication of the Unique Character of the Third Person of the Trinity

As already stated, Augustine attempts to grasp the particular physiognomy of the Holy Spirit by investigating his traditional names, first, the designation "Holy Spirit."[3] But this presents him with an aporia. While the names "Father" and "Son" bring to light what is characteristic of the first and second Persons of the Trinity, the name "Holy Spirit" does not support the presentation of the particularity of the third Person as giving and receiving, i.e., being as gift and being as reception, as word and response – characteristics that are so completely one that unity, not subordination, arises within them. On the contrary, each of the two other Persons of the Trinity could be named in this way. Above all, God himself and as such could be named this way since John 4:24 also states: "God is spirit." Being spirit and being holy is the essential description of God. That is what identifies him as God.

Thus the attempt to gain some kind of concrete understanding of the Holy Spirit in this way only makes him completely unrecognizable. Augustine sees the particularity of the Holy Spirit expressed precisely in this dilemma. When he is named by that which is the divinity of God, by what the Father and Son have in common, then his essence is just that, the *communio* of Father and Son. The particularity of the Holy Spirit is evidently that he is what the Father and Son have in common. His particularity is being unity. The general name "Holy Spirit" is the most appropriate way to express him in the paradox characteristic of him – mutuality itself.

I think that we learn something very important here. The mediation of Father and Son comes to full unity not when it is seen in a universal, ontic *consubstantialitas* but as *communio.* In other words, it is not derived from a universally metaphysical substance but from the per-

3. St. Augustine, *De Trinitate* 5.11.12–12.13. Cf. the excursus of J. Moingt, "Les Noms du Saint-Esprit" in *Oeuvres,* vol. 16, 651-654.

son. According to the nature of God, it is intrinsically personal. The dyad returns into unity in the Trinity without breaking up the dialogue. Dialogue is actually confirmed in just this way. A mediation back into unity that was not another Person would break up the dialogue as dialogue. The Spirit is Person as unity, unity as Person.

From the phrase "Holy Spirit" Augustine takes the definition of Spirit as *communio.* This already has a fundamentally ecclesiological meaning for him, as will be confirmed in the other names of the Holy Spirit. It opens pneumatology up into ecclesiology, and, in reverse direction, ecclesiology into theology. Becoming a Christian means becoming *communio* and thereby entering into the mode of being of the Holy Spirit. But it can also happen only through the Holy Spirit, who is the power of communication – mediating it, making it possible – and is himself a Person.

Spirit is the unity that God gives himself. In this unity, he himself gives himself. In this unity, the Father and the Son give themselves back to one another. The Spirit's own paradoxical and unique property is being *communio,* having his highest selfness precisely in being fully the movement of *communio.* Being "spirit-ual" would thus essentially always have to do with unifying, communicating.

That means that Augustine has secretly also effected an important revision of the notion of spirit as such. A bit of metaphysics of spirit has occurred at the same time. He allows the Johannine sentence "God is spirit" to stand in a purely ontological sense. "Spirit" for him means, first of all, not being matter. On the other hand, one could immediately object that in John it does not have to do with this at all. There the word "spirit" expresses the otherness of God in opposition to worldly matters. The opposite of spirit is not matter but rather "the world."[4] He is not ontological in the Greek sense but axiological, aiming at the specifically religious quality of the wholly Other and in that sense referring to the Holy Spirit as an expression of God's self-determining character, to "the holiness" which expresses this "Other." In many regards, this is an incomparably more radical opposition than the contrast of spirit and matter, since spirit ultimately can also be worldly and does not have to include going beyond the entirety of the innerworldly. Looking at the whole of Augustine's interpretation, one

4. Cf. R. Schnackenburg, *Das Johannesevangelium,* vol. 1 (Freiburg, 1965), 474.

can say that he embraces this view completely, abandoning the ancient metaphysics of spirit precisely because he has to explain spirit not universally and metaphysically but on the basis of the dynamic between Father and Son. *Communio* thereby becomes an essential element of the notion of the Spirit, thus truly giving it content and thoroughly personalizing it. Only one who knows what "Holy Spirit" is can know what spirit means. And only one who begins to know what God is can know what Holy Spirit is. Furthermore, only one who begins to have an idea of what Holy Spirit is can begin to know who God is.

2. The Holy Spirit as Love

The analysis of biblical pneumatology leads Augustine to the thesis that alongside the word "Holy Spirit," the words "love" *(caritas)* and "gift" *(donum)* are also, strictly speaking, names of the Holy Spirit. Let us begin with the analysis of the word "love," which led Augustine to this idea.[5]

(a) The central text from which Augustine develops his thesis is found in the first letter of John: "God is love" (4:16). Augustine determines that, first of all and fundamentally, this statement pertains completely to God as the undivided Trinity but still expresses the unique property of the Holy Spirit. The case is similar to the words "wisdom" and "word," which express qualities of God in a general sense, but also refer in the Bible to the Son in a specific sense. Augustine finds proof for the meaning of *caritas* in the context of 1 John 4:7-16.[6] The textual comparison of verse 12 and 16b with verse 13 is decisive for him:

> Verse 12: If we love one another, God abides in us . . .
> Verse 16b: God is love, and he who abides in love, God abides in him.
> Verse 13: We recognize that we abide in him and he in us because he has given us of his spirit.

In the first instance, love gives abiding; in the second instance, love gives the Holy Spirit. In the above verses, *pneuma* takes the place of love

5. *De Trin.* 15.17.27-18.32.
6. *De Trin.* 15.17.31.

and vice versa. Or literally: "The Holy Spirit, of whom he has given us, causes us to abide in God, and God in us. But love does this. He is, therefore, the God who is love." To clarify, Augustine adds that Romans 5:5 states that the love of God is poured out through the Holy Spirit who is given to us. It appears to me that these observations are correct in principle. The gift of God is the Holy Spirit. The gift of God is love. God communicates himself in the Holy Spirit as love. For Augustine, this reveals a number of very important, meaningful conclusions. First of all, the presence of the Holy Spirit is essentially proclaimed in the manner of love. *That* is the criterion of the Holy Spirit as opposed to the unholy spirit. In fact, that is the presence of the Holy Spirit himself and, in that sense, the presence of God. The basic and central meaning of what the Holy Spirit is and what he effects is ultimately not "knowledge" but love. This makes the expanded notion of spirit, the explanation of which is the Christian understanding of the wholly otherness of God, even more concrete than previously imagined. Admittedly, the full clarity of this statement first comes to light in ecclesiology, where Augustine is forced to address the practical question: "What does love mean as a criterion of the Holy Spirit and therefore also as a criterion of being Christian and of the Church?"

One important clarification immediately results from the analysis of the text of John: the basic criterion of love — its characteristic activity and therefore the characteristic activity of the Holy Spirit — is that it creates abiding. Love proves itself in constancy. Love is not recognizable right at any given moment, or in just one moment; instead, love abides, overcomes vacillation, and bears eternity within itself, which also shows, in my opinion, the connection between love and truth. Love in the full sense can exist only where constancy exists, where abiding exists. Because love has to do with abiding, it cannot take place anywhere except where there is eternity.

From this there emerges the basic framework for a doctrine of the discernment of spirits and a directive for the spiritual life. Clearly, anyone who looks for *pneuma* only on the outside, in the always unexpected, is on the wrong path. He or she fails to appreciate the basic activity of the Holy Spirit: unifying love entering into abiding. This gives rise to a decision of great significance: "Is *pneuma* only to be sought in the discontinuous or does it dwell precisely in 'abiding,' in the constancy of creative fidelity?" If the latter, then it also means that spirit is not present where one speaks "in one's own name" or "seeks one's own fame," thus creating a faction. *Pneuma* is present precisely in remembering (Jn 14:26) and unifying. We will come back to these statements, in which pneumatology, according to Augustine, became a concrete directive for action. But let us first continue with our analysis.

(b) I would like briefly to mention a second passage in which Augustine found his view confirmed, i.e., that the word "love" in Holy Scripture is intended to refer specifically to the Holy Spirit.[7] Augustine contrasts the seventh and sixteenth verses of 1 John 4 and finds in the reciprocal interpretation of the two texts further confirmation of the contrast between verses 12-16 and verse 13. Verse 16 states that God is love. Verse 7 reads: "Love is from God." Love is on the one hand "God," on the other hand "from God." If you put the two together, love is equally "God" and "from God"; in other words, love is "God from God." Together with the previous passage, it seems to explain once again that this "God from God" – God as the power to emerge and become near, as the power of new birth, of a new whither for men and women – is the Holy Spirit and that we may receive what is said about *agape* as an equivalent elucidation of what the Holy Spirit is.

3. The Holy Spirit as Gift

John 4:7-14, i.e., Jesus' conversation with the Samaritan woman, is Augustine's central text for representing the word "gift" *(donum)* as an essential designation of the Holy Spirit. Jesus asks her for the "gift" of water in order to reveal himself as the giver of better water.[8] "If you only recognized God's *gift,* and who it is that is saying to you, '*Give* me a drink,' you would have asked him instead and he would have *given* you living water." For Augustine, the inner logic of this text is supported by Jesus' promise of water at the Feast of the Tabernacles: "If anyone thirsts, let him come to me and drink. As Scripture states, from his body a stream of living waters will flow" (Jn 7:37). The evangelist adds to this passage: "He says this about the Spirit, whom those who came to believe in him were to receive" (7:39). Augustine finds the same pneumatological exegesis of the gift of

7. Ibid.

8. *De Trin.* 15.19.33; cf. 5.14.15-15.16.

living water in 1 Corinthians 12:13: "All of us have been given to drink of the one Spirit." This affirmation of the Spirit in the image of water, as formulated in John 4 and John 7, provides Augustine with the connection between Christology and pneumatology. Christ is the well of living water. That means that the crucified Lord is the generative source of life for the world. The well of the Spirit is the crucified Christ. From him each Christian becomes the well of the Spirit.

It is also important to understand that all the power of the image is joined to pneumatology. Man's ultimate thirst cries out for the Holy Spirit. He and he alone is the fresh water without which there is no life. The mystery of the Spirit becomes visible in the image of the well and of water in a way that is ineffable and cannot be retrieved through reflection, for the water moistens and transforms a desert and encounters man as a mysterious promise. Man's thirst becomes an infinite, radical thirst, a thirst that is not quenched by any other water than that water's refreshment. In this context, Augustine admittedly did not pursue the connection between a theology of the cross and a theology of history, which is suggested especially by John 19 and whose wide influence in patristic theology has been successfully demonstrated by Hugo Rahner.[9]

According to Augustine, the second important result of the connection between John 4 and John 7 is the certainty that the name "gift" is a name of the Holy Spirit so as to make a theology (or, more correctly, a pneumatology) of giving and of gift possible. Conversely, the essence of God as the Holy Spirit is also explained by the idea of gift. On this basis, Augustine can now elucidate the difference between Son and *pneuma.* In other words, he can answer the question about why the Spirit, who also is truly "God from God," is not also "Son." What is different here? Augustine's answer: "He comes from God not as born but as given *(non quomodo natus, sed quomodo datus).* Therefore he is not called son because he is neither 'born' like the 'first-born' nor 'created' as we are *(neque natus . . . eque factus).*"[10] He distinguishes three modes of origin from God: being born, being given, and being created *(natus, datus, factus).* If one can best describe the essence of the Son, his own status with regard to the Father, with the concept of generation, then

9. H. Rahner, *Symbole der Kirche* (Salzburg, 1964), 175-235.
10. *De Trin.* 5.14.15.

that of the Spirit is "giving." The movement of giving is the specifically holy, spiritual movement.

This "being given" *(datus)* is not intended to be a middle position between being born and being created (*natus* and *factus*). It does not at all eradicate the boundary separating creature and God but remains within the divinity. Nevertheless, it still represents an opening to history and to man. Augustine asks whether the Holy Spirit alone has his own gift-being or has his being entirely from the fact that he is "given." Does he have a being independently of being gift and before he turns into gift, or does his being consist precisely of being God's gift? The doctor of the Church from Hippo responds that the Holy Spirit always is in his essence the gift of God, God as the self-donating, God as the self-distributing, as gift.[11] The inner ground for creation and salvation history already lies in this mode of being of the Holy Spirit, being *donum* and *datum,* in fact beginning with salvation history, with God's full self-giving, which appears for its part as the inner ground of creation. On the one hand, the "immanent" doctrine of the Trinity is opened wholly to the "economic." On the other hand, salvation history is referred back to theo-logy. The *gift* of God is God himself. He is the content of Christian prayer. He is the only gift adequate to the divinity. God gives as God nothing other than God, giving himself and with himself everything. Proper Christian prayer does not plead for something or other but for the gift of God which God is, for him. Augustine expresses this beautifully by interpreting as a matter of course the plea of the "Our Father," "*Give* us our daily bread," in terms of the Holy Spirit. *He* is "our bread," ours as one who is not ours, as something completely given. "Our" spirit is not our spirit.[12]

Thus, what really matters is that God as gift is actually God; in other words, that the Holy Spirit is divine. The classical precision of Augustine's formulation can barely be translated into either our own words or our ideas: "There is there (i.e., with God) not a subordinate

11. *De Trin.* 5.15.16.

12. "Spiritus ergo et Dei est qui dedit, et noster qui accipimus. Non ille spiritus noster quo sumus, quia ipse spiritus est hominis qui in ipso est: sed alio modo iste noster est, quo dicimus et: 'Panem nostrum da nobis' (Mt 6:11). Quanquam et illum spiritum qui hominis dicitur, utique accepimus. 'Quid enim habes,' inquit 'quod non accepisti' (1 Cor 4:7)? Sed aliud est quod accepimus ut essemus, aliud quod accepimus ut sancti essemus" (*De Trin.* 5.14.15).

position of being given nor a lordship of the giver but the harmony *(concordia)* of the one given and the giver." Moreover, this point confirms what Augustine previously took from the name "Holy Spirit": "Because he is the one common to both, his own name is what they have in common." This statement also establishes the inner unity of the designations "love" and "gift" with the main designation "Holy Spirit." In this manner, he shows the legitimacy of this unity and integrates the whole into a mutually interpreting unity.

4. The Opening to Salvation History

As already noted, the opening to salvation history results equally from the concepts of love and gift. Two texts shed light and even more clarity on the meaning of the connections.

(a) In *De Trinitate* 15.18.32, Augustine develops the eschatological significance of *pneuma* from the eschatological function of love as judge. *Caritas* is not opposed to justice but is itself the judgment. Love and love alone is the judgment of God. Love separates the left from the right (Mt 25!). The one who loves stands "on his right hand," and the one who does not is directed to the left side. Without love, none of "the Good" is good. Augustine buttresses his argument by turning to the seemingly conflicting preachers of the gospel, Paul and James, the letter to the Galatians and the letter of James, respectively. According to Galatians 5:6, neither circumcision nor uncircumcision counts for anything, only faith working through love. Paul repeats in condensed version what he said dramatically in 1 Corinthians 13:1-3: "Without *caritas* everything else, faith, works, is nothing, absolutely nothing." Paul and James meet at this point because by referring to faith working through love, the apostle separates saving faith, pneumatically inspired faith, from the unsaving faith that the demons also possess (Jas 2:19). Without love, Augustine says, faith can "exist but not save," *esse non prod-esse,* in the inimitable Latin of the bishop of Hippo.

These statements, which interpret *caritas,* i.e., *pneuma,* as the eschatological judgment and thus as the decisive sign of Christian faith, serve as the foundation for the entire sacramental theology and ecclesiology of Augustine, which at this point are reunited with pneumatology. With this conviction, Augustine took on the Donatists. The Donatists had the same sacraments as the Catholic Church, so wherein lies the difference? What is wrong with the Donatists? Taking into account the prehistory of the division, as well as their contemporary form, Augustine responds that they have broken love. They have departed from the true faith because they have placed their own idea of perfection above unity. They have held on to everything that is part of the Catholic Church except that they gave up love when they gave up unity. Without love, everything else is empty. The word *caritas* receives here a very concrete, ecclesiological meaning; and, in fact, in Augustine's language it completely penetrates the concepts, for he says that the Church is love. This, in a sense, is a dogmatic thesis for him. As a creation of the Spirit, the Church is the body of the Lord built up by the *pneuma,* and thus also becomes the body of Christ when the *pneuma* forms men and women for *communio.* This creation, this Church, is God's "gift" in the world, and this "gift" is love. But Augustine sees in this dogmatic thesis a concrete character as well. We cannot build up our Christian identity in sects, in isolation from others. Should this happen, the very soul of the whole would be missing even if one had all the individual parts. Accepting the entire community of believers belongs to Christian identity, i.e., humility, love *(caritas),* and bearing with one another, for otherwise the Holy Spirit, the one who unifies, would be missing. The dogmatic statement "The Church is love" is not merely a dogmatic statement for the manuals, but refers to the dynamism that forms unity, a dynamism that is the force holding the Church together. Thus, Augustine thinks of schism as a pneumatological heresy that takes root concretely in the act of living. To remove oneself from the abiding, which is the spirit, from the patience of love, is to revoke love by revoking abiding and thereby denying the Holy Spirit, who is the patience of abiding, of reconciling. Augustine does not assert that whoever remains in the Church automatically has *caritas,* but rather that whoever does not willingly remain leaves *caritas* behind. Therefore his proposition: one possesses the Holy Spirit to the degree that one loves the Church. Trinitarian theology is the real standard of ecclesiology. The name "love" as given to the Holy Spirit is the key to Christian existence and at the same time interprets love concretely as ecclesial patience.[13]

13. Cf. the presentation of these ideas in my book, *Volk und Haus Gottes in Augustins Lehre von der Kirche* (Munich, 1954), 136-158.

To understand more clearly this summation of an ecclesiological dispute and the pneumatological ecclesiology of Augustine, we should add that the pride of an even greater perfection existed not just at the beginning. The symptoms of this division were stamped with such hate that its diagnosis was obvious. The seed of the separation was the departure from the community of love. A few sentences from F. van der Meer, who vividly depicts the experience of Donatism as it appeared to Augustine, will shed some light on this:

> It was reported that they (the Donatists) destroyed the place where a Catholic had been. And what was worse, they provided angry mobs, bands of embittered workers who perhaps dreamed of an earthly kingdom of God and who attacked over and again the *cellae* (granaries or storehouses) or solitary farms, the country houses, churches, and castles of the Catholics. They plundered the supplies wherever they were not provided, "stealing the dry goods and emptying the liquids," setting fire to the basilicas with books and everything. They mishandled the clerics and later, as their cause declined, threw lime and vinegar in the eyes of the Catholics in order to blind them, "something that did not even happen with the barbarians." They also did not forget to demand letters of debt back, break contracts, extort the liberation of the most terrible good-for-nothings among the slaves, and, when necessary, hitch a resisting lord up to the treadmills.[14]

Thus we have to concede that the identification of Church and love also has its dangers, no matter how grounded in the deepest reasoning and no matter how intelligibly brought forward. There is no doubt that the resultant ecclesial transformation of spirit and love addresses one side of the issue. But it can also lead to dangerous and restrictive consequences. These dangers arise when the designation of the Church as love no longer allows its connection with the Spirit to be the actual standard of the Church (as a practical requirement) but appears in-

14. F. van der Meer, *Augustinus der Seelsorger* (Cologne, 1951), 113; see the entire section, "Die pars Donati und die Ketzer," 109-163. On the historical context of Donatism see H. I. Mattou in *Geschichte der Kirche,* vol. 1, ed. J. Daniélou and H. I. Marrou (Einsiedeln, 1953), 256-260; W. H. C. Frend, "Donatismus," in *Reallexikon für Antike und Christentum,* vol. 4, ed. Th. Klauser, 128-147.

stead as the self-evident content of the institution. In this case, rigidity sets in, a problem that the later Augustine suggested and that subsequently led to the dangerous hardening of positions in the Church during the Middle Ages and modernity.

Perhaps it is also because, in the heretical movements of the Middle Ages and Reformation, the Spirit is considered almost in contrast to the established Church. The opposition that has reemerged in our day between *pneuma* and institution expresses a romanticism that is no longer relevant even in the profane realm. (Germany has dramatically experienced, in this century alone, the power of romantic movements that destroy spirit and body.) This false alternative is all the more incapable of coping with the problem of Church and Spirit. Today the "official Church," or the "empirical Catholic Church," is looked upon as the antithesis of "spirit." Augustine would have denied this and refuted it as a misunderstanding of the Church, which may be forgivable in the pagan, but should be impossible in the believer. The Church that dispenses the sacraments and explains the word of God by listening is not only the "empirical Catholic Church." She cannot be divided up into "spirit" and "institution." The Church is the house of the Spirit, visible and "empirical," in the sacraments and in the word. The Spirit is given precisely in the concrete community of those who derive their support from Christ and bear with one another. The idea that the Spirit appears only in discontinuous and occasional eruptions of self-educated groups would be unthinkable to Augustine. Whoever looks for the Spirit only externally, Augustine would say, misunderstands the fundamental activity of *pneuma:* unifying love entering into abiding. But this opens up an alternative of decisive significance: "Is *pneuma* only in the discontinuous, or precisely in the gift that has been given?"

(b) In this context, Augustine's interpretation of the pneumatology of Ephesians 4:7-12 is important.[15] Here he discovers the notion of Spirit as liberation and the development of "the gift" in the gifts that Paul, among other things, called "charisms" – in other words, the questions that play a decisive role in the contemporary view of *pneuma* as the antithesis of "institution."

Augustine starts with the words from the letter to the Ephesians: "Each of us has received grace according to the measure of the gift of

15. *De Trin.* 15.19.34.

Christ. Thus you find the Scripture saying: 'When he ascended on high, he led captivity captive and gave gifts to men'" (Eph 4:7-8 in connection with Ps 68:18). For Augustine, the key word "gift" identifies the text as pneumatological. It also offers him a dramatic teaching opportunity for the connection between Christ and the Spirit. The gifts of the Spirit, in which the Spirit himself is finally the gift, are the gifts of the victorious Christ, the fruit of his victory, of his ascension to the Father. Two apparently contradictory ways of reading the passage in which the Vulgate paraphrases Psalm 68 are important to Augustine. The first reads: "You receive gifts in men," and the second (which the New Testament follows): "He gave gifts to men." For Augustine, the contrast here represents the ambiguity of the christological mystery itself. Christ, the one who ascended, also remains the one who descended. He stands on the side of both the God who gives and the men and women who receive. He is head and body, giving from the side of God and receiving from the side of humanity. Once again, this is what joins ecclesiology and Christology. In the Church he remains the one who descends. The Church is Christ as the one who descended, a continuation of the humanity of Jesus Christ.

Accordingly, Augustine concentrates here predominantly on the connection between Christ, Spirit, and Church as represented in this text. He concentrates not so much on the individual gifts mentioned in the New Testament as such, but rather on the fact that, in all those gifts, *the* gift – the Holy Spirit – is given. Moreover, Augustine remains faithful to the text and correctly cites 1 Corinthians 12:11 as a parallel to support his view: "But it is one and the same Spirit who produces all these gifts, distributing them to each as he wills." But if the gifts are ultimately *one* gift in many forms, namely the Spirit of God, and if the Spirit is the gift of Jesus Christ (which he gives and receives in men and women), then the innermost finality of all gifts is unity. Thus quite reasonably the related passage from the letter to the Ephesians concludes by setting as the final goal that all of this is "for the sake of building up the body of Christ."

This brings Augustine back to his favorite ecclesiological and pneumatological idea, the idea of building, of abiding, of unity, of love. He finds here a possibility of using it in a new way, which he elucidates by adding Psalm 127:1: "If the Lord does not build the house. . . ." He localizes the Psalm in post-exilic prophecy, which is concerned with building a house "after the captivity." The key word, "captivity," connects Psalm 68 and Ephesians 4: the Lord imprisoned captivity and gave gifts. His gift is the Spirit, and the Spirit is the building that can finally take place after the captivity. This indirectly touches upon the issue of freedom. The imprisoning captivity, which previously impeded building, is the devil. Conversely, the devil is captivity, man's bondage, exile, a luring away from self. The anthropological analysis of *The Confessions* can also be heard in the background. If a man is tempted away from himself, he wanders aimlessly into emptiness. Precisely in this appearance of freedom, he is the exile, the prisoner, the criminal.[16] Once again, Augustine is speaking not just on the basis of a dogmatic or philosophical theory but from the experience of his whole life. In indeterminacy, in the apparent freedom of an existence in which everything was possible but nothing was meaningful, he was enslaved. He was exiled from himself and captured by complete unconnectedness, which was based upon the absence of self and its detachment from its own truth. On the other hand, the gift of the victorious Christ is the homecoming and thereby makes possible the building of the house, and the house is called "Church."

Here the theme of spirit as freedom and liberation plainly comes into play. Although paradoxical to contemporary thought, freedom consists in becoming a part of the house, in being included in the building. This idea is not paradoxical from the perspective of the ancient concept of freedom. For the ancients, whoever belongs to the house is free, and freedom is finding a home.[17] Augustine presupposes this ancient social notion of freedom, but then decisively transcends it in accordance with Christian faith. Freedom stands in an insoluble relation to truth, which is man's authentic way of finding a home.[18] Man

16. Cf. especially St. Augustine, *Confessions* 8.5.12-12.30; particularly 7.16: ". . . retorquebas me ad me ipsum, auferens me a dorso meo, ubi me posueram." See the commentary of A. Soulignac in *Oeuvres,* vol. 14: 543 ("La psychologie augustinienne de la volonté") and vol. 13: 689-693 ("Regio dissimilitudinis").

17. Cf. the thorough study of D. Nestle, *Eleutheria,* Studien zum Wesen der Freiheit bei den Griechen und im Neuen Testament, part 1, *Die Griechen* (Tübingen, 1967); E. Coreth, "Zur Problemgeschichte menschlicher Freiheit," *Zeitschrift für katholische Theologie* 94 (1972): 258-289; on this topic see 264-268.

18. For the connection between freedom and truth, see E. Coreth, "Zur Problemgeschichte," 289.

is free only if he is at home, i.e., if he is in the truth. A movement that distances man from the truth of himself, from truth itself, can never be freedom because such a movement destroys man, alienates him from himself, and thus takes from him his own realm of movement, in which he can become himself. That is why the devil is captivity, and that is why the risen Christ, who involved man and built him into the house, is liberation. Finally, that is why the individual gifts of the Spirit, the charisms, can converge in the idea of building.

In this passage, Augustine takes from the doctrine of charisms the key word "building." As was said previously with the connection between Church and love, such a "narrowing of perspective" has its dangers. It can lead to overlooking the manifold activities of the Spirit in favor of a loyalty to given rules, rules that eventually can be identified with the Spirit. In this respect, these texts do not offer a universally valid pneumatology or a completely balanced teaching on Christian spirituality. But they do make a contribution, and this application of the Bible was indeed quite appropriate in Augustine's time. An overabundance of charisms hardly existed in Augustine's diocese; therefore, the problem was different from that of St. Paul's Corinth. (Incidentally, Paul also concluded that building or love was the single most important charism and singly important for everyone, followed by prophecy or comprehensible proclamation.[19]) That aside, Augustine justifiably calls for the charism that was necessary for a Church torn apart by hate and the formation of sects – the charism to work together to build up the unity of the Church. And he stands wholly on the side of the Apostle when he sees *pneuma* decisively in the affirmative – in the Yes that makes man into "a house" and ends "captivity." The "house" is freedom, not dispersion. The activity of the Spirit is "the house," the granting of the home. Unity. Because the Spirit is love.

Translated by Peter Casarella

19. Cf. H. Schlier, "Ueber das Hauptanliegen des 1: Briefes an die Korinther," in *Die Zeit der Kirche,* 2d ed. (Freiburg, 1958), 147-159; J. Ratzinger, "Bemerkungen zur Frage der Charismen in der Kirche," in *Die Zeit Jesu: Festschrift für H. Schlier,* ed. G. Bornkamm and K. Rahner (Freiburg, 1970), 257-272.

Funeral Homily for Msgr. Luigi Giussani

Dear brother bishops, my dear brother priests: "upon seeing Jesus, the disciples rejoiced." These words from today's Gospel show us the center of the personality and life of our dear Don Giussani.

Father Giussani grew up in a house that was – to use his words – poor in bread but rich in music, so that from the very beginning he was touched, or, better, wounded, by the desire for beauty. He was not satisfied, however, with just any ordinary beauty, with beauty however banal; he sought rather Beauty itself, infinite Beauty, and thus he found Christ. In Christ he found true beauty, the path of life, true joy.

Already as a boy, together with other youths, he started a community by the name of *Studium Christi.* Their plan was to speak of nothing but Christ, because everything else seemed to be a waste of time. Later, of course, he was to overcome this one-sidedness, but the substance for him would always remain the same: only Christ gives meaning to the rest of our life. Fr. Giussani kept the gaze of his life, of his heart, always fixed on Christ. It was in this way that he understood that Christianity is not an intellectual system, a collection of dogmas, or moralism. Christianity is instead an encounter, a love story; it is an event.

This love affair with Christ, this love story that was the whole of Giussani's life, was at the same time quite far removed from any superficial enthusiasm or vague romanticism. Seeing Christ, Giussani truly knew that to encounter Christ means to follow him. This encounter is

---

Published in *Communio* 31, no. 4 (Winter 2004).

a road, a journey, a journey that also passes – as we heard in the psalm – through the "valley of darkness." In the Gospel we heard of the final darkness of Christ's suffering, of the seeming absence of God, of the eclipse of the Sun of the world. Giussani knew that to follow means to pass through a "valley of darkness," to take the Way of the Cross, and all the while to live in true joy.

Why is this so? The Lord himself translated the mystery of the Cross, which is really the mystery of love, by means of a formula that expresses the reality of our life in its entirety. The Lord says, "Whoever seeks his own life will lose it, and whoever loses his life will find it."

Father Giussani truly desired not to have life for his own sake: instead he gave life, and it is precisely in this that he found it not only for himself, but for so many others. He lived out what we heard in the Gospel. He did not wish to be served but to serve. He was a faithful servant of the Gospel. He gave away all the wealth of his heart, he gave away all the divine wealth of the Gospel that permeated him. By this service, by giving his life, this life of his has borne rich fruit, as we can see in this very moment. He has truly become the father of many and by guiding people not to himself but to Christ he has truly conquered hearts, he has helped to make the world better, he has helped to open up the doors of the world to heaven.

The centrality of Christ in his life also brought about in Father Giussani the gift of discernment, of deciphering correctly the signs of the times during an age that is, as we know, very difficult and filled with temptations and errors. Consider 1968 and the following years, when a first group of his followers went to Brazil and found itself face to face with extreme poverty and misery. What could be done? How to respond? And the temptation was great to say, "Just for the moment we will have to set Christ aside, set God aside, because there are more pressing needs. First we have to change structures, fix the external things; first we must improve the earth, and after that we will be able to find heaven again." The great temptation of the moment was to transform Christianity into moralism and moralism into politics, that is, to substitute believing with doing. Because what does it mean to believe? Someone may say: we have to do something right now. By substituting faith with moralism, believing with doing, though, we retreat into particularism. Above all, we lose the criteria for judging and the guideposts that orient us in the right direction. The final result, instead of constructive growth, is division.

Monsignor Giussani, with his fearless and unfailing faith, knew that even in this situation it is Christ, the encounter with Christ, that remains central. Whoever does not give God gives too little; and whoever does not give God, whoever does not enable people to see God in the face of Christ, does not build anything up but rather, wastes human activity in false, ideological dogmatism, and so ultimately only destroys.

Don Giussani preserved the centrality of Christ and it was exactly in this way that he was able, by means of social works and needed services, to help mankind in this difficult world, where Christians bear an enormous and urgent responsibility for the poor.

The believer, too, must pass through the "valley of darkness," the dark valley of discernment, and so also of adversity, opposition, and ideological hostility. He must face even the threat of physical elimination that, by doing away with his own, would be rid of this other voice that refuses to rest content merely with this or that action, but bears a greater message and thus also a greater light.

In the strength of faith Msgr. Giussani passed undaunted through these dark valleys and, given the novelty he brought, also encountered difficulties fitting in within the Church. It is always the case that if the Holy Spirit, in accord with the needs of the times, creates something new – which is in reality a return to the origins – it is difficult to find the right direction and to attain the peaceful unity of the great communion the universal Church. Fr. Giussani's love for Christ was also love for the Church, and thus he always remained a faithful servant, faithful to the Holy Father and faithful to his bishops.

Through his foundations, he also interpreted the mystery of the Church in a new way. "Communion and Liberation" immediately brings to mind the modern era's particular discovery, freedom, while also recalling St. Ambrose's phrase, *"Ubi fides est libertas"* [where there is faith, there is freedom]. Cardinal Biffi drew our attention to the close accord between this phrase of St. Ambrose and the foundation of Communion and Liberation. Focusing on freedom as a gift proper to faith, he also told us that if it is to be a true, human freedom, that is, freedom in truth, then freedom needs communion. An isolated freedom, a freedom solely for the sake of the "I," would be a lie, and would necessarily destroy human communion. To be true, and, therefore, efficacious, freedom needs communion, and not just any communion but ultimately communion with truth itself, with love itself, with Christ, with the trinitarian God. This is the path to communion that creates freedom and brings joy.

The other foundation, *Memores Domini*, brings to mind once more the second Gospel from today:[1] the memory that the Lord gave us in the Holy Eucharist, a memory that is not merely the remembrance of the past, but a memory that creates in the present, a memory in which he gives himself into our hands and into our hearts, and thereby makes us live.

In the last period of his life, Fr. Giussani had to pass through the dark valley of sickness, of infirmity, of pain, of suffering, but here, too, his eyes were fixed on Jesus and so he remained true in the midst of all the suffering. Seeing Jesus, he was able to rejoice; he knew the presence of the joy of the Risen One, who even in the Passion is the Risen One and gives us true light and joy. He knew, too, that, as the psalm says, even passing through this valley, "I fear no evil because I know that You are with me, and I will dwell in the Father's house." This was his great strength, to know that "You are with me."

My dear faithful, above all, my dear young people, let us take this message to heart, let us not lose sight of Christ, let us not forget that without God nothing good can be built up, and that God remains an enigma to us when he is not recognized in the face of Christ.

Now your dear friend Fr. Giussani has reached the other world. We are convinced that the doors of the Father's house have opened, we are sure that now these words have fully come to pass: upon seeing Jesus they rejoiced. He is rejoicing with a joy that no one can take from him. In this moment we wish to thank the Lord for the great gift of this priest, this faithful servant of the Gospel, this father. We entrust his soul to the goodness of his Lord and ours.

Translation provided by Communion and Liberation

1. [The Ambrosian Rite of Milan includes several Gospel readings. – Trans.]

Europe in the Crisis of Cultures

1. Reflections on Today's Contrasting Cultures

We find ourselves at a time of great dangers and great opportunities for man and the world, a moment that also places a great responsibility upon us. During the last century, man's know-how and his dominion over matter have grown in a way that no one could have imagined before. But man's ability to control the world has also given him a power of destruction so great as to be downright terrifying at times. In this connection one cannot help thinking of the new war without borders and without fronts called terrorism. The not unjustified fear that terrorists might get hold of nuclear and biological weapons has led even constitutional states to adopt security measures similar to those that formerly existed only in dictatorial regimes. And yet, when all is said and done, the feeling remains that all these precautions can never really be sufficient, since the sort of world-wide control that would be needed is neither possible nor desirable. Less visible, but not for that reason any less disturbing, are the capacities for self-manipulation that man has acquired. Man has plumbed the recesses of being, he has deciphered the components that make man human, and now he can, so to say, "construct" man by himself. Man, then, no longer comes into be-

---

Published in *Communio* 32, no. 2 (Summer 2005). The lecture was given 1 April 2005 in Subiaco, Italy, upon receiving the St. Benedict Award for the promotion of life and the family in Europe.

ing as a gift of the Creator, but as the product of our action, a product that – for this very reason – can also be selected according to criteria of our own choosing. By the same token, this man is no longer covered by the splendor that comes from his being the image of God, which is what bestows on him his dignity and inviolability, but only by the power of human know-how. He is no longer anything more than the image of man – of which man, though? To this we can add the great planetary problems: inequality in the distribution of the world's goods; growing poverty, indeed, impoverishment; the exploitation of the earth and its resources; hunger; diseases that threaten the whole world; the clash of cultures. All of this shows that the growth of our possibilities is not matched by an equal development of our moral energy. The power of morality has not kept pace with the growth of science, indeed, it has rather diminished. This is because the technological mindset confines morality to the subjective sphere, whereas what we need is precisely a public morality, a morality that can respond to the threats that cast their shadows over everyone's existence. The true, and gravest, danger we face in the present moment is just this disequilibrium between technical capacities and moral energy. The security that we need as a basis for our freedom and dignity cannot, in the last analysis, come from technological systems of control, but can spring only from man's moral strength. Where this strength is lacking, or is only inadequately present, man's power will increasingly transform itself into a power of destruction.

It is true that there is a new moralism today whose key words are justice, peace, and the conservation of creation – words that evoke some of the essential moral values that we do in fact need. But this moralism remains vague and so slides, almost inevitably, into the sphere of partisan politics. It is above all a claim made on others, and is all too little a personal duty for our daily lives. What, in fact, does "justice" mean? Who defines it? What is conducive to peace? In the last decades we have seen in our streets and in our squares how pacifism can deviate into destructive anarchism and terrorism. The political moralism of the 1960s, whose roots are far from dead, succeeded in drawing young people full of ideals. But its basic thrust was wrong, because it lacked a serene rationality and because, in the end, it valued political utopia above the dignity of the individual man; indeed, it proved capable of going so far as to despise man in the name of its lofty goals. The political moralism that we have lived through, and are living through still, not only does not open the way to regeneration, it actually blocks it. The same also holds, therefore, for a Christianity and a theology that reduce the core of Jesus' message, the "kingdom of God," to the "values of the kingdom," while identifying these values with the main watchwords of political moralism and proclaiming them, at the same time, to be the synthesis of all religions – all the while forgetting about God, despite the fact that it is precisely he who is the subject and the cause of the kingdom of God. What is left in his place are big words (and values) that are open to every kind of abuse.

This brief survey of the world's situation leads us to reflect on the situation of Christianity today and, for the same reason, on the foundations of Europe – the Europe that was once, we can say, the Christian Continent, but that also became the starting point of the new scientific rationality that has given us great possibilities and equally great threats. Of course, Christianity did not start in Europe, and so cannot be classified as a European religion, the religion of the European cultural realm. But it was precisely in Europe that Christianity received its most historically influential cultural and intellectual form, and it therefore remains intertwined with Europe in a special way. On the other hand, it is also true that, beginning with the Renaissance, and then in complete form with the Enlightenment, this same Europe also developed the scientific rationality that not only led to the geographical unity of the world, to the meeting of continents and cultures in the age of discovery, but also now, thanks to the technological culture made possible by science, much more deeply places its stamp on what is now truly the whole world, indeed, in a certain sense reduces the world to uniformity. And, in the wake of this form of rationality, Europe has developed a culture that, in a way hitherto unknown to humanity, excludes God from public consciousness, whether he is totally denied or whether his existence is judged to be indemonstrable and uncertain, and so is relegated to the domain of subjective choices, as something in any case irrelevant for public life. This purely functional rationality, to give it a name, has revolutionized moral conscience in a way that is equally new with respect to all hitherto existing cultures, inasmuch as it claims that only what is experimentally provable is rational. Since morality belongs to an entirely different sphere, it disappears as a category in its own right, and so has to be identified in some alternative fashion, since no one can deny that, after all, we still do need morality in one form or another. In a world based on calculation, it is the calculation of consequences that decides what is to count as moral or immoral. And so the category of the good, which Kant had put front and center, disappears. Nothing is good or evil in itself, everything depends on the consequences that can be foreseen for a given action. Although, on the one hand, Christianity found its most influential form in Europe, we must also say, on the other hand, that Europe has developed a culture that most radically contradicts not only Christianity, but the religious and moral traditions of humanity as well. This helps us understand that Europe is going through a true "stress test"; it also helps us understand the radical nature of the tensions that our continent has to face. But also, and above all, what it brings to light is the responsibility that we Europeans have to assume at this moment in history: what is at stake in the debate about the definition of Europe, about its new political form, is not some nostalgic battle at the "rear-guard" of history, but rather a great responsibility for the humanity of today.

Let us take a closer look at this contrast between the two cultures that have marked Europe. This contrast has surfaced in two controverted points of the debate about the Preamble to the European Constitution: Shall the Constitution mention God? Shall it mention Europe's Christian roots? Some say that there is no need to worry, since article 52 of the Constitution guarantees the institutional rights of the Church. However, this means that the Churches find room in European life only in the realm of political compromise, but that when it comes to the foundations of Europe, their actual substance has no room to play any formative role. The arguments given for this clear "No" are superficial, and it is clear that, rather than indicating the real reason, they in fact cover it. The claim that mentioning Europe's Christian roots would offend the feelings of the many non-Christians who live in Europe is unconvincing, since what we are dealing with is first and foremost a historical fact that no one can seriously deny. Of course, this historical observation also implies something about the present, since to mention roots is also to point to residual sources of moral guidance, and so to something that constitutes the identity of this thing called Europe. Who would be offended? Whose identity would be threatened? Muslims, who are typically used as the favorite examples in this regard, do not feel threatened by our Christian moral foundations, but by the cynicism of a secularized culture that denies its own bases. Nor do our Jewish fellow citizens feel offended when Europe's Christian roots are mentioned, since these roots go back to Mount Sinai: they bear the mark of the voice that resounded on the Mountain of God and they unite us in the great basic guidelines that the Decalogue has given to humanity. The same holds for the reference to God: it is not the mention of God that offends adherents of other religions, but rather the attempt to build the human community without any relationship to God whatsoever.

The reasons for this double "No" are deeper than the arguments that have been advanced for it would suggest. They presuppose the idea that only radical Enlightenment culture, which has reached its full development in our time, is able to define what European culture is. Different religious cultures, each enjoying its respective rights, can therefore coexist alongside Enlightenment culture – so long and so far as they respect, and subordinate themselves to, its criteria. This culture is substantially defined by the rights of freedom. Its starting point is freedom, which it takes to be a fundamental value that measures everything else: the liberty of religious choice, which includes the religious neutrality of the state; the liberty to express one's own opinion, as long as it does not call into doubt this canon of freedom; the democratic ordering of the state, hence, parliamentary control over the organisms of the state; the free formation of parties; the independence of the judiciary; and, finally, the protection of the rights of man and the prohibition of discrimination in any form. In this last respect, the canon is still in formation, since the rights of man can also be in conflict, for example, when there is a clash between a woman's desire for freedom and an unborn baby's right to life. The concept of discrimination is being continually broadened, and in this way the prohibition of discrimination can find itself increasingly transformed into a limitation on the freedom of opinion and the freedom of religion. We are not far from the time when we will no longer be allowed to state publicly that homosexuality is, as the Catholic Church teaches, an objective disorder in the structuring of human existence. And the Church's conviction that it does not have the right to give priestly ordination to women is already considered by some to be incompatible with the spirit of the European Constitution. It is obvious that this canon of Enlightenment culture –

which is anything but definitive – contains important values that we, precisely as Christians, cannot, and do not wish to, do without. But it is also obvious that the ill-defined, or even simply undefined, conception of freedom on which this culture rests inevitably entails contradictions. And it is obvious that the actual use of this concept – a use that seems radical – brings with it restrictions on freedom that would have been unimaginable a generation ago. A confused ideology of freedom leads to a dogmatism that turns out to be – more and more – hostile to freedom.

We will, of course, have to come back to the question of the contradictions within the contemporary form of Enlightenment culture. But first we must finish our description of this culture. As a culture where reason has supposedly finally achieved full self-consciousness, it naturally claims universality and imagines that it is complete in itself, with no need to be complemented by any other cultural factors. These two characteristics are abundantly evident in connection with the question about who can become a member of the European Community. This is especially true in the debate surrounding Turkey's possible admission into the European Union. Turkey is a state or, better, a cultural domain that does not have Christian roots, but that has been influenced by Islamic culture. Ataturk later tried to transform Turkey into a secular state, attempting to transplant onto Muslim soil the secularism that grew up in the Christian world of Europe. One can ask whether such an attempt is possible. According to Europe's culture of secular Enlightenment, the norms and contents of this same Enlightenment culture are all that is needed for the definition of European identity, which means that any state that adopts these criteria can belong to Europe. In the end, it does not matter which root system this culture of freedom and democracy is grafted onto. Precisely for this reason, we are told, Europe's roots cannot factor into the definition of its foundations, since they are dead roots that are not part of its contemporary identity. By the same token, this new identity, which depends solely on Enlightenment culture, also implies that God has nothing to do with public life and the foundations of the state.

In this way, the whole affair becomes logical and even, in some sense, plausible. After all, what better outcome could we wish for than universal respect for democracy and human rights? But then we have to ask: is this secularist Enlightenment culture really the culture of a reason common to all men, and has it really proved itself to be definitively universal? Is it really a culture that ought to find access everywhere, even if on a historically and culturally different *humus*? And is it truly complete in itself, and so without need of any root outside of itself?

2. The Significance and Limits of Today's Rationalist Culture

We must now face these last two questions. With respect to the first question – have we attained the universal, at last fully scientific philosophy that brings to expression mankind's common reason? – we have to answer that we have indeed achieved important gains that can claim a general validity: we have achieved the insight that religion cannot be imposed by the state, but can be welcomed only in freedom; respect for the fundamental rights of man, which are equal for all; the separation of powers and the control of power. We must not imagine, however, that these basic values, though generally valid, can be realized in the same way in every historical context. Not every society has the sociological presuppositions for the sort of party-based democracy that exists in the West. By the same token, complete religious neutrality on the part of the state has to be regarded, in most historical contexts, as an illusion. And with that we come to the problems raised by the second question. But first let us clear up the question as to whether modern Enlightenment philosophies, taken as a whole, can claim to speak the last word for reason as something common to all men. Characteristic of these philosophies is their positivism, hence, their anti-metaphysical posture. Consequently, they end up leaving no room for God. They are based on a self-limitation of positive reason, which is adequate in the technical domain, but which, when it gets generalized, mutilates man. It follows from this that man no longer acknowledges any moral authority outside of his calculations, and, as we have seen, even the concept of freedom, which at first sight might seem to expand here without limit, leads in the end to the self-destruction of freedom. Admittedly, the positivist philosophies contain important elements of truth. But these elements are based on a self-limitation of reason typical of a given cultural situation – that of the modern West – and as such cannot be reason's last word. Although they appear to be totally rational, they are not the voice of reason itself, but are themselves culturally bound; bound, that is, to the situation of today's West. They are, then, not at all the philosophy that, one day, might rightfully claim validity throughout the whole world. But above all we need to say that this Enlightenment philosophy, with its corresponding culture, is incomplete. It consciously severs its own cultural roots, thus depriving itself of the original energies from which it itself sprang, the fundamental memory of humanity, as it were, without which reason loses its compass. Indeed, the principle that reigns today says that man is the measure of his action. If we know how to do it, we are allowed to do it. There is no longer any such thing as knowing how to do something without being allowed to do it – such a situation would be contrary to freedom, which is the supreme, absolute value. But man knows how to do many things, indeed, increasingly so, and if this knowledge is not measured by a moral norm, it becomes, as we can already see, a power to destroy. Man knows how to clone men. He knows how to use men as a "warehouse" of organs for other men – and so he does it, he does it because his freedom would seem to require it. Man knows how to build atomic bombs – and so he builds them, which means that he is also willing, in principle, to use them. Even terrorism, in the end, is based on this "self-authorization" of man, and not on the teachings of the Qu'ran. Enlightenment philosophy's radical severing of its roots becomes, when all is said and done, a way of doing without man. Man, at bottom, has no freedom, the spokesmen of the natural sciences tell us, thus contradicting completely the starting point of the whole discussion. Man must not believe that he is anything special with respect to any other living being, and so he ought to be treated as they are – so we are told precisely by the most advanced spokesmen of a philosophy cleanly cut off from the roots of humanity's historical memory.

We had asked ourselves two questions: Is rationalist (positivist) philosophy strictly rational, and so universally valid? And is it complete? Is it self-sufficient? Can, or even must, it relegate its historical roots to the domain of the mere past, and so to the domain of the merely subjectively valid? We have to answer all of these questions with a clear "No." This philosophy does not express human reason in its fullness, but only a part of it, and because it thus mutilates reason, it cannot be considered rational. By the same token, it is also incomplete, and it can heal only by re-establishing contact with its roots. A tree without roots withers.

In making this claim, we are not denying all the positive and important things that this philosophy has to say. Rather, we are simply stating its need for completeness, its radical incompleteness. The act of setting aside Europe's Christian roots is not, after all, the expression of a superior tolerance that respects all cultures equally, and refrains from privileging any of them, but rather the absolutization of a way of thinking and living that stands in radical contrast, among other things, to the other historical cultures of humanity. The true antithesis that characterizes today's world is not that between different religious cultures, but that between the radical emancipation of man from God, from the roots of life, on the one hand, and the great religious cultures, on the other. If we eventually find ourselves in a clash of cultures, it will not be because of the clash of the great religions — which have always been in conflict with one another, but which, in the end, have always managed to coexist — but it will be because of the clash between this radical emancipation of man and the major cultures of history. In this sense, the refusal to mention God is not the expression of a tolerance that would protect the non-theistic religions and the dignity of atheists and agnostics. It is rather the expression of a mindset that would like to see God erased once and for all from the public life of humanity and relegated to the subjective sphere maintained by residual cultures from the past. Relativism, which is the starting point for all of this, thus becomes a dogmatism that believes itself in possession of the definitive knowledge of reason and of the right to regard everything else as a mere stage of humanity's development that has been fundamentally superseded and that is best treated as a pure relativity. What this really means is that we need roots to survive and that we must not lose sight of God, at the cost of the disappearance of human dignity.

3. The Permanent Significance of Christian Faith

Is this a simple refusal of the Enlightenment and of modernity? Absolutely not. From its very beginning, Christianity has understood itself as the religion of the *logos,* as the religion according to reason. It found its precursor, not primarily in the other religions, but in the philosophical enlightenment that cleared the way of traditions in order to devote itself to the pursuit of the true and the good, of the one God who is above all the gods. As a religion of the persecuted, as a universal religion that reached beyond states and peoples, Christianity denied the state the right to regard religion as a part of its own order, and so claimed freedom for faith. It has always defined men, all men without distinction, as creatures of God and images of God, and has always in principle proclaimed their equal dignity, albeit within the inevitable limits of given societies. In this sense, the Enlightenment is of Christian origin and it is not an accident that it came to birth precisely and exclusively in the domain of Christian faith. True, in that very domain Christianity had unfortunately contradicted its own nature by becoming a state tradition and a state religion. Despite the fact that philosophy, as a quest for rationality – including the rationality of faith – had always been the prerogative of Christianity, the voice of reason had been too much tamed. The merit of the Enlightenment was to insist once again on these original values of Christianity and to give reason back its voice. The Second Vatican Council, in its constitution on the Church and the modern world, reasserted this deep correspondence between Christianity and enlightenment. It sought to achieve a true conciliation between Christianity and modernity, which is the great inheritance that both sides are called upon to protect.

That having been said, the two parties need to reflect on themselves and to be ready for self-correction. Christianity must always remember that it is the religion of the *logos*. It is a faith in the *Creator Spiritus,* the source of all reality. This faith ought to energize Christianity philosophically in our day, since the problem we now face is whether the world comes from the irrational, and reason is therefore nothing but a "byproduct," and perhaps a harmful one, of its development – or whether the world comes from reason, so that reason is the world's criterion and aim. The Christian faith tends towards the second position. From the purely philosophical point of view, then, it has a truly strong hand to play, despite the fact that many today consider the first position alone to be "rational" and modern. But a reason that springs forth from the irrational and that, in the end, is itself irrational, is no answer to our problems. Only creative reason, which has manifested itself as love in the crucified God, can show us the way.

In the necessary dialogue between Catholics and the secular-minded, we Christians have to take special care to remain faithful to this basic principle: we have to live a faith that comes from the *logos,* from creative reason, and that is therefore open to all that is truly rational. But at this point I would like, as a believer, to make a proposal to secular folk. The Enlightenment attempted to define the essential norms of morality while claiming that they would be valid *etsi Deus non daretur*, even if God did not exist. In the midst of confessional conflict and the crisis of the image of God, the attempt was made to keep the essential moral values free of contradiction and to undergird them with evidence that would make them independent of the many divisions and uncertainties of the various philosophies and confessions. The idea was to secure the bases of coexistence and, in general, the bases of humanity. At that time, this seemed possible, inasmuch as the great basic convictions created by Christianity still held and still seemed undeniable. But this is no longer the case. The quest for a reassuring certitude that could stand uncontested beyond all differences has failed. Not even Kant, for all of his undeniable greatness, was able to create the necessary shared certainty. Kant had denied that God is knowable within the domain of pure reason, but, at the same time, he thought of God, freedom, and immortality as postulates of practical reason, without which it was impossible to act morally in any consistent way. Doesn't the situation of the world today make us wonder whether he might not have been right after all? Let me put it differently: the extreme attempt to fashion the things of man without any reference to God leads us ever closer to the edge of the abyss, to the total abolition of man. We therefore have good reason to turn the Enlightenment axiom on its head and to say that even those who are unable to accept God should nonetheless try to live *veluti si Deus daretur*, as if God existed. This was the advice that Pascal gave to his non-believing friends; it is also the advice that we would like to give to our non-believing friends today. Thus, no one's freedom is restricted, but everything human gets the support and the criterion it so urgently needs.

What we most need at this moment of history are men who make God visible in this world through their enlightened and lived faith. The negative witness of Christians who spoke of God but lived against him obscured his image and opened the door to unbelief. We need men who have their eyes fixed straight on God, and who learn from him what true humanity is. We need men whose intellects have been enlightened by the light of God and whose hearts have been opened by God, so that their intellects can speak to others' intellects and their hearts can open others' hearts. God returns among men only through men who are touched by God. We need men like Benedict of Nursia. In a time of dissipation and decadence, he plunged into the most extreme solitude, and then was able, after all the purifications he had to undergo, to reemerge into the light, to return and to found, at Monte Cassino, the city on the hill that, in the midst of so many ruins, brought together the energies from which a new world took shape. In this way Benedict, like Abraham, became the father of many peoples. His recommendations to his monks at the end of the Rule still show us the way that leads on high, beyond the crises and the massacres:

> As there is a bitter zeal that leads us away from God and leads to hell, so there is a good zeal that leads us away from vices and leads to God and to eternal life. And it is in this zeal that the monks must train themselves with the most ardent love: let them outdo one another in honoring one another, let them put up with one another's physical and moral infirmities with supreme patience. . . . Let them love one another with brotherly affection. . . . Let them fear God in love. . . . Let them put nothing before Christ who is able to lead all to eternal life. (Chapter 72)

Translated by Adrian J. Walker